Horror

Genre Fiction and Film Companions

Volumes

The Gothic
Edited by Simon Bacon

Cli-Fi
Edited by Axel Goodbody and Adeline Johns-Putra

Horror
Edited by Simon Bacon

Forthcoming

Sci-Fi
Edited by Jack Fennell

Monsters
Edited by Simon Bacon

Transmedia
Edited by Simon Bacon

HORROR

A Companion

Edited by Simon Bacon

PETER LANG
Oxford • Bern • Berlin • Bruxelles • New York • Wien

Bibliographic information published by Die Deutsche Nationalbibliothek. Die Deutsche
Nationalbibliothek lists this publication in the Deutsche National-bibliografie; detailed
bibliographic data is available on the Internet at http://dnb.d-nb.de.

A catalogue record for this book is available from the British Library.

Library of Congress Cataloging-in-Publication Data:
Names: Bacon, Simon, 1965- author.
Title: Horror : a companion / Simon Bacon.
Description: Oxford ; New York : Peter Lang, 2019. | Series: Genre fiction
 and film companions ; 3 | Includes bibliographical references and index.
Identifiers: LCCN 2019005212 | ISBN 9781787079199 (alk. paper)
Subjects: LCSH: Horror in literature. | Horror tales--History and criticism.
 | Horror films--History and criticism. | Horror television
 programs--History and criticism.
Classification: LCC PN56.H6 B33 2019 | DDC 809/.9164--dc23 LC record available at
https://lccn.loc.gov/2019005212

Cover design by Peter Lang Ltd.

ISSN 1422-9005
ISBN 978-1-78707-919-9 (print) • ISBN 978-1-78707-920-5 (ePDF)
ISBN 978-1-78707-921-2 (ePub) • ISBN 978-1-78707-922-9 (mobi)

© Peter Lang AG 2019
Published by Peter Lang Ltd, International Academic Publishers,
52 St Giles, Oxford, OX1 3LU, United Kingdom
oxford@peterlang.com, www.peterlang.com

Simon Bacoh has asserted his right under the Copyright, Designs and Patents Act, 1988, to
be identified as Editor of this Work.

All rights reserved.
All parts of this publication are protected by copyright.
Any utilisation outside the strict limits of the copyright law, without
the permission of the publisher, is forbidden and liable to prosecution.
This applies in particular to reproductions, translations, microfilming,
and storage and processing in electronic retrieval systems.

This publication has been peer reviewed.

Printed in Germany

Contents

Acknowledgements — ix

Simon Bacon
Introduction — 1

PART I Approaches to Horror — 9

Murray Leeder
David Robert Mitchell's *It Follows* (2014) – The Limits of Knowledge — 11

Gerry Canavan
Dan Trachtenberg's *10 Cloverfield Lane* (2016) – Inconceivable Horror — 19

Xavier Aldana Reyes
Jaume Balagueró and Paco Plaza's *[REC]* (2007) – The Affective Approach to Horror — 27

Darren Elliott-Smith
Brad Falchuk's *American Horror Story* (2011–present) – Queer Horror and Performative Pleasure — 35

PART II Media and Mediums of Horror — 43

Lorna Jowett and Stacey Abbott
Victor Fresco's *Santa Clarita Diet* (2017–present) – Television Horror — 45

Julia Round
Joe Hill and Gabriel Rodriguez's *Locke & Key*
(2008–2013) – Horror Comics　　　　　　　　　　　　　53

Christian McCrea
Kojima Productions' *P.T.* (2014) – The Game of Horror　　　61

Jeffrey Andrew Weinstock
Michael Jackson's 'Thriller' (1982) and Stanley Kubrick's *The
Shining* (1980) – The Sound of Horror　　　　　　　　　　67

Alexandra Heller-Nicholas
Joseph DeLage and Troy Wagner's *Marble Hornets* (2009–2014) –
New Media Horror　　　　　　　　　　　　　　　　　　75

PART III　Categories of Contemporary Horror　　　　　　83

Steve Jones
Spierig Brothers' *Jigsaw* (2017) – Torture Porn Rebooted?　　85

Elizabeth Parker
Alex Garland's *Annihilation* (2018) – Eco-horror　　　　　　93

Thomas Fahy
The Duffer Brothers' *Stranger Things* (2016–present) –
Horror and Nostalgia　　　　　　　　　　　　　　　　　103

Steffen Hantke
Alex Garland's *Ex Machina* (2014) – Science Fiction and Horror　111

Stacey Abbott
James DeMonaco's *The Purge: Anarchy* (2014) –
Post-millennial Horror　　　　　　　　　　　　　　　　119

Stephanie A. Graves
Jordan Peele's *Get Out* (2017) – Smart Horror — 127

PART IV National and Cross-Cultural Horror in the Twenty-First Century — 135

Tracy Fahey
Jeremy Dyson, Mark Gatiss, Steve Pemberton and Reece Shearsmith's *The League of Gentlemen* (1999–2017) – Contemporary Folk Horror — 137

Ian Olney
Julia Ducournau's *Raw* (2016) – Euro Horror — 143

Katarzyna Ancuta
Sadako Yamamura and the *Ring* Cycle (1991–present) – Asian Horror — 151

Cristina Santos
Mariana Enríquez's *Things We Lost in the Fire* (2009/2017) – Argentinian Horror — 159

Gina Wisker
Tananarive Due's *Ghost Summer: Stories* (2015) – African American Horror — 167

Gail de Vos and Kayla Lar-Son
Cowboy Smithx's *The Candy Meister* (2014) – First Nations Horror — 175

Meheli Sen
Prosit Roy's *Pari* (2018) – Bollywood Horror — 181

Dana Och
Jalmari Helander's *Rare Exports* (2003–2010) – Transnational Horror — 191

PART V   Horror Authors and their Contemporary Afterlives   199

Dara Downey
Laeta Kalogridis' *Altered Carbon* (2018–present) – Edgar Allan Poe   201

Carl H. Sederholm
Crafteon's *Cosmic Reawakening* (2017) – H. P. Lovecraft   211

Todd S. Garth
Damián Szifron's *Relatos salvajes* (2014) – Horacio Quiroga   219

Kristopher Woofter
Caitlín R. Kiernan's *The Drowning Girl* (2012) – Shirley Jackson   227

Simon Brown
Stephen King's *Full Dark No Stars* (2010) – Stephen King   235

Bibliography   241

Notes on Contributors   265

Index   273

Acknowledgements

Many thanks to Laurel Plapp and the team at Peter Lang for all their help and assistance along the way, and the invaluable suggestions of Reader #2. And, as always, the never-ending patience of Mrs Mine, Eben and Majki and the support of Mam i Tata Bronk.

Simon Bacon

Introduction

Defining Horror

Horror brings to mind a world of extremes: dark and sinister locations, dreamlike environments, sudden shocks and surprises, extreme violence and gore, transgressive sexuality, threats to life and limb and, of course, the presence of terrifying monsters. Horror narratives are also typically filled with frightening characters (vampires, mad-scientists, unstoppable killers, aliens, mutated animals), jarring and evocative music (high-pitched and 'stabbing' violins, throbbing base-notes, medieval chanting) and mysterious objects (Ouija boards, phones with no signal, esoteric books, cryptic symbolism), which shock, scare and excite us out of our everyday lives.[1]

However, trying to define and explain the genre of horror itself is actually far more difficult. As described above, we quite often know horror when we encounter it, yet there are different kinds of horror, both in terms of type (violent, supernatural, slasher, etc.) and origin (European, Asian, Indian, etc.). And further, why does the work of certain authors of horror seem to be as important now as it was when it was written ten, fifty, or 100 years ago? How does horror change when it is read in a book, watched on a screen, listened to as music, or engaged with online? Horror then is not one thing but the coming together or over-laying of many.

As horror theorist Brigid Cherry observes, 'the [horror] genre should perhaps be more accurately thought of as an overlapping and evolving set of "conceptual categories" that are in a constant state of flux' (2009: 3). This

---

[1] In fact, a recent study claims that we purposely seek out such thrills as a way to prepare ourselves for real-world situations, see Jacobs 2019.

introduction will outline key approaches to horror to give a sense of these overlapping concepts and how we might understand them. Since the book needs to be selective, it will focus on those theories of horror that have particular relevance to the aim of this volume in describing where the genre is now, in the twenty-first century, and the possible influences on its future.

An oft-quoted starting point is Ann Radcliffe, one of the original Gothic novelists, who saw a clear distinction between terror and horror, where the former can be more akin to the sublime of Edmund Burke and possessing an almost spiritual quality, whereas horror is something of a more mundane experience (Radcliffe 1826: 145–52).[2] This definition is not without its problems and, as Kevin Costorphine writes, 'This famous distinction suggests that horror is merely an affect' (2018: 4). Yet, as he goes on to note, this does not prevent horror, and horror stories, from allowing for 'an imaginative engagement with the monstrosity that plagues our existence [which] can allow for an exploration of what this might mean to us, and an establishment of some kind of order' (2018: 7).

Noël Carroll, in his seminal book *Philosophy of Horror* (1987), goes a step further by distinguishing between two types of horror, which he calls 'natural-horror' and 'art-horror'. The former is evoked through ecological disaster or acts of terrorism (51) and the latter appears in cultural expressions such as film, art, literature, etc. There is still much of the affective nature of horror in Carroll's definitions and, whilst he does much to separate the two they are, as seen in the essays later, inevitably entangled. Theorists like Julia Kristeva in the slightly earlier work *Powers of Horror* (1980) see forms of real-life revulsion, emotional excess, and abjection being configured in ways that provide frameworks for literary and artistic interpretation.[3] Kristeva's theoretical framework is born

---

2   Edmund Burke wrote *A Philosophical Enquiry into the Origin of Our Ideas of the Sublime and Beautiful* in 1757 describing the aesthetic differences between the beautiful and the sublime where beauty is well-proportioned, pleasing and calming but the sublime is inspired by that which threatens to destroy us.
3   In a sense this flow between natural and art Horror is reversed in Adriana Cavarero's idea of Horrorism (Horror/Terrorism) where the experience of real-world events and violence are refracted through the visual saturation of art-horror in popular culture (see Cavarero 2011).

from the work of Mary Douglas's *Purity and Danger* (1966), where the abject and the 'horror-full', or horror-inducing, are cultural constructs designed to 'protect' society, which suggests a normalizing function to even the most transgressive horror. Therefore, art-horror as an imaginative, societal creation is inherently meaningful, speaking of the fears and anxieties of a particular cultural and historical moment. These are never singular or separate events but part of an ongoing, evolving process that sees subsequent expressions of horror narratives as sharing similar characteristics, features and tropes which can be grouped together under the heading of the horror genre.

Andrew Tudor defines genre as 'a special kind of subculture, a set of conventions of narrative, setting, characterization, motive, imagery, iconography' which possesses its own 'language' (1991: 5–6). This does not mean that the edges of a genre, or indeed, the 'ritual or ideological function[s]' (Altman 1998: 26) it serves are rigid. Ken Gelder notes that one must always be aware of not homogenizing the horror genre and seeing all manifestations of it as performing the same kind of tasks. The 'field of horror' is a fractured, many-faceted thing, and critical dispositions not only depend on what is being looked at, and when, but will determine what is being looked at (and what is deemed inappropriate, irrelevant, and so on) in the first place (Gelder 2000: 4). In this sense, the complexity of what can be included within the category of horror is simultaneously simple and complicated. Lists of possible literary works, films, comics, artworks, etc., that can be included within the genre is constantly shifting and not only intersects with other genres but also shifts in relation to its context and audience. Context can refer to something as obvious as where the text was watched/read/played and who with – for instance, watching a horror film alone at night can be very different from that when seeing the same film in a cinema full of horror fans – but also extends to, as noted by Cherry, 'the social and political anxieties of the cultural moment' (Cherry 2009: 214).

Cherry also notes how horror films can 'speak' to an audience and 'elicit a range of responses in the viewer, these responses being created through cinematic and aesthetic cues that trigger or tap into psychological states or cognitive processes' (2009: 214). Further, Cherry sees these affective states – both bodily (Sobchack 2004) and psychological (Aldana Reyes 2016) – as capable of imparting types of ideological messages 'over and above meeting the basic desire in the viewer to be scared, the horror genre seems to be a form that is easily adaptable at addressing, and imparting, a range of ideological issues' (Cherry 2009: 214). This adaptability of horror can lead to many and varied kinds of interpretation and approaches, some of which will be considered next.

Approaches and Types

Interpretative approaches to horror, of which there are many, fall approximately into three categories: psychoanalytic, cognitive and affective. Psychoanalytic interpretations stem from Freudian interpretations and continues through Carl Jung, Jacques Lacan and Slavoj Žižek. While there are limitations to this approach (see Clasen 2010: 114), it is often used to fascinating effect in revealing possible repressed or sublimated meanings in horror texts, which are wholly appropriate in works often founded upon cultural anxieties. Many important feminist and queer interpretations of horror are founded on such an approach, such as Barbara Creed's *The Monstrous Feminine* (1993), Carol Clover's *Men, Women, and Chainsaws* and Barry Keith Grant's *The Dread of Difference* (1996), to name but a few.

Cognitive readings focus more explicitly on the ways in which the text interacts with its audience by way of its conscious, intellectual abilities, to create horror. Through 'the disturbance of cultural norms, both conceptual and moral, it provides a repertory of symbolism for those times in which the cultural order – albeit at a lower level of generality – has collapsed or is perceived to be in a state of dissolution' (Carroll 1987: 214). Matt Hills summarizes this as the provocation of emotions, causing 'fear, disgust, cognitive dissonance, and cognitive reflections on evil' (Hills 2005: 23), but also points out that the focus on negative reactions in such readings often downplays the pleasurable or comedic aspects of horror.

Affect theory relies on the work of philosophers Gilles Deleuze, Baruch Spinoza, Friedrich Nietzsche and Henri Bergson, though the interpretation of horror films may go beyond their work. Hills and Xavier Aldana Reyes see affect theory, or affect studies, as a way of examining the somatic and emotional responses induced by horror films, but which can, largely, be extended to other works of horror (Hills 2005: 23; Aldana Reyes 2016: 5). This is not just about the normal 'shocks' often involved within the genre but extends to all visual and aural aspects of a text. As such it can work as an extension of cognitive interpretations and describe dread, anxiety and foreboding of the unseen, unknowable and inconceivable. Whilst psychoanalytic interpretations approach horror as an artefact produced by a cultural as an expression of its fears and anxieties – if only to diffuse them through comedy, etc. – cognitive and affective ones tend more to focus on the relationship between a text and its audience and the resultant intellectual, emotional and/or bodily responses.

Of course, not everyone experiences such texts in the same way, which can complicate readings if not taken into consideration. Such problematics can be seen to apply when looking at horror texts from other countries and/or cultures. The cultural milieu is the vitalizing component of art-horror, which affects the kinds of artworks produced as well as audience responses. This is ever more important in an age of increasing globalization and the continuing influence of Hollywood, not just through its aggressive production and marketing initiatives – including the prevalence of remakes of non-Hollywood 'foreign' films – but also through its historical links to the construction of the horror genre itself (Och and Stryer 2014: 1).

Indeed, affected by what might be termed the over-Hollywoodization of film, horror film has shown a greater dependence on CGI (computer-generated imagery) and expensive special effects. This has often led to an over-dependence on what might be called the 'trappings of horror' – a bland repetition of genre tropes and characters – and an associated self-awareness that sees a knowing, if not necessarily inventive, referencing of earlier texts in the genre. Costorphine sees this as an example of what he calls the postmodern mode, which 'can potentially serve to remove any sense of genuine dread' (2018: 16). This approach, while creating an extremely 'slick' or highly produced surface texture to horror films, often also sees them lacking in narrative intricacy, or forms of conceptual or existential dread that can resonate with an audience. Darryl Jones calls this category *Unhorror*, which

> resembles horror, and deploys, often in a very self-conscious and accomplished way, many of horror's tropes. Its vampires are better looking and have sharper fangs. Its

metamorphoses are seamless, using computer-generated imagery to transform its monsters in a way which comprehensively outdoes the attempts of the previous generation of make-up and visual effects artists. Its monsters are bigger and more destructive. (Jones 2018: 141)

A good example of this is the ongoing *Underworld* series of films (2003–present), where the vampires are largely young and good looking, the werewolf (lycan) transformations flash flawlessly before our eyes and the hybrid monsters get increasingly larger and outrageous with each installment.

In contrast to this is the appearance of what is being labelled by some as *Smart Horror* or *Elevated Horror*,[4] which emphasizes the more cerebral aspects of horror, without losing the shocks and jumps that have always been central to the genre. This often sees a return to the centrality of stories and plot to the horror genre and a deeper sense of the cultural concerns of the audience/reader and the anxieties of the times they live in, rather than a pandering to what is often seen as instant sensations and quick monetary returns. The film *Get Out* (2017) is a good example of this type of horror, as discussed later in this volume.

Horror, then, is an ever-transforming, repeating and re-inventing genre that continuously refers to the past as it evolves into the future. Revealing our darkest fears and anxieties whilst trying to restore a sense of order to a world that seems to imminently on the verge of destruction and spinning out of control.

The Shape and Aims of this Volume

This companion is made up of twenty-eight essays which focus on important approaches, mediums, categories, cultural contexts, and seminal authors and filmmakers within the horror genre to examine what horror is now, in the twenty-first century, and how it has been influenced by the past. Each essay uses

4   See Virtue 2018.

a contemporary example (e.g. novel, comic, or film) as a lens to looks at the wider implications of its chosen topic as a way not only to examine certain aspects within that subject but to purposely focus on its implications in the present.

The volume begins with 'Approaches to Horror', which highlights some selected ways of interpreting art-horror texts. Essays examine the ideas and philosophies behind some of the most popular recent horror narratives, that of seen and unseen dread and the horror that cannot be understood or dispelled ('The Limits of Knowledge' and 'Inconceivable Horror'). These are followed by considerations of two ways of engaging with and experiencing of contemporary horror ('The Affective Approach to Horror' and 'Performative/Queer Horror'), which describe how bodily responses and queer positioning can re-create horror and its possible meanings in ever new forms.

'Media and Mediums of Horror' is the second part and focuses on important developments in the genre that are fuelled by the inherent properties of certain technologies which have helped shape current horror. Subsequently, there are essays on horror in television, comics, gaming, music and new media, all of which examine how the medium itself not only carries horror narratives to its audience but is part of the story itself.

The third part, 'Categories of Contemporary Horror', looks at smaller topics and sub-genres within horror that continue to influence the direction of the wider genre as a whole. Considerations of 'Torture Porn', 'Eco-horror', 'Horror and Nostalgia', 'Science Fiction and Horror', 'Post-millennial Horror', and 'Smart Horror', reveal the dependence of the genre on its past but in ways which switch its focus to new directions.

'National and Cross-Cultural Horror in the Twenty-first Century' is the penultimate part and looks at the different cultures and traditions of horror and the varying ways they intersect, resonate with, or resist globalization. Essays on 'Contemporary Folk Horror', 'Euro Horror', 'Asian Horror', 'Argentinian Horror', 'African American Horror', 'First Nations Horror', 'Bollywood Horror' and 'Transnational Horror' discuss each area's specific cultural contexts and their expression through the horror genre. More importantly, they touch on ways in which other cultural or minority groups counter or embrace outside influences as they develop new and/or shared ways forward.

The final part, 'Horror Authors and their Contemporary Afterlives', selects seminal authors from the genre to reveal horror's continual connection to its past and how it is continuously adapted and transformed into the future. Listed in chronological order, essays on figures such as 'Edgar Allan Poe', 'H. P. Lovecraft', 'Horacio Queroga', 'Shirley Jackson', and 'Stephen King' pinpoint the ongoing influence of spectres from the past, their sudden and violent explosions into everyday life and the horror of the ordinary.

The companion takes readers on a path touching on theoretical frameworks and sub-genres, mediums and media, seminal authors and filmmakers, and different cultural contexts. As mentioned earlier, it is necessarily selective in the material covered but discusses its chosen topics in such a way as to meaningfully engage the reader and encourage further exploration. Indeed, horror, as an ever-evolving aspect of cultural anxiety and production, is by its nature never fully comprehensible. The nature of horror is glimpsed in Julia Kristeva's description of abjection:

> There looms, within abjection, one of those violent, dark revolts of being, directed against a threat that seems to emanate from an exorbitant outside or inside, ejected beyond the scope of the possible, the tolerable, the thinkable. It lies there, quite close, but it cannot be assimilated. (Kristeva 1980: 1)

This resistance to assimilation is important as it hints at the continual impetus towards individuality and evolution: horror is the inconceivable, the intolerable and the impossible of the future, often taking forms we cannot yet imagine.

Part I
Approaches to Horror

Murray Leeder

David Robert Mitchell's *It Follows* (2014)

In recent decades, more has been done to recognize that H. P. Lovecraft's works are not only reflective of Lovecraft's own personal philosophy, but that he constitutes a philosopher in his own right, particularly concerned with weirdness of the unhuman world and its challenge to humanocentrism (Harman 2011). In particular, Lovecraft is a pessimist deeply concerned with epistemology – what can be known, and especially what lies beyond knowledge. His story 'The Unnamable', written in 1923 and published in 1925, concerns a discussion between two men, Lovecraft's proxy Carter, a writer of weird fiction, and Manton, a high school principal. They debate whether or not it is possible for anything to be truly 'unnamable' – not just unnamed but so removed from human experience that it is impossible to name. Manton, a hard-headed Bostonian whose worldview interestingly combines Christian faith and scientific rationality, argues that Carter's fondness for the use of terms like 'unnamable' and 'unmentionable' and ending stories that left their protagonists without words to explain what had befallen them were 'puerile … quite in keeping with my lowly standing as an author' (Lovecraft 2008b: 256). In other word, Manton's belief system puts a considerable faith in human reason and its system of classifications. But Carter defends his works and the idea of the unnamable:

> so far as aesthetic theory was involved, if the psychic emanations of human creatures be grotesque distortions, what coherent representation could express or portray so gibbous and infamous a nebulosity as the spectre of a malign, chaotic perversion, itself a morbid blasphemy against Nature? Moulded by the dead brain of a hybrid nightmare, would not such a vaporous terror constitute in all loathsome truth the exquisitely, the shriekingly *unnamable*? (260)

By the end of the story, Manton has an encounter that brings him around to Carter's way of thinking: 'It was everywhere – a gelatin – a slime – yet it had shapes, a thousand shapes of horror beyond all memory. There were eyes – and a blemish. It was the pit – the maelstrom – the ultimate abomination. Carter, *it was the unnamable!*' (261, original emphasis). On some level, Manton is a straw man who exists solely to be proven wrong. It would be a mistake, however, to think of 'The Unnamable' as solely didactic; it is also among Lovecraft's most atmospheric tales, conveying a vivid sense of place. It takes place in Arkham, Lovecraft's pseudo-Salem, where a gloomy past is evident everywhere. The key debate is precipitated by Carter's observations on a gigantic willow tree that has nearly engulfed an ancient slab in a historic Arkham cemetery. This insistence on the primacy of the natural world, a world fundamentally indifferent to the objectives of human, provides a key counterpoint to its philosophical pursuits.

Let us compare a scene in *It Follows* (2014), one that seems almost incidental and yet reveals the film's core concerns. Jay (Maike Monroe) and her friends are trying to track down the man she knew as Hugh (Jake Weary), who purposely slept with her to 'infect' her with a curse that now threatens to kill her. Leaving their affluent Detroit suburb, they pass a landscape of post-industrial urban decay: run down houses, impoverished streets, and overgrown empty lots. They reach Hugh's house, an abandoned ruin, and, in an evocative, almost wordless sequence they survey its contents (see Figure 1).

Figure 1: Urban decay. *It Follows*, dir. David Robert Mitchell (RADIUS-TWC, 2014).

Hugh has boarded up the windows and left empty bottles and cans hanging in front of each one as a makeshift warning system. The bathroom sink is smashed and a wall collapses; the bedroom is a lone mattress and a stack of soft-pornographic magazines, the light coloured by pages from old comic books pasted in the window in place of curtains. Hugh, we understand, was striving to keep something out – the 'it' of the title – but the space has instead given way to a rot from within.[1]

The house becomes a microcosm for Jay's own life. Protected by race and class privilege, she has maintained a life of wilful ignorance of the decaying, enervated city that surrounds her. Of her friends, only Yara (Olivia Luccardi), the film's resident philosopher, comments on this situation directly as she describes the slow realization as to what her parents' restrictions on her movements through Detroit truly meant, and throughout the film Jay and her friends need to venture beyond their white enclave in order to investigate and combat Jay's curse in a variety of ways – all with ambiguous results at best.

The foe in *It Follows* does not neatly fold into the categories of 'villain' or even 'monster'. It is not gelatinous or slimy like the beast encountered by Manton, though it is fitfully abject (dripping with urine in an early appearance, and staging incest in another); it does not quite seem 'impure' in the sense outlined by Noël Carroll in his own philosophical treatment of Horror (1990). It amalgamates other kinds of horror figures: akin to *Invasion of the Body Snatchers* (1956), it can look like anyone, familiar or otherwise, and it is also invisible like Dr Griffin in *The Invisible Man* (1933) or the unseen rapist in *The Entity* (1981), a clear influence on *It Follows*. Though its motivations are speculated about, it ultimately has no clear qualities beyond what the title expresses: it follows. Perhaps it is more the kind of demon described by Eugene Thacker in terms of 'everywhere but nowhere ... fully immanent, and yet never fully present ... at once pure force and flow, but not being a discrete thing in itself, it is also pure nothingness' (Thacker 2011: 35–6). Like that other 'It,' that of Stephen King, *It Follows*' foe is a powerful, supernatural force with many guises. But unlike Pennywise, it has no name, no backstory and no Achilles heel. Barbara Creed draws attention to the frequency with which

---

1 For a more socioeconomic reading of this sequence and the film in general, see Kelly (2017).

defeating a monster involves naming it or otherwise comprehending it, learning the rules of its existence and therefore its weak points and the means of its destruction (Creed 1993: 29) – the Rumpelstiltskin narrative is exemplary in this regard. Once one knows what a vampire or a werewolf is, when one 'names' it, it becomes possible to fight it. But 'it' is part of a counter-tradition that Lovecraft contributed to, and which has a particular significance in the modern world. As John Clute writes,

> Horror is born at point when it has begun to be possible to glimpse the planet Itself as a drama: a very dangerous time in the history of the West, because it is at this point that … Enlightened Europeans were beginning to know it all, were beginning to think that glimpsing the world was tantamount to owning it. Horror is (in part) a subversive response to the falseness of that Enlightenment ambition to totalize knowledge and the world into an imperial harmony. (Clute 2006: 88)

In presenting its monster as intangible and unknowable (and generally unseeable), *It Follows* corresponds to this tradition of horror providing commentary on the limits of human knowledge and rationality. And yet it is also the perfect horror film for its contemporary moment, functioning as a sort of cinematic counterpoint to the millennial body of 'new horror theory' emblematized by Eugene Thacker's *In the Dust of This Planet* (2011). Thacker writes,

> The world is increasingly unknowable – a world of planetary disasters, emerging pandemics, tectonic shifts, strange weather, oil-drenched seascapes, and the furtive, always looming threat of extinction … it is increasingly difficult to comprehend the world in which we live and of which we are a part. (Thacker 2011: 1)

For Thacker, '*"horror" is a non-philosophical attempt to think about the world-without-us philosophically*' (9, original emphasis).

It can hardly be said that *It Follows* forgoes the human world and thinks about the unhuman world on its own terms; rather, it presents the unhuman as an implacable challenge that human prerogatives are simply not up to facing. Despite its small scope, *It Follows* is fixated on the notion of extinction. Early on, Yara reads a passage from Dostoyevsky's *The Idiot* from a clamshell-shaped personal device: 'I think that if one is faced by inevitable destruction – if a house is falling upon you, for instance – one must feel a great longing to sit down, close one's eyes and wait, come what may'. Later, herself wounded during a hare-brained attempt to defeat 'it,' she recites another passage which argues that the greatest agony of a wounded person is the knowledge of impending death: 'knowing for certain that within an hour, then within ten minutes, then within half a minute, now at this very instant – your soul will leave your body and you will no longer be a person, and that is certain; the worst thing is that it is certain'. Both quotes apply to the curse of death that hangs over Jay, but also broaden to the death sentence facing the human species itself in an age that promises extinction, whether it comes quickly or slowly.

It Follows borrows from films like *Night of the Demon* (Tourneur, 1957) and *Ringu* (Nakata, 1998) in presenting a transmittable curse, where those afflicted can save themselves by passing it to someone else. There is a marked difference, however, in that *It Follows* presents a curse that is not fully escapable: transmission merely buys time, reduces priority in 'its' unwritten hit list. It cannot be 'handed back', as in *Night of the Demon*, and there is none of the techno-utopian potential of *Ringu*'s ending, where it becomes clear that nobody need die so long as a careful network – the titular 'ring' – assumes and passes on Sadako's curse in turn by copying and watching the videotape. In *It Follows*, the curse is transmitted sexually, which suggests a generic link with the traditional role virginity and sexuality have had in the horror film, regarded as 'symptoms of a culture which is fascinated with sex but which still thinks of it in terms of guilt and transgression' (Ryan and Kellner 1998: 191). And yet it is difficult to read 'it' in any uncomplicated way as a 'walking STD,' since STDs cannot be avoided through more sex and there's little sense that 'frivolous' sex is its sole means of transmission.

Nonetheless, sexuality is extremely important to *It Follows* in its entanglement with death. It seems possible to read *It Follows* as a Heideggerian fable on ways of facing death, rather as Gilberto Perez has read *Nosferatu* (1922; Perez 2000: 123–48). In *It Follows*' striking opening sequence, Annie Marshall (Bailey Spry) flees her own suburban home and prepares for death alone on a lakeshore. She might represent a sort of authentic version of Heidegger's *Dasein* or 'being-towards-death' such as Perez finds in the sexualized self-sacrifice that ends *Nosferatu* – essentially the condition of accepting the inevitability of one's own death. Yet the spectacle of her mangled corpse challenges any notion of Annie's fate as a 'good death', and in any event, all the other characters fall short. Jeff (posing as 'Hugh') contrives to pass on a death sentence to save himself.

Of the two men who sleep with Jay to relieve her of her curse, Greg (Daniel Zovatto) – the character most akin to Manton from 'The Unnamable' – fails to acknowledge the danger and dies for his wilful ignorance, literally fucked to death by an image of his mother. While Paul (Keir Gilchrist) cares for Jay's wellbeing and instinctively trusts and believes her, his 'nice guy' demeanour shelters, as it so often does, a patriarchal sense of ownership over her. Both Jay (in desperation) and Paul (more calculatedly) seem to consciously pass the curse on, Jay to three men on a party boat and Paul to prostitutes in another seedy neighbourhood. Both offer up other human lives in order to buy themselves more time.

In the film's last scene, Paul and Jay walk hand in hand down a suburban street – they are apparently a couple now (the purchase of his self-sacrifice?) and yet their stiff body language demonstrates no contentment, no affection. The anxious tone that has attended most of the film has not fled; there is no non-diegetic music, yet the sounds (a man raking leaves on his lawn, children playing somewhere nearby) are uncomfortably high in the mix, adding to the tone of self-consciousness and anxiety lurking beneath the ordered appearance. In the penultimate shot, a male figure walks in their direction behind them: 'its' return (at centre frame, in 'its' traditional location) or simply a reminder that they can never feel safe again? The screen turns black, the droning, John Carpenter-inspired electronic soundtrack roars, and the name/description; 'It Follows' appears on the screen. Like the allegorical Sword of Damocles popularized by Cicero, death now seems prepared to drop on them at any moment ... or never.

In the film's uneasy non-closure lurks a set of questions linked to Yara's Dostoyevsky quotations: is it better to die at once or be killed by degrees? How does one live with the knowledge of death? Are Jay and Paul now living inauthentically, since their lives have been purchased at the expense of others? And yet these ethical questions seem ultimately secondary to the film's broader concerns with the implications of the unhuman, the unnameable and the unthinkable related to Lovecraft's philosophy of 'cosmic indifferentism.' As James Campbell writes, Lovecraft 'created a new kind of horror story by shifting the focus of traditional supernatural dread ... to a new crushing realisation that he and all mankind, far from occupying the centre of the cosmic stage even on earth, are scarcely important enough or long-enduring enough to occupy the stage's shabbiest corners' (Campbell 1996: 169). In *It Follows*, the promised fate of Jay and Paul is the promised fate of their species, an inglorious extinction that will consume the guilty and the innocent alike and render all philosophical quandaries moot. They – and we – cannot save themselves, but merely buy a meaningless stay of execution in the face of the usurpation of the human world. It draws to mind another Lovecraft quote, from 'The Call of Cthulhu': 'The most merciful thing in the world, I think, is the inability of the human mind to correlate all its contents. We live on a placid island of ignorance in the midst of black seas of infinity, and it was not meant that we should voyage far' (Lovecraft 2008a: 355). And it was always that way, but as we move deeper into what may prove humanity's last century, that ignorance grows harder and harder to maintain.

Gerry Canavan

Dan Trachtenberg's *10 Cloverfield Lane* (2016)

'Ours is indeed an age of extremity', writes Susan Sontag in her foundational essay on 1950s and 1960s science fiction film, 'The Imagination of Disaster'. 'For we live under the continual threat of two equally fearful, but seemingly opposed, destinies: unremitting banality and inconceivable terror. It is fantasy, served out in large rations by the popular arts, which allows most people to cope with these twin spectres' (Sontag 1965: 42). Sontag saw the science fiction cinema of her day as operating within a dialectic between escapism and normalization, with a single gesture 'inuring' us to the very horrors it distracts us from thinking about. She finds that such films follow an intensely formulaic pattern, with the alien invasion variety proceeding like clockwork from 'the arrival of the thing' to confirmation of its incredible powers in an act of mass destruction to the declaration of national emergency to the last-chance deployment of a countermeasure and finally the 'final repulse of the monsters or invaders', followed by the ambiguous worry: 'But have we seen the last of them?' (42–3). In the end, though, these films are all about the same thing: not science but disaster, 'the aesthetics of destruction, with the peculiar beauties to be found in wreaking havoc, making a mess' (44). Sontag's wide reading of the genre, with examples ranging from *The Thing from Another World* (Nyby, 1951) and *This Island Earth* (Newman, 1955) to *It Came from Outer Space* (Arnold, 1953), *Attack of the Puppet People* (Gordon, 1958), and *The Brain Eaters* (VeSota, 1958) and many more – which remarkably declares that 'there is absolutely no social criticism, of even the most implicit kind, in science fiction films' (48) – views them all as entirely symptomatic of larger social forces, as an understandable but wholly 'inadequate response' to the 'almost unsupportably psychologically' contemporary situation in which 'collective incineration and extinction ... could come at any time, virtually without warning' (48).

A Sontagian reading of the Cloverfield franchise would thus seem almost to write itself. The throwback 2008 sleeper-hit original, *Cloverfield* (Reeves), centred on a Godzilla-style kaiju monster attack on New York City, draws heavily from the chaotic, found-footage imagery of 9/11 rather than nuclear attack, but otherwise tracks Sontag's alien-invasion formula quite closely, right down to the breathy, terrified 'it's still alive' played over the ending credits. That the film itself deployed a marketing strategy designed to inculcate excitement and confusion in its potential audience – including the release of a teaser trailer that did not even give the name of the film – contributed to its eerie sense of a disaster that could suddenly and spectacularly erupt anywhere, at any moment. This 'surprise' branding would become the key to the Cloverfield franchise: *10 Cloverfield Lane* (Trachtenberg, 2016) was filmed in secret under a fake name, with its first trailer dropping less than two months before release, while the third movie in the franchise, *The Cloverfield Paradox* (Onah, 2018) was released unexpectedly on Netflix late in the evening on 4 February 2018, after first being advertised that same day, in an unannounced Super Bowl ad, with even the actors themselves not knowing the release strategy until that morning.

Both *Cloverfield* and *The Cloverfield Paradox* rely heavily on explosive science fictional spectacle for their internal narrative propulsion – but *10 Cloverfield Lane*, the middle film, is something of an outlier in the franchise. Not directly connected to the events of the original, but seen as a sort of spiritual sequel by the production company, Bad Robot, *10 Cloverfield Lane* begins with a wordless scene of Michelle (Mary Elizabeth Winstead) frantically packing up an apartment, while occasionally checking her phone or glancing through the blinds out the window. But despite the eerie depiction and the creepy sounds on the soundtrack – or the fact that a picture in the room seemingly blows over by itself, as if responding to the sway of the camera or a half-perceived sonic boom outside – she's not actually fleeing in the face of a monster attack; she's just leaving a bad relationship. Likewise, the report she hears on her car radio about widespread blackouts in the South is just a perfectly ordinary natural disaster, not a token of some larger science fictional catastrophe. Our knowledge that we are watching a Cloverfield film, and our familiarity with the wider genre of science fiction monster movie with which the franchise is in conversation, may reflexively cause us to scan the horizon, looking from signs of trouble – but there's no trouble to be found.

But then everything changes. T-boned by another car, Michelle's car flies off the road and she blacks out, while we smash-cut to the title: 10 CLOVERFIELD LANE. When she wakes up, she finds herself chained to a bed in an unfurnished cellar in a cast that immobilizes her leg. The gruff man who has brought her there – Howard (John Goodman) – offers bizarre responses to her questions and speaks in a disturbingly flat affect, and so we quickly revise our genre assumptions; now we are in *that* kind of movie instead, the kidnapping, the abduction. Michelle has seen such movies too, and (a born survivor) quickly takes action to protect herself, improvising a fire in the air duct that causes Howard to return to the room that is serving as her cell, at which time she attacks him with a wooden crutch she has cleverly sharpened into a weapon. Howard barely resists the attack and, after subduing her, explains that she is only there in the bunker at all because he has chosen to save her life: there has been some sort of massive attack on the surface, which is now contaminated by fallout; they have only survived because Howard built a bunker for just such a contingency. He is, he says, her rescuer, not her captor.

It all sounds crazy to Michelle, but another man trapped in the bunker with them, Emmett (John Gallagher Jr), believes Howard; Emmett is wearing a cast on his arm, he says, not because he got hurt trying to get out but trying to get *in*. Michelle isn't having any of it – until, during an escape attempt, she reaches the airlock on the surface and sees a deranged woman outside the bunker, visibly suffering the chemical or radiological effects of some sort of hyper-technologized attack, who frighteningly bashes her own head against the window when Michelle won't open the door. The ghastly scene persuades Michelle that Howard has been telling the truth all along. Having wrong-footed its audience over and over through its first third, constantly teasing plot developments that do not come to pass, in its second third *10 Cloverfield Lane* now settles into an odd sort of habituated, even old-fashioned domesticity; we see the three survivors doing puzzles, playing board games, eating together, and watching old movies over a montage set to the poppy, bubblegum original 1967 version of 'I Think We're Alone Now,' later covered by Tiffany in 1987 – a brilliant song choice that evokes the uncanny way that the newly domesticated sphere of the bunker evokes the childhoods of both Goodman and Winstead's characters simultaneously. Despite the occasional rumble in the distance, and the periodic ominous shaking of the world above, it's a reasonably good life for the three of them underground: an awkward but unexpectedly comfy ersatz family (see Figure 2).

Figure 2. Not even the end of the world can stop family fun night. *10 Cloverfield Lane*, dir. Dan Trachtenberg (Paramount Pictures, 2016).

Still, this is a Cloverfield film, and the relaxed mood cannot last; it turns out that despite apparently being right about the attack outside Howard is *also* a creepy kidnapper after all, as Michelle and Emmett find evidence that he had previously kidnapped a missing teenager from the area and forced her to live with him in the bunker as a replacement for the daughter he lost in a divorce. This discovery corresponds with the abusive childhood revealed to be part of Michelle's own backstory, a trauma she says she has relived whenever she was unable to help a child being yelled at by a father in a grocery store and which she is now finding inflicted upon her own person. The menace that had infused Howard's earliest presentation in the film now returns with a vengeance, imbricated with his newly dad-ish persona (nicely playing on Goodman's most famous role as the father on *Roseanne*) – perhaps most stunningly in an intense game of charades played among the three survivors that vacillates between amusing and terrifying and back again. Meanwhile, using Michelle's design knowledge and materials pilfered from Howard, she and Emmett are able to construct a hazmat suit to allow one of them to escape to the surface and look for help without being exposed to the fallout – but Howard discovers their work and murders Emmett, disposing of the body in a vat of sulphuric acid he has in the bunker. Now Howard switches his affect from creepy father to creepy husband, shaving, neatly combing his previously unkempt hair, and dressing nicely as Michelle is trapped only with him; he offers her ice cream before dinner, ambiguously noting 'I thought we'd change things up tonight. And have dessert before dinner. After all, we can do whatever we want now' – a creepy hint of the breakdown of the incest taboo in the face of nuclear war as depicted in such early Cold War works as Ward Moore's 'Lot' (1953) and 'Lot's Wife' (1954). Before things progress too far in this direction, however, Michelle is able to turn the tables and escape; recovering the hazmat suit, she incapacitates Howard and makes it to the surface, starting a catastrophic fire that ultimately destroys the bunker in the process. Behind her, a wounded and mutilated Howard bellows: 'You're going to walk out on me? After I saved you? And kept you safe? This is how you repay me?' We have swung all the way around to the other side of Sontag's extremities. It is the domestic sphere, the unending cycle of bad dads terrorizing frightened children that becomes the real horror, whether suburban or subterranean; the true nightmare is not that the apocalypse will upend the quiet misery of our lives together but that nothing, not even the apocalypse, ever could.

10 Cloverfield Lane has a final surprise for us, however. Despite the initial relief and serenity of returning to the surface, it turns out Howard's most paranoid theories were entirely true, despite his larger mental illness; the surface *is* held by grotesque alien invaders who are ravaging the surface, using roving drones and a mysterious green gas to exterminate any humans left. Michelle (truly a consummate survivor) soon takes down a large alien exterminator with an improvised Molotov cocktail, and steals a car to safely get away. A female voice on the car radio announces that a battle is being raged against the invaders, and the humans are winning; she says that any human survivors should head to Baton Rouge, which is said to be a sanctuary from the war – but adds that able-bodied people with combat or medical experience are needed in Houston to continue the fight. After a brief moment of contemplation, Michelle chooses

Houston, resolving now to be the sort of person who intervenes to help the innocent where she can (something she never could before the apocalypse); the film ends as we see her driving away towards her destiny, while a lightning flash ambiguously illuminates massive alien ships in the distance, directly in her path, threatening to render her steadfast heroic determination quickly and completely moot.

10 Cloverfield Lane trades on our familiarity with the 1950s monsters-from-space genre and its grim nuclear ideological subtext in multiple meta-textual ways: first, by exploiting our supposition that such narratives belong to a ridiculous past that no longer holds sway over us, and second by making them unexpectedly urgent and terrifying after all. Trading the old-style male scientist of Sontag's archive for a would-be fashion designer in Michelle, the switch from distinguished older man to younger, marginally employed woman belies a much more progressive social transformation in this sort of science fiction spectacle than a surface glance would suggest. Michelle's ability to survive extends beyond mechanical invention to an incredible ability to read and manipulate people; perfectly aware of a woman's stereotypical role in such stories as the one in which she now finds herself, she is able to swing fluidly from damsel-in-distress to flirty coquette to doting daughter to steely warrior woman and back again as the situation demands, to get what she needs out of the men around her. (Emmett's one attempt to move through personas the way Michelle can, in contrast, gets him killed almost immediately). Meanwhile, in Howard the masculine hero turns sour: adaptive, knowledgeable, and always prepared, having anticipated and planned for every contingency and in his own bizarre way a genuine genius, he is nonetheless the true monster of the picture, a toxic figure who views the world exclusively through the prism of his own wounded resentment and entitlement and destroys everything he encounters. Thus, Howard's cleverness and ingenuity only empowers him to build himself a sterile and miserable tomb, while Michelle finds ways to heal her own pain and (at least provisionally) reconnect to the larger world of collective life.

In his 1971 essay 'Metacommentary', Fredric Jameson remarks upon Sontag's essay and finds a path out of her hopeless dialectic between banality and terror through a different reading of the films with which she is concerned; the essay provides an early glimpse of the utopian theory with which Jameson would become so closely associated. Jameson identifies a utopian impulse beneath the surface level banality of such stories, which 'uses the cosmic emergencies of science fiction as a way of reliving a kind of wartime togetherness and morale, a drawing together among survivors which is itself merely a distorted dream of a more humane collectivity and social organization' (Jameson 1971: 17). Such a drawing together is teased first in the bunker, only to be poisoned by Howard's broken masculinity – and then teased a second time in Michelle's ambiguous sharp turn towards both the battle for Houston and those mysterious floating warships. I suspect that for many viewers the genre classification of *10 Cloverfield Lane* – whether it is 'really' a science fiction movie or a horror movie – may hinge in the end on that deeply ambiguous image: whether one concludes Michelle will soon be coming for those ships, or rather that they will soon be coming for her.

Xavier Aldana Reyes

Jaume Balagueró and Paco Plaza's *[REC]* (2007)

The early twenty-first century has seen a distinct move away from the psychoanalytic leanings that once dominated the academic analysis of horror film and towards the possibilities offered by more empirical approaches. This is not to suggest that studies like those by Robin Wood (1984), Carol J. Clover (1992) and Barbara Creed (1993) have become redundant or that there have been no psychoanalytically inflected horror studies in the new millennium. Some of the theoretical constructs put forward by the work of psychoanalytic critics during the 1980s and early 1990s have, in fact, become staples of horror criticism ('the return of the repressed') and even part of the general vocabulary utilized in the analysis of the genre's engagement with, for example, gender (the 'final girl', the 'monstrous-feminine', 'abjection'). As for new studies, a collection like Steven Jay Schneider's *Horror Film and Psychoanalysis* (2004) shows that the genre may still be productively mined for meaning using methodologies that favour notions like the uncanny or perverse pleasure. The recent embrace of the experiential realms of phenomenology, cognitivism and affect rather stems from a desire for more quantifiable means through which to study the subjective nature of viewership, an aspect that has been perceived to be ignored by psychoanalysis's essentialization of the figure of the spectator, not to mention his/her psychosexual straitjacketing. Naturally, such a view has been coloured by a more widespread rejection of abstract theory in film criticism, spearheaded in the 1980s and 1990s by David Bordwell and Noël Carroll, and a concerted effort to develop alternative strategies for the reading of films. As Bordwell and Carroll themselves note in the introduction to their landmark collection *Post-Theory* (1996), cognitivist approaches have the benefits of being pluralistic in their attempt 'to understand human thought, emotion and action by appeal to processes of mental representation, naturalistic processes and (some sense of) rational agency' (Bordwell and Carroll 1996: xvi), so that they appear as discrete stances rather than a Grand Theory.

Noël Carroll's influential 1990 study *The Philosophy of Horror, or Paradoxes of the Heart* (1990) took a significant first step towards what would become an affective mapping of horror by proposing a cognitive approach in its theorization of 'art-horror' as a type of literary or cinematic experience defined by emotion and thought processes connected to the figure of the monster. A more active viewer was also implicit in the work of Steven Shaviro (1993) and Cynthia Freeland (2002) and demanded by Matt Hills in his meticulous exploration of the pleasures of horror (2005: 13–32). Gilles Deleuze's thoughts on affect and affection, very much opposed to the psychoanalytic and structuralist underpinnings of Freudian and Lacanian theory, formed the backbone of Anna Powell's *Deleuze and Horror Film* (2005). Although this study was more evidently interested in thinking horror ideas through Deleuze's work – and the philosopher's writings are not themselves exempt from abstract ideas that often eschew scientific or empirical proof – Powell did much to reinscribe the body and its sensorium into the horror experience. Julian Hanich's *Cinematic Emotion in Horror Films and Thrillers* (2010) was a veritable turning point in terms of the development of a solid cognitivist and phenomenological methodology. His systematic breakdown of the various types of emotions associated with horror film (and some thrillers) – direct horror, suggested horror, cinematic shock, cinematic dread and cinematic terror – is an important reminder that horror does not always operate in the same way and that films are highly reliant on all the key elements that separate the cinematic medium from literature. Cinematography, sound and editing are only some of the key examples. My own *Horror Film and Affect* (Aldana Reyes 2016) attempted to think through the various affective layers encompassed by the horrific cinematic encounter and established at least three levels of interaction between the bodies of viewers and those of the horror film: representation (cultural), emotion (cognitive/phenomenological) and somatics (phenomenological). My aim in this book was to show that horror is not a simple emotion, but is actually made up of various sensorial and cerebral processes that are as culturally defined as they are governed by filmic spectacle. At the heart of cinematic horror, I argue, lies the thought of physical threat, of vulnerability (Aldana Reyes 2016: 49–54). Disentangling the various ways in which affect operates necessarily entails more than one approach: cognitivism (thought processes), phenomenology (emotion as connected to our perception of the world and ourselves) and the study of reflexes and instincts (somatics). In what follows, I use the Spanish film *[REC]* (2007) to illustrate how the affective approach can help us understand the mechanics of horror cinema.

Representationally, *[REC]* plays with the iconography of the horror film, more specifically with those of the haunted house and of the zombie film subgenres. The setting, a quarantined building in the centre of a generally sunny and touristy Barcelona, quickly becomes the 'terrible place' (Clover 1992: 30): its various rooms are rendered claustrophobic spaces where predatory creatures roam the dark; its structure is almost labyrinthine. Some of the rooms, like the attic, do not just play on tropes like that of 'the madwoman in the attic', developed by the nineteenth-century novel, but also operate as secret passages leading to higher octane horrors. The actual effects that these spaces can elicit on viewers are the more direct domain of cinematography, lighting and sound, yet, even at the level of surface and imagery, *[REC]* cannot help but invoke a long tradition in Western literature and film of old dark houses that harks back to the ominous castles of Gothic novels like *The Castle of Otranto* (1764) or *The Mysteries of Udolpho* (1794). Such buildings often represent a twisted version of the home and the domestic space (as indeed does *[REC]*), conjuring up a series of signifiers that are both defined by the cinematic medium and culturally specific. The rabid humans are not technically zombies, since they are not undead but possessed, and still they operate as the undead do in zombie films: they act instinctually, are incapable of coherent speech, pose a direct threat and signify danger and contagion. Any film seeking to make zombie-like creatures one of their foci of attention needs to engage with the representational history of the zombie film (see Figure 3). This is not to say that expectations of horror figures are not subject to revision – quite the opposite. Precisely because monsters, like any other motif in horror, are connected to a long filmic tradition that is alive in the popular imagination, filmmakers must either seek to innovate, retain certain parameters while changing others or simply copy extant models.

It is crucial, however, to disentangle representation from emotion, especially because this is precisely the move that several psychoanalytic approaches do not make. Rather than read the body of the monster as inherently bound up by psychosexual structures, it is of more experiential import to turn to aesthetics and formalism, especially as these come together to create specific affective moods and effects. This entails moving away from the zombie as interstitial, abject threat that conjures up certain feelings and reactions *per se* and towards the zombie as cinematic figure within a framework that includes framing (camera shots and angles), colour, lighting, editing, sound, costuming, set design and narrative pace, and which aims to generate a number of particular emotions. In the case of *[REC]*, the rabid creatures are obviously sources of threat, and the film plays with its reality TV and found-footage aesthetic to bring viewers closer to the action and, thus, to a potential alignment with the camera as victim. Little is known or shown of cameraman Pablo; this enables the viewer to inhabit the visual space of the camera in a way that replicates first person shooter games and survival horror. The soundscapes are intended to be jarring too. Animal cries dub the screams of the infected, humans shout in confusion and the lack of intradiegetic music allows for the atmospheric use of thuds and noises. The constantly moving handheld camera creates visual disorientation and displacement, most strongly on a first viewing, and can even cause motion sickness. These shooting techniques and postproduction work also make the film more realistic, imitating the mechanics of, for example, mobile phone video recording technology. The emotive mechanics of *[REC]* and found-footage horror are, on the whole, more complicated than I can cover comfortably in this article (see Aldana Reyes 2015a; 2015b), but they do not operate in isolation. Horror films attack viewers perceptually, and this means more than merely generating dread or suspense, as *[REC]* does by placing the main characters, especially Ángela (Manuela Velasco), in life-threatening situations. Emotions and thought processes are closely connected to proprioceptive or kinaesthetic processes – that is, somatics.

Emotions such as dread are complex and can be enhanced by even more thought-invested self-reflexive emotions like guilt or shame. Somatic reactions to cinema are no less complicated, but they are certainly not 'thought through',

Figure 3 (background image). Representationally, *[REC]* borrows from the haunted house and zombie horror subgenres. *[REC]*, dir. Jaume Balagueró and Paco Plaza (Filmax International and Castelao Productions, 2007).

as they rely on instinct and reflexes. If, in *[REC]*, the infected attacking the camera can make viewers jump, this is because they are perceived as a direct threat by the body/mind of the viewer, even if the latter is aware that what is being watched is fictional. Horror exploits the human sensorium in various ways: films often use bursts of loud, high-pitched noise micro-seconds before a jump scare in order to enhance the 'startle' reaction; they play with pacing (slow build-ups, the generation of dread) and composition (scares tend to come from corners or barely visible spaces within the frame, when not from directly outside it); they use (centre) framing to concentrate assaults on the area where vision is likely to focus or rest; they may even employ 3D technology to enhance the illusion of immersive interaction and thus of being under direct attack. Somatic reactions in horror film operate irrespectively of the representational value of the source of threat (which can even be a fluke, as in the cat scene in *Alien* (1979)), although this can also enhance impact, as can a narrative and emotional investment in the characters. In order to maximize intended effects, horror films, as in *[REC]*, tend to align viewers with the victims, rather than the perpetrators. Many films also utilize elaborate editing and multi-perspectival shooting (like cutting from killer to victim) to guarantee maximum affect (see Figure 4).

There is much more work that needs to be carried out in the field of Affect Studies and horror. Mathias Clasen has shown how evolutionary theory, especially how biological defence mechanisms that have evolved in humans throughout time, may help us bridge the gap between somatics and the cultural readings of horror. In his words, incorporating evolutionary theory can 'account for the ways in which specific works of horror reflect or engage with sociocultural issues' while 'locat[ing] such analysis within a framework' 'sustained and constrained by converging evidence from a wide range of disciplines and sciences' (2017: 5, 3). A concerted effort to draw attention to physiology, emotion and their relationship to cinema has made it possible to write about what were previously perceived as unimportant aspects of the filmic experience (the startle effect), but more interdisciplinary research needs to be carried out if we are to successfully marry neuroscience and horror cinema. Certain challenges arise from this enterprise: the contexts in which we watch horror and their effect on us vary from culture to culture and are changing substantially as new viewing practices (subscription streaming systems like Netflix) allow

Figure 4. An affective approach to *[REC]* would focus strongly on the emotional responses and somatic reactions that the film attempts to generate through, for example, its cinematography, sound and editing. *[REC]*, dir. Jaume Balagueró and Paco Plaza (Filmax International and Castelao Productions, 2007).

us to watch horror from tablets or mobile phones. Julian Hanich (2018) has begun to focus attention on the dynamics of the collective cinematic experience, albeit from a more general point of view that explores emotions that do not necessarily predominate in horror: laughter, tears and anger. Still, little research has been carried out on how spaces amplify or reduce horror effects, or how watching horror with other people can alter our subjective experiences. Phenomenological, cognitivist and affective approaches have sidestepped the main failings of psychoanalysis by focusing on the intended mechanics of the films themselves, rather than on a universal (normally passive) viewer. Such readings, including my own in this chapter, rely on what Carl Plantinga has called 'cooperative' viewers, that is, 'viewers who allow the film to do its intended emotional work' (Plantinga 2009: 97) and do not actively fight it. Such an approach does not establish a specific and unique form of reception, but rather focuses on the mechanics of cinema as an audiovisual medium and puts the emphasis on how films intend to function (their internal structures, scene dynamics, alignments and so on).

Another connected and overlooked aspect of affect in Horror Studies is the behaviour of those who love the genre. To propose that horror films operate in specific ways that rely on a number of affective strategies – even to suggest that these strategies are inflected by biology and human threat perception – does not offer any insights into how horror films live on beyond the screen. In other words, a shift is also needed from the experiential to the discursive, especially since horror audiences are some of the most loyal (horror festivals abound, as does merchandising for certain franchises) and fans of the genre are likely to behave differently from general viewers. For example, they might celebrate, rather than fear, the antics of a specific monster (the killers of the slasher film) or creatively engage in the storyline of given films (say, the *Jigsaw* series's fans who invent new death traps in blogs). Fan Studies are a growing subfield garnering increasing attention. Scholars have analysed the engagement of digital communities with specific texts and their related creative and critical practices (Cherry 2010; Booth 2011). Fan studies have also begun to pervade Film Studies more generally, becoming significant tools to be used in the historicization and contextualization of specific films. Kate Egan's excellent book *Trash or Treasure?* (2007), which analyses the history and reception of the video nasties, dedicates three chapters to exploring the afterlives of these films in fan communities. Cultural memory is as important as a renewed emphasis on form. Considering the ways in which fan culture and collectors relate to specific films today contributes to our understanding of the social and historical meanings of horror. Audience discourses, which may centre on challenging censorship or on celebrating specialist knowledge (Hills 2005: 71–107), cannot be ignored, and their study may well demonstrate that showing appreciation for the craft behind horror filmmaking does not necessarily have to be incompatible with the pleasurable consumption of its affective scenarios. The acknowledgement of fan practices can be productively understood as a continuation of broader cognitivist and phenomenological efforts to reinstate the value of the viewer to the cinematic experience while respecting personal difference and subjective specificity.

Finally, what is still missing from the affective picture is a stronger emphasis on what Matt Hills has termed 'empirical audience investigation' (2014: 105). Turning to fan discourses, especially their shared practices in open fora, is not quite the same as undertaking qualitative and quantitative audience research.

I mean very specifically the analysis of data, such as significant traits of those who watch horror films (age, gender, class, motivation), and of its study alongside targeted interviews. In the very few instances where the quantitative side of audience research has been carried out, as in Stephen Follows's *The Horror Report* (2017), this has come from an industry perspective. More research with audiences, like that of James B. Weaver and Ron Tamborini (1996) and of Brigid Cherry (1999), is needed, and the samples of participants need to be broader and more representative. There are obvious reasons why such studies have been few and far between: Film Studies scholars are not always trained to develop the type of sociological and anthropological skills necessary to tackle this type of research effectively. In short, Affect Studies is sure to benefit from truly interdisciplinary approaches to the study of audiences (who watches horror, how and why) as it continues to prod its workings for biological and perceptual primers.

Darren Elliott-Smith

Brad Falchuk's *American Horror Story* (2011–present)

In my recent book, *Queer Horror Film and Television* (Elliott-Smith 2016), I outline that post-2000 queer horror film and television renders the long-standing monstrous metaphor of queerness more explicit. These 'out' (but not necessarily proud) texts are largely created by queer-identified directors and producers; and contain narratives and characters that are unambiguous in their presentation of sexual difference. As a result, the symbolic value of monstrousness as a metaphor for the threat that homosexuality poses to heteronormativity, ceases to be coded and, instead, becomes open. Similarly, Stacey Abbott and Lorna Jowett remark in *TV Horror* (2014) that in recent years there has also been a noticeable boom in TV horror as part of a New Golden Age of television content.[1] Due to the diversification of cable channels and streaming platforms like Netflix, HBO Go and Amazon Prime, TV content has arguably become equally varied in its portrayal of non-normative and marginal characters, its presentations of diverse and alternative sexualities, and in its visualization of often taboo-breaking, visceral horror. The TV horror explosion demonstrates a merging of horror with other genres, an embrace of genre fusions that suggests a 'loosening up' of generic tropes and conventions marking a shift away from fixed genre forms (see *The Walking Dead* (Darabont, 2010–present) and *Preacher's* (Catlin, 2016–present) embrace of Western/Horror traits and *Bates Motel's* (Bloch, 2013–17) conflation of teen-drama/slasher elements). Such a thematic shift can also be seen in recent

---

1   See for example the discussion of the boom in TV Horror in Jowett, Abbott, Elliott-Smith, and Janicker (2016).

TV Horror's depictions of non-essentialist representations of gendered and queered identities.

The central text for analysis in this chapter is anthology Gothic horror series *American Horror Story* (henceforth *AHS*) which appropriates and pays nostalgic homage to a number of horror texts drawn both from TV and cinema. Across its (currently) seven seasons, the show has garnered a cult following in the LGBTQ+ community and attracted a wealth of interest in queer academic circles.[2] I argue that the appeal of *AHS* as the Queer Horror TV show *par excellence* lies specifically in its anti-essentialist queer appropriation of both gender *and* genre. The show's focus on the concept of identity-as-costume, allows the queer fans of *AHS* to experience a jouissance-filled immersion in genre, gender, identity and temporal forms that are all effectively shown to be constructed, culturally imposed and therefore, able to be assumed and rejected at will.

Co-creators Brad Falchuk's and Ryan Murphy's prior collaborative work[3] can be said to contain queer content whether in the form of LGBTQ+ characters themselves, or in stylistically camp melodramatic moments. However, *AHS* marks peak queerness within the Murphy and Falchuk canon. The show is undoubtedly queer in terms of its themes, its characters, and arguably its very narrative architecture. Each season of *AHS* contrives to present a self-contained story while utilizing the same stable of actors and actresses (very much like a theatre ensemble) playing different characters in a recognizably excessive and grotesquely camp style. The show, to a greater or lesser extent, also exudes a queer sensibility in its explicit focus on alternate sexualities but perpetuates the penchant for the 'performative'[4] via an emphasis on shifting and fluid identities and the inclusion of 'drag' or 'dress up' within its narratives and aesthetics. While horror clearly dominates as the overwhelming generic, formal, thematic and aesthetic choice, it shifts (often outrageously) between

---

2   See, Janicker 2017, Geller and Banker 2017, and Sevenich, 2015.
3   These include medical drama *Nip/Tuck* (Murphy, 2003–10) and the queer infused high school musical *Glee* (Brennan, 2009–15)
4   Judith Butler's seminal work on gendered bodies and performance theory rejects stable categories of gender and addresses how subjects 'perform' sexuality and gender identity. She claims that gender is socially constructed and entirely performative. Butler writes that, 'Gender reality is created through sustained social performances' (1990, 192–3).

gross out comedy, period melodrama, reality-TV pastiche (*AHS: Roanoke* (2016)) and even the musical (*AHS: Asylum* (2012–13), *Coven* (2013–14) and *Freak Show* (2015) feature blatant instances of musical pilfering and explicit musical performances).

AHS also captures the zeitgeist of other successful TV dramas in its embrace of the trend towards fetishistic nostalgia[5] featuring frequent flashback/forwards to dates and places announced via black and white Rennie Mackintosh-style inter-title cards. Across the first three seasons, each created 'world' has been self-contained, ranging from the story of a family moving into a house overwhelmed with ghosts on the outskirts of present-day Los Angeles (*AHS: Murder House* (2011)), to *AHS: Asylum*'s (2012–13) tale of a Massachusetts mental institution, Briarcliffe, which is largely set in 1964, to the history of the slave trade and a war between white witchcraft and black voodoo in New Orleans as seen in *AHS: Coven* (2014) with a timeline that is more excessively fractured. Season four *AHS: Freak Show* (2015), set in one of America's last Freak Show carnivals in 1950s Florida, marks a shift in the approach to the canon of *AHS*. The creators from this point onwards outwardly acknowledged, with the reappearance of a character from a previous season, namely Pepper (Naomi Grossman) from *AHS: Asylum*, that the series takes place in a multiverse of sorts which has led to 'Easter egg' style reappearances of characters from seasons past.

Each season speaks to distinctive American social, cultural, and political tensions (still felt today), being set in different decades in American history from the 1950s/60s to the present day. *AHS*'s narrative architecture serves to reinforce the queerness of its characters,[6] as they are contained in an eternal diegesis subject to the thematic anxieties of the cycle. This means that they are simultaneously self-contained yet endlessly layered and excessive, subject

---

5   See for example Niemeyer and Wentz 2014.
6   Explicitly queer characters range from: *Murder House*'s gay interior designer Chad Warwick (Zachary Quinto); the 'outed' investigative reporter Lana Winters (Sarah Paulson) and her girlfriend Wendy (Clea Duvall) in *Asylum*; Stanley (Dennis O'Hare), closeted gay 'strongman' Dell Toledo (Michael Chiklis) and his lover Andy (Matt Bomer) in *Freak Show*; Lady Gaga's bisexual vampire the Countess, her lovers Ramona Royale (Angela Bassett), Tristan (Fran Wittrock) and Dennis O'Hare's iconic queer bar-tender Liz Taylor in *Hotel*.

to timelessness and spacelessness, operating within *AHS*'s queer narrative design. The pleasure of identity-queering 'dress-up' that *AHS* showcases then extend to what Geller and Banker note is a form of 'temporal drag' (Geller and Banker 2017: 37), whereby the show effectively 'wears the clothes' of the period it re-presents in often stylistically excessive ways. While the 'performative' appropriation of period, gender and genre allows for self-assertion that draws attention to the constructed-ness of mainstream generic and heteronormative gender forms; it can also operate as a form of *self-divestiture*. The jouissance implied in this *self-loss* is afforded to the subject via an immersion in appropriation, 'role play', performance, adaptation and in the self-reflexive layering of the texts themselves.

AHS's capacity to appropriate cultural forms, and its tendency towards repetition and mimicry, operates to oppose essentialism. By highlighting the constructed-ness of genre, of gender and of identity *per se* but it also functions to *deconstruct* that same meaning. The appeal of such performative Queer Horror is also due to an obsessive identification with character types, gestures, music, narrative and the aesthetics that are borrowed from the genre, and that there is an insatiable compulsion to repeat such adaptation and appropriation over and over via parody and pastiche. Kamilla Elliott writes that Gothic screen parodies often work due to 'the attention parody draws to film forms [which] heightens awareness of their constructedness and, by extension, the discursive constructedness of the Gothic' (Elliott 2007: 223). While the appeal of *AHS* clearly lies in its own recurring self-reflexivity, the show's compulsion to repeat effectively creates a familiar/unfamiliar *mise-en-abîme* effect both *within* and *across* each season.

As a cult television show, *AHS* arguably combines what Sarah Gwenllian-Jones calls 'immersive and interactive logics' (Gwenllian-Jones 2002: 89–90) via its performative and self-referential structures. The show has even inspired its own interactive theme park attraction at Universal Studios Florida and Universal Orlando Resort in the form of a 'walk through maze'[7] homage to past seasons. Gwennllian-Jones continues that cult television often queers the

---

7 As part of its 'Halloween Horror Nights' Universal Orlando and Universal Studios publicized immersive theatre sets based on the previous *AHS* seasons prior to 2017, see LeBar 2017.

rigidity of heteronormativity via its presentation of camp, alternative sexuality, excess, and *immersive* performance. Further to this I would argue, that *AHS* encourages a spectatorial experience akin to that found in immersive theatre.[8] The concept of 'temporal drag' is central to the appeal of *AHS*'s immersive horror. Geller and Banker continue that, temporal drag has 'all of the associations that the word "drag" has with retrogression, delay, and the pull of the past on the present', as such the term arouses a typically queer subversion of gender norms, via the drag-like-performance of shifting identities seen in *AHS*, while also 'suggesting a queer relationship to time and history' (Geller and Banker 2017: 39). I want to extend upon the exaggerated theatrical adornment of particular time periods, to include the cultural borrowing of iconic queer oriented pop-cultural artefacts and influential horror film/TV imagery and soundtracks.

In its opening two seasons, *AHS* runs riot in its queer appropriation of the horror genre, with its pop-cultural pastiche ranging from: *Rosemary's Baby* (Polanski, 1968), *The Entity* (Furie, 1982), *The Brood* (Cronenberg, 1979), *The Shining* (Kubrick, 1980) in *Murder House*; *The Exorcist* (Friedkin, 1973), *The X-Files* (Carter, 1993–present), *One Flew Over the Cuckoo's Nest* (Forman, 1975) and *Carrie* (De Palma, 1976) in *Asylum*; *Freaks* (Browning, 1931) inspires *Freak Show*; and *The Hunger* (Scott, 1983) *Se7en* (Fincher, 1995) and *House on Haunted Hill* (Malone, 1999) are among the narrative and visual influences in *Hotel*. *AHS* continues with its heteroglossic revelry with the quoting of recognizable audial motifs and scores from iconic horror films comprising: soundtracks from *Psycho* (Hitchcock, 1960), *Vertigo* (Hitchcock, 1958) and *Twisted Nerve* (Boulting, 1968); *Bram Stoker's Dracula* (Coppola, 1993), *Carrie* (1976) and *Candyman* (Rose, 1992). This then shifts to explicit musical performance in *AHS: Coven* with its explicit reference of Fleetwood Mac in the diegesis, and the appearance of Stevie Nicks playing herself as a white witch who performs several numbers including 'Seven Wonders' and 'Sara'. Musical performativity of *AHS* becomes overwhelmingly palpable in *Freak Show*'s introduction of regular performance slots in which various characters entertain and sing on and off-stage. Jessica Lange's fading diva Elsa Mars is a draggy

---

8 Consider such 'walkthrough' immersive productions such as *The Masque of the Red Death* (2007), *Sleep No More* (2009 and 2011) *The Drowned Man: A Hollywood Fable* (2013) by Punch Drunk Theatre Company, which is often referred to as *promenade theatre*.

send-up of Marlene Dietrich's star persona (see Figure 5) complete with her thick, exaggerated German accent, peroxide blonde wig and androgynous suits.

Figure 5. Elsa Mars in Dietrich-drag. *American Horror Story*, created by Brad Falchuk and Ryan Murphy (20th Century Fox Television, 2011–present).

Parodying Dietrich's distinctive off-key singing voice, Mars atonally delivers many of the show's queer-uncanny cover versions including Bowie's 'Life on Mars?' and 'Heroes'. The queer jukebox of songs and scores referenced in *AHS* perhaps finds its most obvious centre in one episode from *Asylum*. 'The Name Game' (Series 2, Episode 5) draws attention to the queer Gothic's potential for performative pleasures and outrageous camp in its presentation of a shambolically choreographed dance scene to a cover of 'The Name Game' by Shirley Ellis. Here Sister Jude (Jessica Lange) fantasizes singing with her fellow inmates at the mental asylum, and during the performance various characters' names from the show are effectively 'queered' via the lyrics' recurring rhymes:

> Pepper-Pepper bo-Pepper,
> Banana-fana fo-Feffer,
> Me-mi, mo-Mepper,
> Pepper!

Brad Falchuk's *American Horror Story* (2011–present)   41

In doing so, Jude effectively invites the gathered crowd, and the spectator of *AHS* to take part in the songs (and the show's) queer identity play. 'The Name Game' efficiently represents the appeal of the *self-loss* afforded by performative oriented Queer Horror that is depicted via on-screen and off-screen identity play and fluidity.

The show perhaps reaches its intertextual peak in its sixth season, *Roanoke*, where the very structure of the series begins to disintegrate into parody and pastiche of various clichéd reality horror and paranormal TV programming. The lines become continually blurred between the various fictional reality shows: the first third of the series follows 'My Roanoake Nightmare' (the original interview/reconstruction documentary), before moving onto another *show-within-a-show* 'Return to My Roanoake Nightmare' (a self-referential, 'found-footage' style show where the actors who portrayed the 'real life' people in the previous show's story go back into the haunted house with their 'real' counterparts). The final sections of the season are given over to 'Crack'd' (a show mimicking the true-crime reality series format following Lee Harris (Adina Porter) the sole survivor of the original Roanoke story), clips from 'Spirit Chasers' a parody of paranormal investigation serials; and finally, 'The Lana Winters Special', where central protagonist Lee Harris is interviewed by *AHS*'s returning 'celebrity journalist' character Lana Winters (Sarah Paulson). Dawn Keetley describes this narrative and thematic dilapidation as 'entropic Gothic', whereby the show's 'trajectory [moves] towards exhaustion and stasis … as entropy transforms energy from useful to useless and ordered to disordered' (Keetley 2013: 97). *Roanoke* reaches the most frenetically queer entropic exhaustion in its self-aware *mise-en-abîme* conceit, even making a reference to *AHS's* own cult followings at various pop-culture conventions, such as Comic Con. In 'Chapter Ten' (Season 6 Episode 10) the 'cast' of 'My Roanoke Nightmare' appear on stage at a fan convention to reveal stories behind the headlines and are introduced and interviewed by *RuPaul's Drag Race* (Logo/VH1 2008–present) alumna Trixie Mattel. *AHS* takes the concept of the entropic literally as its multiple overlapping storylines (and timelines) are concluded, characters killed off one by one and the narrative thrust moves towards a post-coital climax, before its seasonal reset where the rebirth and recasting of certain actors and characters continues in queer-uncanny form: unfamiliar turned familiar.

In conclusion for its queer fans, the lure of *AHS* lies precisely in the show's predilection for chaos and collapse. In its drag-like embrace of clichéd genre tropes, iconic horror film and TV references, and its adoption of fluid, performative gender traits; *AHS* confronts and challenges the essentialist notions of subjective *authenticity*. Queer Horror shows like *AHS* represent modes of imitation, mimicry and immersion that develop from LGBTQ culture's queering of binary gender norms and heteronormativity via 'performative' play. In terms of the fragility of gender Butler concludes that the possibilities for a transformation of identity can be found in a 'failure to repeat, a de-formity, or a parodic repetition' (Butler 1990: 192). This notion of the fragile surface coupled with the foregrounding of that same surface performance in order to draw attention to the constructed-ness of cultural identity is precisely what *AHS* utilizes in its parodic costumery and intertextual references. In drawing *deliberate attention* to the pleasures of excess, camp performance and mimicry, *AHS*'s unoriginal repetition works precisely *because* of this failure to convince as entirely original.

Part II
Media and Mediums of Horror

Lorna Jowett and Stacey Abbott

Victor Fresco's *Santa Clarita Diet* (2017–present)

In October 1996, *The X-Files* (Carter 1993–2002, 2016–18) broadcast one of its most notorious episodes, 'Home' (4.2). With themes of incest, infanticide, and extreme bodily deformity, the episode was met with audience complaints and was never reshown on Fox. It continues to be listed as one of the scariest examples of TV Horror (Tallerico 2017). In 2017, the global on-demand streaming service Netflix launched an original series *Santa Clarita Diet* (2017–), a half-hour sitcom about middle-aged realtors Sheila (Drew Barrymore) and Joel Hammond (Timothy Olyphant) who must cope with the discovery that Sheila has become a zombie, with the requisite hunger for human flesh ('So Then a Bat or a Monkey' 1.1). With its California location, sunny lighting, and warm colour scheme, this series could not seem more different from 'Home', an episode that pushes *The X-Files*' iconic chiaroscuro to horror-laden extremes. Yet both, broadcast over twenty years apart, use horror to deconstruct themes often central to horror and to TV: family, gender, suburbia, and home. Their focus upon the domestic demonstrates that television is an ideal location for horror and the genre has been integral to television history, particularly in the USA and UK. *Santa Clarita*, however, highlights a changing landscape in which horror has reached unprecedented visibility and popularity across multiple broadcast platforms; takes a multitude of forms and formats; and is aimed at diverse audiences. Twenty-first century TV horror continues to transgress the boundaries of genre, gender, acceptability, good taste and, even platform, spilling out from our screens onto laptops, tablets and phones, making *Santa Clarita* an ideal starting point for examining television horror.

Since releasing its first 'original production', *House of Cards* (Willimon 2013–18), Netflix has become the go-to site for talked-about TV. It is hardly a coincidence, then, that its second original series was *Hemlock Grove*

(McGreevy, 2013–15), a horror series since followed by a range of horror TV such as *Mindhunter* (Penhall, 2017–), *iZombie* (Ruggiero/Thomas 2015–), *Black Mirror* (Brooker, 2011–13 and 2016–), *Dark* (Odar, 2017–), and *Stranger Things* (Duffer, 2016–). Some are Netflix productions, others originated elsewhere before being bought by Netflix, and yet others are canned products snapped up by the streaming service. *Black Mirror* is British while *Dark* is the first German-language (and German-produced) Netflix original series, and a Turkish vampire series *Immortals* (another first for Netflix) was launched in 2019. The abundance of horror television available via Netflix demonstrates how horror has bled from traditional TV into a convergent, multimedia world, finding new (global) models and operating as transmedia.

Netflix plays with the forms of TV horror in series like *Santa Clarita* and those mentioned above. *Stranger Things* taps into 1980s retro-nostalgia through music, narrative detail and visual design, with the award-winning title design influenced by earlier eras of horror. Michelle Dougherty, of credit sequence designers Imaginary Forces relates, 'When [series creators] the Duffers came to us, they wanted it to feel like Halloween in the Eighties…' The Duffer Brothers were, according to Dougherty, eager to evoke typefaces from 1980s horror novel covers, specifically Stephen King books (*Telegraph* reporters, 2017). Pre-launch season 2 promotion included a Twitter campaign #strangerthursdays which featured mash ups of old horror movie posters such as *The Evil Dead* (Sam Raimi 1981), *Firestarter* (Mark L. Lester 1984), and *Nightmare on Elm Street* (Wes Craven 1984). Promotion for *Santa Clarita* has not been as elaborate, though it combines genre imagery: crisp images of the main characters are bathed in California sunshine, presenting an idyllic suburban family until you notice the blood – a spatter, a drip, a smear. Without attentive study, the images could easily be taken at face value as promoting a white picket fence sitcom.

Less well-known examples exploit distinctiveness and the potential of multiple platforms. Canadian web series *Carmilla* (Hall, Ouaknine and Bennett, 2014–), comprising multiple seasons, inter-seasonal content, and a movie, is a highly successful digital adaptation or reimagining of Sheridan Le Fanu's 1872 novella with episodes averaging 1 million YouTube views. Translated into twenty languages, with viewers in 193 countries, the web series demonstrates the flexibility of horror and television, tapping into new technologies and media forms by telling its story via the vlog of university student Laura. *Carmilla*'s contemporary campus setting inflects and updates how the characters – almost all non-binary/non-heteronormative – operate within the story. In a less overt fashion, *Santa Clarita* introduces the Hammonds as middle-class, professional, heterosexual, white suburban dwellers – but the normative is subverted once Sheila becomes a zombie. Horror unsettles and destabilizes; on TV it plays with pleasure and transgression in terms of content and the televisual, often by juxtaposing genres.

Genre hybridity is inherent in television drama and plays a significant role in contemporary TV horror, as evidenced by the integration of horror with the police procedural (Zuikker, *CSI*), psychic investigation (Caron, *Medium*), zombie apocalypse (Darabont, *The Walking Dead*) and detective fiction (Thomas, *Veronica Mars*) in *iZombie*. The focus on character development led to George Romero describing *The Walking Dead* as a 'soap opera with a zombie occasionally' (cited by Han 2013). Today's competitive media often structures long-form serial narrative upon a hybrid genre matrix and Netflix uses micro-genres to appeal to many potential audiences, as argued by Stella Gaynor (2018), and seen in *Hemlock Grove* and *Stranger Things*, as well as *Santa Clarita*. *Hemlock Grove*'s hybridity merges family melodrama, teen TV, romance, Gothic and horror in the tradition of *True Blood* (Ball, 2008–2014) and *The Originals* (Plec, 2013–17); *Santa Clarita* is one in a line of supernatural sitcoms beginning in the 1960s with *The Munster's* (Haas/Liebmann, 1964–6), *The Addams Family* (Levy, 1964–6) and *Bewitched* (Saks, 1964–72) where 'staple Gothic characters [were presented] as "just plain folks," taking the American-Gothic family-centric narrative and image repertoire into the suburban world of the white picket fence and the Ladies League' (Wheatley 2006: 126). Like these earlier series, *Santa Clarita* merges family sitcom with horror and teen comedy to attract multigenerational audiences. The mainstream success of *The Walking Dead* signals the crossover potential for horror – no longer exclusively targeting established horror fans but drawing viewers through its character melodrama – and *Santa Clarita* maximizes this with parallel narratives focused on Joel and Sheila dealing with the changes to Sheila's zombified body in relation to work and their marriage, alongside arcs tracking how daughter Abby (Liv Hewson), accompanied by geeky friend Eric (Skyler Gisondo), develop a maturing understanding of her parents' fallibility and mortality. The first two seasons follow

Abby's transition from wanting to do 'cool' things like her parents (including killing people and disposing of bodies), to taking on a productive role within the family, high school, and society by protecting her parents from discovery ('Strange or Just Inconsiderate' 1.7), saving Eric from a zombie-girlfriend ('The Queen of England' 2.4), defending a fellow student from bullying ('The Queen of England'), and rescuing Santa Clarita from fracking ('Going Pre-Med' 2.5).

While the show takes ground covered by earlier supernatural sitcoms, the incorporation of the zombie allows a more abject and inherently unstable presence to erupt into the familiar sitcom landscape. Lily Munster (Yvonne DeCarlo), Morticia Addams (Carolyn Jones) and Samantha Stephens (Elizabeth Montgomery) regularly disrupted the traditional family home and offered transgressive gender depictions, yet their monstrous nature was contained by network sitcom conventions. The zombie, however, is physically and metaphorically abject, and Sheila transgresses physical, emotional, psychological and moral boundaries. Every time she seems to be narratively contained, by a cure or by chains in the basement, she breaks free, even if that means dislocating her thumbs to get out of handcuffs ('No Family is Perfect' 2.1). Thus, she has much in common with Kieran Walker, the zombie-protagonist of BBC series *In the Flesh* (Mitchell, 2012–14) who disrupts the status quo of his home town Roarton by overturning zombie truisms and queering the genre. In *Santa Clarita*, the abject zombie signals the overt transition of the supernatural sitcom from Gothic to graphic body horror, transgressing expectations and aesthetic boundaries.

In *TV Horror* we argued that 'from the early days of television to the present, industrial and broadcast restrictions encourage horror creators to use stylistic excess to convey the macabre, the abject, the gothic and the uncanny, and to generate fear or unease' (Jowett and Abbott 2013: 13). This stylistic excess continues in *Penny Dreadful*'s (Logan, 2014–16) wallowing in the aesthetics of nineteenth-century Gothic classics, and *American Horror Story* (Falchuk/Murphy, 2011–) embeds visual and aural citations to classic horror films such as *Freaks* (Browning, 1932), *Psycho* (Hitchcock, 1960), and *The Hunger* (Scott, 1983) within its sumptuous aesthetic design. More significantly, the shift from the 1950s-80s network era to the on-demand era of the 2010s has witnessed an increasing liberalization of television that has rendered horror far more visible;

the excessive styles of *Penny Dreadful* and *American Horror Story* incorporating graphic blood and gore. This is evident by the positioning of *The Walking Dead*, initially developed for NBC, on cable channel AMC, who, in 2010, were far more receptive to the visceral requirements of zombie TV. By 2013, however, NBC were broadcasting *Hannibal* (Fuller, 2013–15), a series featuring weekly depictions of serial murder and cannibalism that merged art-house stylistic excess with graphic splatter. *Santa Clarita* demonstrates the next stage of this liberalization, integrating comedy and horror but emphatically *not* using comedy as a substitute for gore nor to render the horror safe. Instead, the series, like Starz' *Ash vs Evil Dead* (Raimi, 2015–18), liberally splatters the screen with blood and bodily excretions, daring the audience to laugh, recognizing and successfully navigating the fine line between horror and comedy.

The first episode, 'So Then a Bat or a Monkey' includes two graphic set pieces. The first is when Sheila, showing a house to prospective buyers, unleashes a torrent of green vomit onto a bedroom floor, first in medium close-up as vomit spews toward the camera, then moving to long shot, emphasizing its spread and consistency. Further highlighting the simultaneously disgusting and humorous nature of this moment, Sheila plays out the rest of this scene with vomit entangled within her hair and smeared across her face. The second set piece has Sheila's colleague Gary (Nathan Fillion) make unwanted sexual demands; she responds by first licking his fingers but then biting two off. As blood fountains from Gary's hand, Sheila, covered in blood, tells him, 'I know: weirdest foreplay ever'. This marks her final transition into a zombie: once she has tasted human flesh there is no going back, as reinforced by the episode's final image when Joel comes home to find Sheila kneeling over an eviscerated Gary. With bits of flesh and sinew dripping from her mouth, she tells Joel, 'I really want to make this work'. The graphic gore in this episode and throughout the series signals Sheila's, and the show's, transgression. Repeated images of Sheila covered in blood challenge conceptions of normality. This is, after all her 'new normal' (as Barrymore describes it in one interview)[9] and the comedic use of blood and gore insists that Sheila cannot be recuperated into traditional gender roles.

9   Shoen 2018: n.p.

Themes of identity, power, the body, and voyeurism ensure that gender is a key factor in horror. Increasing attention to how media products are made, and by whom, means that horror is now debated in terms of women behind as well as in front of camera: Barrymore's role as executive producer of *Santa Clarita* and her performance as Sheila indicate a high level of engagement with the series, despite her reluctance to accept the role initially (Shoen 2018: n.p.). Recent research has shown that horror is the genre where female characters speak most and have most screen time ('The women ...' 2017). Of course, greater screen time doesn't mean women are represented positively. Peter Hutchings argues that horror 'functions as a potentially queer space for its audiences, one that offers illicit and transgressive (especially sexually transgressive) identifications and pleasures, if only ultimately to recuperate and contain these' (Hutchings 2004: 89). Therefore, horror allows for gender fluidity, and is prepared to celebrate transgression of social norms, rules and limitations.

Lorna Jowett has argued elsewhere that horror speaks to women and girls because of the horrors of female lived experience (see horror's rape revenge subgenre, for instance; Jowett 2018). In order to survive this, it helps to have a support network, and *Santa Clarita* is a neat example of this. Horror often presents the mother as monster, but Sheila is no abject monstrous female – or not in a bad way. The fate of the predatory Gary indicates that *Santa Clarita* celebrates the monster as a release from social expectations. This is seen increasingly during season 2 where Sheila works off zombie energy by boxing with sheriff's deputy Anne (who is one half of a lesbian couple); Eric's would-be girlfriend Ramona is content with her lack of 'normal' emotion; and Abby addresses social media harassment by publicly hitting the offender in the face with a tray ('The Queen of England'). The positive relationship between Sheila and her daughter is given significant screen time: in season 1 they enjoy mother-daughter time ('The Book!' 1.9) and in season 2 when Sheila is chained in the basement Abby joins her and Joel in bed, thinking it isn't right for her to be alone ('No Family is Perfect'). As a female monster, Sheila is accepted by those who love her, and none of the characters are under the illusion that they, or the events they now experience as every day, are normal (unlike the supernatural sitcoms of the 1960s).

Given how Sheila relishes her release from social conventions, the series' representation of masculinity is also affected. Joel often laments the loss of normality and elements of gender reversal are apparent in his 'hysterical' responses to ongoing events (shrieking, nervousness, especially when having to distract others from zombie goings-on). Sheila's energy and the gore that surrounds her, coupled with Joel's screams and bizarre postures suggest that neither can neatly 'fit' gender or other social categories, both burst through attempts to confine them to particular roles or behaviours. Their ability to adapt to and embrace non-normative identity indicates an openness to new ways of being also reflected in their acceptance of Gary's decapitated-but-conscious head (now free of machismo, presumably because he is equally free from patriarchal social structures), and of Ramona and Mr Ball Legs (the organ vomited up by new zombies, which later grows legs), while their selection of neo-Nazis as ideal victims ('Moral Gray Area' 2.3) slyly suggests that they still have recognizable standards.

Barrymore and Olyphant appearing on breakfast TV to promote *Santa Clarita*, signals its mainstream success along with the ubiquitous nature of horror on twenty-first-century television. But as we have shown this ubiquity does not necessarily mean that horror on television cannot, or does not, continue to push boundaries. In fact, it signals the degree to which TV horror continues to transgress and cross thresholds into the home in new and unsettling ways.

Julia Round

Joe Hill and Gabriel Rodriguez's *Locke & Key* (2008–2013)

Horror as a literary and cinematic genre revolves around the shocking, grotesque and obscene. It sits in counterpoint to other forms of Gothic such as terror, which is defined by Radcliffe as the threatening, obscured and unknown. Many past horror comics combine these two strategies, moving from unseen threat to shocking reveal (EC Comics and Warren Publishing) and contemporary works also range between these two poles, from the explicit and violent (*Crossed*, Ennis and Burrows 2008–10) to the implicit and psychological (*Adamtine*, Berry 2012). Both types of fear are well suited to the comics medium, whose stylized art and staccato panels enable grotesque images and horrifying reveals. The medium also exploits terror's imaginative potential as events can be hidden between panels and the reader must also interpret the shown content.

Critical interpretations of horror and Gothic have often applied psychoanalysis (Schneider 2001). In such readings the spaces of horror blur the psychological and physical. Settings are both iconographic and symbolic and often stand as metaphors for the text's themes or characters. Dr Frankenstein has his 'workshop of filthy creation'. Castle Dracula is isolated, foreign and mysterious – full of long passageways and closed doors. Buffalo Bill has a secret, feminine sewing room. Eleanor 'come[s] home' to Hill House, Mrs Rochester has her attic (referencing concealment and mental disturbance), and Charlotte Perkins Gilman's narrator has her yellow wallpaper, its 'bars' a symbol of her imprisonment. Each of these spaces represents and reinforces the character's mental state and the text's themes.

This chapter explores how Joe Hill and Gabriel Rodriguez's *Locke & Key* (IDW, 2008–13) uses space to construct horror and to reflect on its psychological interpretation. It first examines the comic's spectral and uncanny qualities, which are created by markers from cinematic and literary horror such as serial killers, possession, and transformation. I then look more closely at spatial tropes such as the abyss and the haunted house. I argue that, despite numerous literary markers, *Locke & Key* privileges physical places and literal meaning over symbolic or metaphorical interpretations. The comic responds to closed psychoanalytic approaches with intertextual citations and by literalizing horror symbols and their psychoanalytic meanings into physical, spatial forms.

Locke & Key is about the three Locke children, Tyler, Kinsey and Bode, who move to their ancestral home, Keyhouse, after their father's murder. They discover that Keyhouse's doors offer a range of powers when they are unlocked with special keys. These include transformation of various types (animal, gender, ethnicity, size, and even corporeality), healing, control over shadows and animals, and so forth. The keys have been made from a substance called 'whisp'ring iron' by various Locke generations since the eighteenth century. This iron is the physical form of demons that have tried to enter our realm through a portal called the Black Door without being able to attach to a human soul. Soon the siblings are engaged in a war to prevent the Black Door from being opened by Dodge, a possessed character who was once their father's friend.

Locke & Key initially marks itself as horror by including visual motifs from horror cinema. In Volume 1 Sam and Tyler's fight is shown in heavily shadowed images, arranged as jumbled snapshots on an otherwise black page, representing the intermittent flashes of light from Sam's gunshots (1.25–6).[1] This draws on established horror cinema tropes noted by Stephen King (1982: 216) in films such as *Night of the Living Dead* (Romero, 68) and *The Birds* (Hitchcock, 1963), where a 'strobe' effect arises from the use of limited light from a single source, creating 'a nightmare dreamscape of shifting, swinging shadows'. The effect is repeated later in the same volume (1.108–9) when Bode converses with Dodge while flicking a flashlight on and off.

Other sub-genres of cinematic horror are also referenced. The story opens with a home invasion that ends in Rendell Locke's murder by student Sam Lesser, referencing classic horror movies such as *Straw Dogs* (Peckinpah,

---

1   These references refer to Volume 1, 25–6.

1971) and *When a Stranger Calls* (Walton, 1979). Nina Locke kills Sam's accomplice with his own hatchet in a splash page that evokes the rape-revenge genre – her torn clothes and scratched body recalling the publicity images from *I Spit on Your Grave* (Zarchi, 1978). The comic is also scattered with visual and verbal references to other horror subgenres and titles. Dodge climbs out of the well in a scene reminiscent of *Ringu*'s notorious television incident (see Figure 6), and archetypes such as vampires (4.9) and werewolves (4.16) are cited.

Figure 6. Intertextual references. *Locke & Key: Welcome to Lovecraft*, Joe Hill and Gabriel Rodriguez, 2011 (1.110). © IDW. Image presented under Fair Use legislation.

Julien Wolfreys (2016: 643) claims that 'Literature is citation. Literature is spectral' and so these intertextual markers can also be read as a kind of spectrality, where other texts haunt the one we read. Alongside these nods to horror cinema tropes, *Locke & Key* situates itself as literary horror in paratextual and intertextual terms. Its author Joe Hill is Stephen King's son, and dedicates Book 5 'To Alan Moore and Neil Gaiman', two of the most writerly names in comics. Literary namechecks also abound within the story: from the town Lovecraft to the family's 'Uncle Machen' (6.163). The comic's structure is also self-consciously literary as the opening issues of the first volume are focalized through each main character in turn: Tyler, Bode, Kinsey, and antagonist Sam. Echoes of the literary Gothic are also apparent in its paratexts, which include 'The Known Keys': extracts from the diaries and correspondence of generations of the Lockes, drawn as aged scraps of paper.

At first glance, the story's content also seems to privilege the literary by using traditional horror symbols and metaphors. For example, much is made of the uncanny potential of shadows, reflections and mirrors. Kinsey speaks about not recognizing her own image (1.62, 1.81) and all the children spend a deal of time staring at their reflections. The medium emphasizes this through repetition and page layout, for example as Tyler imagines different versions of himself (1.10). Mirrors have special power: they can show the real rather than an illusion, for example Dodge's reflection as a decaying corpse (1.59). Mirrored page layouts (1.125) and panels pairing, or doubling characters are also used to underline this (6.147). Other traditional horror tropes are also present. Possession and transformation underpin the story as characters use the Animal Key, the Skin Key, or the Gender Key to change their appearance. The visual aspects of the medium of comics are well-suited to this and layout is also used for emphasis: the first time Tyler uses the Giant Key the panels become splash pages, changing size to echo his enormous stature (3.96–110).

Figure 7. Injured and injurious eyes. *Locke & Key: Clockworks*, Joe Hill and Gabriel Rodriguez, 2012 (5.22). © IDW. Image presented under Fair Use legislation.

Horror has often lurked in the darkness: its 'ghosts come alive in the shadows' (Brown 2005: 161). In Volume 3 the children find a crown that allows control of shadows. This is expressed particularly well by the medium of comics where a menacing shadow within a panel requires the reader to search for it (1.112) rather than being alerted by movement or extratextual signs. The visuality of the medium also privileges shadows at various points, bringing in another marker of horror, the eyes. Injured and injurious eyes are a common motif to both horror and comics (Waller 1986, Round 2014). At many points characters (particularly Tyler) are drawn with cavernous or shadowed eyes (see Figure 7)[2] and eyes also mark the Black Door, transforming from stone carvings to alert, open and yellow as it opens (see Figure 7).[3] When Dodge surveys the house using the Philosophoscope Key his eyes appear as ghostly red images (4.90).

2   See also Locke & Key 1.76, 1.96, 1.99, 4.75.
3   See also Locke & Key 5.27, 5.102.

Freud argues that the uncanny not only relates to doubles, doppelgangers and reflections, but also to the involuntary repetition of acts. *Locke & Key* often repeats panel compositions within scenes, creating an uncanny atmosphere. Each issue contains an average of three sequences where the same image is repeated across three panels or more.[4] These sequences often continue for pages at a time, privileging the physical space of the story by representing the locations as static and unchanging places within which time passes (2.113, 2.29). The technique is used particularly in scenes of death and sadness. For example, at their father's funeral (1.13–15) a layout of the same long thin horizontal panels repeats across two pages as various family members comfort Tyler. Another double page sequence of repeated panels follows when Bode demonstrates his use of the Ghost Key to Kinsey (1.70–1).

Freud also notes the uncanny potential of womb phantasies and haunted homes (Creed 1993: 53) and so spaces such as the abyss and the haunted house are of particular interest. The abyss 'inspires anxiety, terror and awe' and exists as a pole of both attraction and repulsion to characters, 'embodying an ambiguity that is central to the Gothic' (Edwards 2016: 4). The Well-House and the Drowning Cave (location of the Black Door) are both examples of the abyss and the site of significant story events, as the catalyst for the tale is when Bode releases Dodge from the well.

The Drowning Cave in particular is a good example of symbolic horror. Creed (1993: 27) argues that the horror film is an ideological project of patriarchy, and so a common image of horror is 'the voracious maw, the mysterious black hole'. This is the site of the archaic mother, representing 'the blackness of extinction – death' (28). It evokes the desire for non-differentiation; to return to the womb, described as 'the desire to merge' which then 'gives rise to a terror of self-disintegration, of losing one's self or ego ... the obliteration of self' (28). This is apt as the demons that come through the Black Door have this same purpose: to merge with a human soul and consume its identity.

Critics also argue that the haunted house is a symbol of the uncanny in horror. Doane argues that the house 'becomes the analogue of the human body' (Doane 1987: 72) and Creed reads it as another space where identity

---

4   Based on random sampling of ten issues.

can collapse, and the womb may be symbolized. Haunted houses contain cruel secrets and have witnessed terrible deeds (Creed 1993: 55) and thus are symbolic spaces where three primal scenes (conception, sexual difference, and desire) are played out. Superficially this seems to apply to Keyhouse, as Sam Lesser's ghost tells Rufus: 'This may look like an old house, but … It's a battlefield. The fighting has claimed many lives' (4.84). The children and other characters also reflect on Keyhouse's haunted qualities, for example musing 'Nice place … For a medieval torture chamber' (1.99, also 5.46). But in actual fact, although the house *is* the site of many battles, it is not in itself uncanny. In *Locke & Key* it is the Lockes' old home in San Francisco that is the site of murder and rape. Dodge's malevolent spirit is relegated outside Keyhouse, to the Well-House. Instead Keyhouse is a place where the children can literally unlock and examine their memories (using the Head Key) and heal themselves (with the Mending Key).

The temptation in psychoanalytic readings of horror is to hone in on the metaphorical import of motifs like these. Punter suggests that metaphor creates the uncanny: 'saying both more and less than it knows' (Punter 2007: 8). *Locke & Key*'s themes and symbols all invite a reading of the comic as a symbolic horror based around uncanny doubling and haunted caverns – nicely woven, but nothing new. However, new approaches to contemporary horror and Gothic argue against closed psychoanalytic readings like these, suggesting instead that these narratives exist in an intertextual space and thus offer many possible interpretations and subject positions to their constructed reader (Buckley 2018).

Locke & Key enacts this revisionist approach to horror by undermining psychoanalytic readings, for example by using phrases that sound metaphorical but are actually literal. When Nina says, 'I swear the locks in this house have minds of their own' (1.112) she is more right than she knows – the whisp'ring iron keys have both agency and power. When Kinsey realizes 'Ideas can't really be killed. Not for good' (5.40) she isn't speaking in the abstract but is referring to her memories and emotions that exist as tiny anthropomorphized characters and live on despite drowning. When Dodge claims 'Your father … unlocked my thoughts and took my memories' he is, again, speaking literally (1.139) – the Head Key allows for things to be put in and taken out of people's heads.

This literalization creates a metatextual commentary on the use of metaphor in horror that relies primarily on the use of space. Taken as a whole, *Locke & Key* is a story about psychological healing: a 'resolving' horror of the type identified by Jancovich (1992). It reverses and rejects literary metaphor by literalizing the abstract processes of psychoanalysis. Doors are opened and memories are removed and put back again. Tyler literally locks up his negative emotions and memories in his head (5.43), but this type of repression is not the answer. After she has removed her Fear and Tears, Kinsey injures herself (2.99), nearly kills her friends in the Drowning Cave (3.36–51), and disastrously places her trust in Dodge without a second thought – unable to hear her Fear warning her: 'You need me! ... He's daaaanger!' (2.115). The 'key to being a complete person' is not just believing in oneself (1.80), but literally exists and can be used to return a person's personality and memories (6.176).

The trajectory of the story depends on this manipulation of the spiritual and physical, which transform into each other throughout the text. Demons turn into iron and characters' emotions take on tangible, physical form. At the story's close Dodge attempts to describe 'the place spirits go':

> You ever find a cat sleeping in a ray of sun?
> There's a *sound* over there. It's a *golden* sound. That's the only way to describe it. It's a *bright* sound, and it has little flecks of music in it, drifting like motes of dust.
> (6.172–3)

Here the visual becomes the audible, just as throughout the text the abstract has become the physical. Traditionally, critics have argued that 'horror uses image and metaphor to embody what we fear' (Wisker 2005: 38). But rather than using symbolism, *Locke & Key* makes horror metaphors and clichés into literalizations that form the basis for its fantastic plot: a strategy particularly suited to the visual medium of comics.

Christian McCrea

Kojima Productions' *P.T.* (2014)

When games first emerged, horror was there to greet them. From the earliest arcade games, even in mechanical pre-digital forms, there they were – the zombies, ghouls and ghosts we needed to slap, shoot and punch down for a few points. Yet it has never been that clear at the arcade, underneath the television or in front of the computer whether what you are experiencing is just ever truly horror. Film genres are defined in all sorts of obvious and naturalized ways, and by what is crudely called 'content' in games parlance, while games have come to be more closely organized by their style of play (Andersen and Shimabukuro 2013: 89). Or, more to the point, that is how they've come to be consumed much of the time.

Full-tilt horror games *per se*, where both the gameplay and what we see and hear are all heavily coded as belonging to the genre, are only part of the story of horror videogames. Tapping into what makes this arrangement so strange and special in games is not just about the obvious question of interactivity. More accurate, as Tanya Krzywinska outlines, videogames expand on moments of doing and not doing, where a player experiences non-interactive sequences between bursts of action (Krzywinska 2002: 13). For example, in *Resident Evil* (Shinji Mikami, 1996), players would navigate the rooms and areas with several cut-scenes of non-interactive action, menu screens, often challenging the player to a reaction from an unfamiliar angle in 3-dimensional space after a cut-scene. The horror is heightened by the tension of the moment, and the way that responsibility for action comes in and out of your control. Krzywinska calls this 'a resonant rhythm between self-determination and pre-determination' (13), which can be applied both at the physical level and the thematic – as supernatural horror, high-concept action horror scenes, and 'survival' horror stake out the generic landscape of horror games since the beginning of the PlayStation era in the 1990s.

Histories of horror games often refer back to *Sweet Home* (Tokoru Fujiwara: 1989) on the original Famicom/Nintendo Entertainment System as an important moment in the genre; the game had you collect items and then puzzle through a set of difficult encounters with monsters to ensure your characters would survive – once one of them was killed, they were gone forever, and the rest had to push on. Since *Sweet Home*, and certainly since *Resident Evil* (on which producer Fujiwara also worked heavily), feelings of dread, tension and anticipation are fed by gameplay as much as the audio-visual environment. *Sweet Home* is also interesting for releasing alongside a film, *Sweet Home* (Kurosawa, 1989) that straddles high camp and teen schlock but still uses intense psychological effects. The game and film shared plot elements and setup, as Kiyoshi helped supervise the project with Fujiwara at the game company Capcom.

As a point of distinction, the company Konami set about producing an alternative to the Resident Evil games with *Silent Hill* (Toyama, 1999). In the first game, a grim environment and high tension take the place of *Resident Evil*'s more direct jump scares and zombie chases. Ewan Kirkland discusses how the survival horror genre is generally seen as less narrative-centred but analyses how games like the *Silent Hill* series elude such an easy distinction by pulling away from expectations, and shattering long-held critical distinctions about narrative, agency and action (Kirkland 2009: 64–5).

As the series developed, and the Japanese videogame industry's interest in horror began to increase in the early days of the PlayStation 2 (largely 2001–6), Konami took a chance on a different style of game again and developed *Silent Hill 4: The Room* (Murakoshi, 2004). In this iteration, you play Henry Townshend, who is trapped in his apartment for much of the story. You look across to other apartment buildings to witness far-off events, in clear reference to *Rear Window* (Hitchcock, 1954). In the apartment, you play in first-person, and once you travel to the supernatural zones, in third-person – a macroscopic variant of the 'resonant rhythm' of control.

Survival horror games on home game consoles became less popular over time, especially in the wake of a few unpopular titles and changing appetites for hardware in the post-smartphone era in 2007–8. Or perhaps, more accurately, the changes to videogame production that occur with each change of console hardware have required a shift in economics – as costs increases to produce more photorealism and other growths in costs, games have to scale up to produce more income through initial sales or later in-game purchases. During this time it was PC games such as *Amnesia: The Dark Descent* (Grip, 2010), which had more abstract visuals and more focus on stealth than combat, that started to develop reflexive audiences on YouTube. Fans of YouTubers would watch them get scared during a game – spectating the picture-in-picture effect as a kind of dual horror pleasure.

Once early 2014 arrived, the PlayStation 4 was launching around the world and with it, what is termed an 'early' survival horror game for the console – *Outlast* (Morin, 2013). Even though the game was already available on PC, it had an outsized impact as an early and anticipated horror game for the console. It combined plenty of action sequences and gratuitous body horror with classic survival horror tropes – you control a video camera rather than a gun, as was the case in *Michigan: Report from Hell* (Suda, 2004) and in close reference to *Fatal Frame* (Shibata, 2001), which featured a still camera. In August 2014, during an internationally covered game event Gamescom in Germany, Konami released an enigmatic teaser video for a downloadable game called simply '*P.T.*'. The game was immediately available to download that day on PlayStation 4s around the world. No internal company information was released, and initially no developer names or even clarity about what 'P.T.' stood for.

Within a few hours, the game's puzzles were solved and the first few players to complete P.T. were uploading the ending to YouTube. It was a 'Playable Teaser' for Silent Hills, a new game in the series – but this time co-directed by Guillermo del Toro (*Blade 2*: 2002 and *Hellboy*: 2004 amongst others) and game designer Hideo Kojima. Kojima was a full-time employee of Konami Corporation during this time and was responsible for a lesser-known science fiction robot action series *Zone of the Enders* (2001) and one of the biggest franchises in games, Metal Gear, known by its main incarnation *Metal Gear Solid 1–5* (1998–2014). These games have a critical and public reputation for baroque politically informed and conspiratorial plots, complex narratives, obtuse humour, and expansive yet exacting gameplay modes. He is also videogame design's pre-eminent auteur figure – a reputation both exhaustively encouraged through aggressive media tactics and borne out by the games' bombastic approach to narrative.

Once you load up *P.T.*, it lacks the traditional parade of production company logos, software partner logos and traditional title screen. Instead, a brief calibration screen to check you are going to be playing in a dark enough environment with the contrast on your television tuned low enough – essentially, to not see absolutely everything. The screen fades up from black; you are in a first-person view – sideways, on the ground. A dark cellar. An unusual-looking cockroach, or is it two? The camera moves without your prompt to a standing position, slowly and unevenly, emulating grogginess. A blur comes over the image now and then. You see a wooden door. Now in control of the game, it waits for you to press up on the right control stick of the controller – by now, this the traditional gesture for movement in first-person games released on home consoles. You move towards the door, and once close enough, the door opens.

It opens into a well-lit hallway in what appears to be an American house in the country – something about the scale and high ceiling. This small hallway turns right, and has two small alcoves, and one horrendous bathroom. This is all of *P.T.* This hallway is the game. Every event in the hours of gameplay you experience will be here.

You move through the hallway and look for things to do. You can zoom in your sight/camera and no more. The dark recesses around a filthy cabinet seem to hold some scribblings, but nothing obvious. The front door of this house is on the right; it is locked. After the corner, there is another door at the far end. You approach it, and finally something happens, it opens up to a dark room with small set of stairs leading down towards another door. You trundle down and open the second door. Horror. You're back at the beginning of the same hallway (see Figure 8).

So, it is that over the course of your time with *P.T.*, you push through this hallway time and again. The universe inside deteriorates as the ashtrays fill up with debris, the rain outside gathers pace, the lights flicker. The radio chatter changes, the paintings become dirtier. After a few times through, the bathroom door is open and a grimy, mewling foetus (or is it a rat?) is writhing around in what was once a bathroom sink. It seems like a reference to *Eraserhead* (Lynch, 1977) in some respects, but could also be distant collage

Figure 8. The open door at the end of the hallway in *P.T.*: A new cycle awaits. *P.T.*, created by Hideo Kojima and Guillermo del Toro (7780s Studio/Konami, Playstation 4, 2014). © Konami. Image presented under Fair Use legislation.

of lesser horrors – cheap tricks in music videos, scribbles in the margin of a teenager's sketchbook. At several points through each walk through the hall, there is a chance of a jump-scare as a demonic figure appears in your sightline without warning and takes you down to the ground. You then reset in the first room, but appear in the 'version' of the hallway you were up to. Sometimes the denizens are certain to attack, other times you are sure how to trigger them. As you push through the horror and deteriorating environment, you hear of murders in the house through the radio, distorted chatter and nearby ambient gurgling. The universe unravels into high-concept full-sensory demonic horror as you progress, a staple of the *Silent Hill* games. There are easy filmic comparisons to make; the circular spatial reference of the Red Room environments in *Twin Peaks* (Lynch, 1990–1) or the invisible threshold in *The Exterminating Angel* (Bunuel: 1962). But a repeating hallway in a videogame scenario is relatively unremarkable – it is the presentation, approximation and verisimilitude that give it fresh life in *P.T.*

What makes *P.T.* such an interesting historical market of horror videogames is that it exemplifies the design traditions changing, the technological conditions in flux, and the spectatorship modality shifting all at a crucial point. Just a few weeks prior, *Five Nights At Freddy's* (Cawthon, 2014) was released for computers, and mobile/tablet versions were released in the same August/September phase as *P.T.*'s success. In that game, the player monitored cameras to keep watch over haunted animatronic animal attempting to make their way to the player. The game's resonant rhythm of control and inability was very different; you can see a lot more, but can control less in comparison. Both games, however, found that their approaches to flinching jump scares, incremental supernatural horror and lurid audio design were perfect for the YouTube/Twitch content creators and channels who had already become central, if not yet entirely domineering of videogame consumption and spectatorship.

Five Nights At Freddy's would go on to spawn sequels, toys and merchandise and become a mainstay of iPad games culture in the following years. *P.T.*'s fate was more interesting – as Hideo Kojima wrapped up work on *Metal Gear Solid 5* (2014–15), he left Konami in a secretive dispute, and *Silent Hills* was cancelled. His old company Konami quickly moved to take *P.T.* off the PlayStation Store, and went so far as to disallow re-downloading for those who had previously done so. While films and literature have their own problematic material conditions, nothing compares to the strange fate of releases like *P.T.*: a wholly designed self-contained experience that changed the history of the medium, but is now near-impossible to propagate and disowned by the rights holders.

Instead, Kojima (as director) and del Toro (as motion-capture actor) would re-emerge in 2016 with a trailer for a new game, *Death Stranding* (unreleased) indicating a mix of horror, high-concept science fiction and supernatural elements. The link between *P.T.* and that new project illuminates the strange fate of partnerships and collaborations in the gaming milieu. Games that progress many years into production can be abandoned at the last minute, but the working practice often finds a way – even a carefully written history can only give a surface reading of the relationship between game creators as a result. For this reason, P.T. is in the middle between a supergroup concept album and a lawsuit deposition – representative of the medium of videogames in general. The commercial constraints, the rapid technological pace, the twists of genre appreciation, and the submerged history of collaborations – all the shocks and scares waiting for us in the corridor.

Jeffrey Andrew Weinstock

Michael Jackson's 'Thriller' (1982) and Stanley Kubrick's *The Shining* (1980)

'Horror music,' broadly construed, arguably functions in two main capacities: to convey meaning and to evoke affect. Usually, these two capacities are intertwined. In the service of conveying meaning, horror music can lyrically tell a horrific tale or, when accompanying visual images, inflect our understanding of what is being represented as the music provides cues guiding interpretation. Horror music may also seek to evoke affective responses associated with horror such as suspense, discomfort, fear, or disgust through aural qualities including key, timbre, tempo, effects, and so on. To address these functions, I will first consider Michael Jackson's song 'Thriller' and then the soundtrack to Stanley Kubrick's 1980 film *The Shining*.

While Michael Jackson's hit song 'Thriller' from his 1982 album of the same name is difficult to disentangle from the famous 14-minute video directed by John Landis, when the 5:57-minute long song is considered on its own, it is clear that the horror aspect is primarily conveyed through lyrical content. While the song includes sound effects such as a wolf howl and thunder, and instruments such as a pipe organ and Theremin that are associated with the horror genre, stripped of its lyrical content, this disco-funk song in a major key would have little in terms of its musical qualities to evoke sensations or emotions associated with horror. Indeed, the bright synthesizer chords that open the song and the funk beat that then kicks in signal right away that it is intended not for scaring but for dancing. Its categorization as horror music instead depends upon the story it tells, and the allusions it makes to the horror genre through instrumentation and particularly the monologue delivered by horror screen legend Vincent Price, as well as the visuals that accompany the song when the video is viewed.

The lyrics to 'Thriller' are packed with horror film images and motifs. Addressing the listener with the second-person 'you,' the song initially situates the listener at midnight confronting a supernatural menace. Unable to scream, 'you' are initially paralysed before fleeing; the scene then shifts to a deserted house where a door slams, trapping 'you' – also now gendered as 'girl' – inside as a monster approaches. The song lyrics unleash a barrage of horror film antagonists – the walking dead, aliens, demons – before then revealing that the listener is only vicariously threatened by the 'terror on the screen' from which Michael Jackson will provide safety, even as he promises thrills of a different kind.

That the song is a playful homage to the horror genre and the kind of 'terrible thrills' (to borrow from *Rocky Horror*) that consumption of such media can elicit is then made clear through the monologue by horror movie icon Vincent Price. Price's monologue in the second half of the song completes the transition from the listener's being *in* the scene to the listener's *watching* the scene as Price takes us to the movies. In the monologue, it is again almost midnight as vampiric predators corner unwary souls and 'grizzly ghouls from every tomb / Are closing in to seal your doom'. The song then ends by foregrounding the 'evil of the thriller' as the music stops and we are left with more than ten seconds of Price's trademark evil laugh.

The auditory horror of 'Thriller' is thus primarily conveyed through lyrical content, supplemented by 'codes' of the horror film that depend to a certain extent on the listener's conversance with the conventions of horror. The listener's recognition, for example, that Price – despite a career spanning many genres – made a name for himself particularly in the 1960s and 1970s by playing sinister characters in horror films directed by William Castle, Roger Corman, and many others, colours interpretation of the song through those associations. Similarly, awareness of the roles of the Theremin and church organ in horror media helps to situate the song in relation to genre, despite the incongruous disco and funk elements.

Of course, 'Thriller' the song is difficult to disentangle from 'Thriller' the video, the premiere of which in 1983 was a landmark event in music video history. Directed by John Landis – whose horror film *An American Werewolf in London* was released two years earlier – the video overlays an additional narrative onto the song. Prior to the song beginning, a teenaged Michael is shown

Figure 9. Michael's yellow eyes. 'Thriller', dir. John Landis (Epic Records, 1983).

transforming into a kind of werecat and threatening his female companion; this is then revealed to be a scene in a Vincent Price horror film called *Thriller* that Jackson is enjoying with a date who finds it terrifying. The music begins as the two leave the theatre and zombies begin to emerge from a graveyard. Jackson himself transforms into a zombie and, after some vigorous dancing, chases his date to an abandoned house. As zombie Jackson reaches for her throat, she awakens and realizes it was all a dream. But, in a final twist, Jackson turns back to the camera as he is leaving, revealing his yellow werecat eyes from the opening scene as Vincent Price offers his echoing laugh (see Figure 9).

Before considering the soundtrack music to *The Shining*, it is worth mentioning that the initial scene of the 'Thriller' video that takes place prior to the music beginning is shot using the conventions of the horror film, including soundtrack – horror – music intended to create an ominous mood and suspense. As Michael, who has been walking with his date down a dark country road starts to confess that he is unlike other guys, the moon emerges from behind a cloud to arpeggiating wind instruments and harp – a convention of horror films signalling a shift away from the real world and into fantasy or the supernatural. When Michael begins his horrific transformation, a deep plodding baseline in a minor key is added conveying menace. This is supplemented by diegetic sounds of the girl screaming in terror, agonized groans and growls from the transforming Michael, and 'sticky' sounds of the transformation itself. The music swells as the transformation progresses, becoming ponderous and dramatic – a kind of requiem – and then sharp staccato string 'stingers' become prominent. There is a dramatic pursuit accompanied by staccato orchestral bursts and a minor key string section melody, before beast-Michael converges on his prey to the sound of swirling strings. Contrasting with the later part of the video in which there is arguably a disjunction between musical style and narrative (both visual and lyrical), the music present in the initial scene is horror music in the sense that its qualities seek to coordinate with onscreen image to direct audience response and evoke horror affect – suspense, fear, horror. The minor key, the staccato 'stingers' (most immediately associated with the famous shower scene from Hitchcock's 1960 *Psycho*), the ponderous bass line, the swift tempo during the chase, and the other musical qualities combine to amplify the emotion fear modelled by the female actor menaced by the monster.

Jackson's 'Thriller' is a useful starting point for a discussion of horror music, because the disjunction between scary story and funky pop music offers a clear contrast between horror music as conveyer of meaning and horror music as generator of affect. More commonly, particularly in heavy metal, death metal, and goth music, but also extending to other genres, we anticipate congruence between lyrical content and musical qualities as both work together to align affect with interpretation. In other words: we expect 'dark' music to go along with a scary, disgusting, or violent story – which is almost always the case with soundtrack music that seeks to amplify the intended affect and to cue the audience on how to respond.

The distinction between horror music that conveys meaning in the sense of telling a horrific tale and horror music that primarily seeks to evoke affect can be illustrated by juxtaposing Jackson's 'Thriller' with the soundtrack to Stanley Kubrick's 1980 film, *The Shining*, which 'makes abundant use of radically dissonant, sonorously extreme modernist musical languages' (Code 2010: 133) in order to evoke what Barham refers to as 'psychological horror' as it attempts to 'embody the omnipresent but unseen malevolence of the alien "other"' (Barham 2009: 137). Interestingly, for the soundtrack to *The Shining*, Kubrick chose to rely heavily on (or to 'repurpose') existing compositions by Béla Bartók, György Ligeti, and Krzysztof Penderecki, as well as to feature prominently the medieval chant *Dies Irae* ('Day of Wrath' from the Requiem Mass) – the last a favourite of the horror genre in general. For present purposes, I will focus on Wendy Carlos and Rachel Elkind's adaptation of the *Dies Irae* chant during the film's initial helicopter shots of Colorado Rockies, and then on Bartók's *Music for Percussion, Strings, and Celesta* – a piece that is used at three key moments in the film.

Kubrick's film opens with a 'portentous synthesizer adaptation' (Code 2010: 133) of *Dies Irae* that accompanies stunning helicopter shots tracking the Torrance family car as it makes its way through rugged Rockies terrain toward the Overlook Hotel. As Donnelly observes, this arrangement of the ponderous, minor key chant includes 'wailing synthesizer sounds as the title of the film appears on the screen, mixing Carlos's synthesizer with Elkind's mewling vocals' (Donnelly 2005: 47). The plodding, step-like progression of the chant creates a sense of inevitability as the car progresses, while the overhead shots that swoop and tilt vertiginously as they fly across the landscape convey a sense of vulnerability as some unseen force seems to track the tiny Torrance family across the sublime landscape even before they arrive at their destination. Music thus combines with image to evoke a sense of *menace*. The *Dies Irae*, writes Donnelly, is 'one of the key musical signifiers of doom, evil and death' and, as *The Shining*'s opening piece, 'leaves audiences in no doubt about the character of the ensuing film' (48). Code refers to this sequence as 'one of the most blatant imaginable instances of music's power to act as independent generic signature' (Code 2010: 133): this is the essence of horror music as 'low pedal tones and manic shrieks around the grimly repetitive tread of the chant tune ... clearly [tell] us what kind of film we are watching, and [signal] the crescendo of horrors lying ahead' (134).

The foreboding sense of menace evoked by the opening sequence is then echoed and amplified by Kubrick's use of Bartók's *Music for Strings, Percussion, and Celesta* at three key moments in the film: when Jack looks across a model of the hotel's hedge maze and appears to see his wife and child within it (see

Figure 10); when Danny first attempts to enter room 237 and fails; and when Danny asks the increasingly unstable Jack if he would ever hurt him and his mother. Donnelly's thorough overview of the Bartók piece used by Kubrick describes it as including 'two vertiginous sounds of "dissolution"' (Donnelly 2005: 48). In the first, 'the strings play microtonally, creating a shimmering effect as some drop minutely in pitch. This is accompanied by some twangy plucked string glissandi. This leads into a strong melody played in unison on strings and piano that is not "tuneful" in the accepted sense' (48). 'On the second run through', Donnelly continues,

> the melody rises in pitch and tension, reaching a climactic point, which is then held, whereupon a passage of three rising piano chords followed by deep timpani rumbles is repeated twice. The piece then goes into a second pitch 'dissolution', which is a dizzy building in intensity dominated by celesta arpeggios accompanied by a cacophony of strings. (48)

Figure 10. Jack surveys the model hedge maze. *The Shining*, dir. Stanley Kubrick (Warner Brothers, 1980).

Descriptions such as Donnelly's above of course primarily benefit those who know the piece well or who are listening to it at the same time (and it helps to have some musicological training). Donnelly's descriptive language however – 'vertiginous', 'dissolution', 'shimmering', 'dizzy', 'cacophony' – may help convey a sense of the affect evoked by the piece. In each of its three iterations, the disquieting feel of Bartók's composition transports the listener to a fantasy world of supernatural menace. In its first use, echoing the opening credits, Jack becomes the unseen force looking down on the Torrance family and the Overlook hotel as Danny and Wendy enter a maze that mirrors the twisting hallways of the hotel itself (and through which Jack will chase Danny in the end); in the second, Danny is liminally positioned at the doorway to the world of malevolent spirits; and in the third, Danny cautiously confronts the father he suspects is not well and possibly meditating harm to his family. In each case, the Bartók piece evokes and accentuates the feelings of menace and dread, conveying the sense that all is decidedly not right with the world. Donnelly proposes that *The Shining*'s score goes beyond being 'simply film music' and can rather be described as 'non-diegetic sound effects': 'It can be interpreted as sounds that express the supernatural world of the film, yet emanate from outside the diegetic world the film has created' (45). The music thus participates in evoking from us the horror the film seeks to inspire. This is horror music as affect generator.

Of course, even given Donnelly's claims that music plays such a significant role in *The Shining* that, rather than being considered background music it should be construed as 'foreground music' (36) and that music in the film 'seems to dominate the image' (43), it remains the case that the music is intended to work in conjunction with both the image and diachronic sound to convey meaning. As Code notes of the opening sequence of *The Shining*, were it not for the adaptation of the *Dies Irae* as soundtrack, there would be little to distinguish the scene from an 'expensively produced car commercial' (Code 2010: 134). So the music, while evoking affect, simultaneously inflects interpretation. The qualities of the music, as well as – particularly in the case of the *Dies Irae* – its history and the associations attached to it, direct the audience's understanding of specific scenes as well as generic categorization more broadly. We know a horror film when we hear one!

If we imagine a continuum of horror music stretching from pure meaning to pure affect, it seems unlikely that we could linger at either extreme for more than a few moments. Even something like 'Thriller', which is horror music only in the sense of telling a story (meaning), will evoke an affective response – perhaps even in response to the story told. And even on its own, absent of any lyrics or visual accompaniment, music we might describe as dark, creepy, scary, and so on by virtue of its qualities will inevitably be made meaningful by the listener, if perhaps only in a fuzzy or abstract way. Those who craft effective horror music understand this as they seek to coordinate musical qualities – in some cases with lyrics, images, or both – in order to manipulate auditors into hearing horror.

Alexandra Heller-Nicholas

Joseph DeLage and Troy Wagner's *Marble Hornets* (2009–2014)

There has always been a tightly forged relationship with new and emerging media technologies and the supernatural imagination. This premise underscores Jeffrey Sconce's foundational book *Haunted Media* (2000), who argues that 'tales of paranormal media are important ... not as timeless expressions of some underlying electronic superstition, but as a permeable language in which to express a culture's changing social relationship to a historical sequence of technologies' (Sconce 2000: 10). Across his many case studies, he provides vital insight into the sense, experience and capacity for fear that the rise of what at any given historical moment could be defined as 'new media' in a lengthy discussion of Orson Welles's notorious 1938 Halloween radio broadcast of H. G. Wells' science fiction novel *The War of the Worlds*. Formatted as a 'real', live new broadcast, the radio programme famously caused many listeners to believe it was true, resulting in a widespread panic. As Sconce notes:

> More than a cautionary tale about irresponsible broadcasting or gullible audiences, *War of the Worlds* continues to fascinate by reminding us of the repressed potential for panic and disorder that lies just behind the normalizing functions of media technology, a terror that is at once terrifying and yet suggestively enticing. (Sconce 2000, 116–17)

When considering the relationship between 'new media' as it is understood today – pertaining specifically to commonly interactive digital technologies broadly connected to the internet, but also including videogames, VR, home entertainment technologies (DVD, Blu-ray, etc.) and augmented reality. The term is loosely accompanied by a cache of widely held assumptions: new media helps us keep in touch with each other through things like social media, while granting us access to information and entertainment faster and more varied than ever before. As Sconce suggests with *War of the Worlds*, however, the re/presentation of 'scary' narratives to concretely address the dark side of new media – whatever the era of production – has a long history.

Most recently, the found footage horror subgenre that made its dramatic public debut with *The Blair Witch Project* (Myrick and Sánchez, 1999) spiked in popularity with films like Jaume Balagueró and Paco Plaza's *[REC]* (2007), George A. Romero's *The Diary of the Dead* (2007) and Oren Peli's *Paranormal Activity* (which received wide distribution in 2009). As I have written at length elsewhere (Heller-Nicholas 2015), of course, the roots of found-footage horror as it is understood today stem back at least to the Welles' *War of the Worlds* broadcast, through to the road safety films of the Highway Safety Foundation of the 1950s and 1960s, the 'snuff fictions' (fictional films about the existence of 'real' snuff movies) that blossomed in popularity in the 1970s in particular, and 'reality' styled fictional horror narratives on television in the 1980s and 1990s, especially Jean-Teddy Filippe's French series *The Forbidden Files* (1989) and the notorious BBC *Ghostwatch* broadcast in 1992 which, again – like the Welles radio show – greatly confused its viewers in terms of its ontological status, many believing the reality-styled teleplay they saw on screen was actually happening in real life.

In recent decades, horror has embraced similar kinds of anxieties around media technologies Sconce had identified in *Haunted Media*. The popular J-horror *Ringu* films (and their American remakes), from 1998 onwards, pivot around the idea of a haunted video cassette that curses those who view it to an imminent death unless they show the tape to someone else, passing on the curse – viral media, indeed. Television and VCR technology had already been explored in films like *Poltergeist* (Hooper, 1982), *Videodrome* (Cronenberg, 1983), and *The Video Dead* (Scott, 1987). Similarly, cell phones have also been identified as a source of horror in a range of horror movies, including Takashi Miike's 2004 J-horror film *One Missed Call* and its range of sequels and remakes, the South Korean film *Phone* (Ahn, 2002), *Pulse* (Sonzero, 2006), Tod Williams' 2016 adaptation of Steven King's novel *Cell*, and even the more arthouse-aligned *Personal Shopper* (Assayas, 2016) pivots around spooky, mysterious messages sent from a potential-spectre to that films haunted protagonist, played by Kristen Stewart. Movies about murderous videogames stem back at least to *Brainscan* (Flynn, 1994), *How to Make a Monster* (Huang, 2001), and *Stay Alive* (Bell, 2006), while the potential perils of VR are explored in *The Lawnmower Man* (Leonard, 1992) and *Arcade* (Pyun, 1993).

But if there has in recent years been a dominant new media fascination in horror cinema, it is surely the internet, with a particular emphasis on anxieties surrounding the invasiveness and danger of social media. Stemming back at least to *The Collingswood Story* (Costanza, 2002), films like *Vlog* (Butler, 2008), *Megan is Missing* (Goi, 2011), *The Den* (Donohue, 2013), *Unfriended* (Gabriadze, 2014), *Ratter* (Kramer, 2015), *#Horror* (Subkoff, 2015), *Friend Request* (Verhoeven, 2016), *Smiley* (Gallagher, 2012) and *Chatroom* (Nakata, 2010) are a small handful of the many films released around this theme. As the titles of Yōhei Fukuda's 2010 films *Death Tube: Broadcast Murder Show* and its quickly churned-out sequel *Death Tube 2: Broadcast Murder Show* alone indicate, video hosting websites like YouTube have also not been immune to this trend of literally demonizing new media in a horror context.

Rather than simply making a traditional horror film feature about YouTube, in 2009, three young filmmakers in Alabama spent $500 on the first series of their YouTube-based horror series *Marble Hornets*. As it came to an end in 2014, it had almost 400,000 subscribers on its YouTube channel, and its introductory episode alone – lasting for less than two minutes total runtime – is at the time of writing sitting close to 4.5 million views. At the peak of its popularity, *Marble Hornets* was synonymous with the internet's 'Slender Man' mythos, a so-called 'creepypasta' – internet-specific supernatural or horror folktales – whose real-world repercussions became terrifyingly clear in May 2015 when two 12-year-old girls in Wisconsin stabbed a classmate nineteen times, almost killing her, claiming they were under orders of Slender Man. With a feature film adaptation of the web series released in 2015 by director James Moran under the title *Always Watching: A Marble Hornets Story*,[1] it

---

1   In August 2018 - after this chapter was originally submitted – a bigger-budget, more mainstream horror film was released based on the same mythology, simply called Slender Man [in italics]. Directed by Sylvain White, the film grossed over $50 million internationally; however, both critical and audience responses were extremely negative, with Jaz Sinclair even receiving a Worst Supporting Actress nomination at the 2019 Golden Raspberry Awards for her performance.

Figure 11. Slender Man graffiti, Mingo Park Logan, Ohio, 2016. Photo: © Dan Keck (via Creative Commons).

should have been a phenomenon, but the stabbing saw the project reduced to a barely straight-to-DVD release made on a shoestring and effectively brushed under the carpet (see Figure 11).

The horror of the Wisconsin stabbings and its tragic bringing into 'our' world the Slender Man legend in an odd way aligns neatly with precisely what it was about the *Marble Hornets* YouTube phenomenon that made it so addictive for so many of its online fans. With its roots deep within the countercultural underbelly of the internet on the Something Awful forums – the birthplace of the notorious 4chan imageboard (which itself begat hacktivist group Anonymous and the Project Chanology anti-Scientology movement) – Slender Man was born through a creepypasta-themed Photoshop thread on the Something Awful that included two black-and-white images by user 'Victor Surge' in 2009. Otherwise innocuous photos of kids that had superimposed amongst them the now-iconic Slender Man figure: tall and thin with tentacle like limbs in a black business suit with a blank face. From the hotel proprietor in Salvador Dali's dream sequence for Alfred Hitchcock's *Spellbound* (1954) to René Magritte's *The Lovers* (1928) to the cover of Korn's self-titled debut album (1994), the iconography of the Slender Man has historical roots, but *Marble Hornets* – renaming the figure 'The Operator' – breathed new life into the image, making it an internet phenomenon that spawned a series of other Slender Man-centric web series like *EverymanHYBRID* and *TribeTwelve*, as well as videogames. In terms of broader folklore, although an internet-age phenomenon, the wider category of 'bogeyman' transcends national and historical borders, from the Saudi Arabian *Dojairah and Umna al Ghola* and the Guyanan *Jumbi*, to the *khokhan* from Azerbaijan and the *Bau-bau* from Romania. Like Marble Hornets' variation of the figure, although a fledgling mythology the function is effectively the same: to warn children and adolescents against bad behaviour (in this instance, having 'secret' lives online, clearly articulated here as a decision that only results in danger and death).

Narratively, *Marble Hornets* follows Jay (creator and co-director Troy Wagner) and his concerns about his old school friend Alex (co-director Joseph DeLage) who has left behind a cache of videotapes that ostensibly tracked a low-budget indie feature he had been working on called Marble Hornets. Alex dropped the project suddenly and moved away, telling Jay that he could have the tapes if he wanted them but strongly recommended he 'burn them'. The three series of short videos – generally around ten minutes in length – track Jay's investigations along with others who have been roped in, such as Tim (Tim Sutton) and Jessica (Jessica May).

With the addition of each video to the YouTube channel announced on Twitter, *Marble Hornets* is a transmedia found-footage horror success story explicitly about anxieties and fears surrounding new media technologies. Rather than merely a tool to update, promote and disseminate information new episodes, the Twitter account became an active storytelling tool: 'Jay' would often give brief updates on his safety and mental state, and the Twitter account would often be 'hacked' by a mysterious figure called 'To The Ark', who would link to highly abstracted, even experimental, short films on a separate YouTube channel in a kind of response to Jay's videos. Aesthetically, the *Marble Hornets*' YouTube videos are marked strongly by a low-budget, low-fi found-footage horror aesthetic, aligning its audience on a visceral level with Jay (and later Tim's) investigations and encounters with both Alex and the omnipresent figure of the Operator.

The power of *Marble Hornets* lies within gaps and ellipses such as this, riddled with an ever-present paranoia that at its most aggressive stops any of its characters from talking openly about The Operator. Unable to trust one other and paralysed by their own paranoia, this silence in effect means there is little screen time spent where the series' characters even openly talk to each other about what is happening to them: Tim and Jay in particular venture to use only vague terms, such as when in Entry #66, Tim's long-anticipated back-story includes a reference to The Operator only as 'that person in the background or whatever it was'. Despite Tim, Alex, Jessica and Jay's lives all being destroyed by the Operator, they cannot bring themselves to discuss him openly on camera. They do not trust technology.

This failure of trust and fear to speak through technology about the secrets that plague them effectively constructs *Marble Hornets* as a modern folkloric manifestation that takes place at the intersection of technology and teen isolation. In the digital age where adults so vocally express their anxieties about their children's hidden-to-them lives online – be it sexual predators or cyber bullies – *Marble Hornets*' interpretation of the broader Slender Man mythos presents a significant instance where youth culture has itself created its own bogeyman to tell stories about the dangers of having secrets online: it is – if one can leave the real-life horrors of the Wisconsin stabbing out of things for a moment – a profound instance of the robust self-protection strategies young people can make by themselves, and for each other (see Figure 12).

The core narrative tension within *Marble Hornets* stems from its protagonists' fundamental desire to reconcile the past with the present: to unravel the secrets that first revealed themselves in the digital archive of Alex's failed film project, and to identify the links between them and the violence of the present. At the centre of this lies the appearance of the Operator himself, a figure who announces his presence through digital distortion: the Operator is, at his core, a *corruptor* of our faith in the archive as a method to decipher 'truth' (whatever that may be). Due no doubt in large part to the money its creators made from *Marble Hornets*' success as the series progressed, the material construction of the Operator himself shifts from what at first appears to be a puppet-like, tangible real-world presence to something increasingly more ephemeral and digitized. Whether a conscious decision on the part of the series' creators or not, this is crucial: as the series progresses through to the final episodes of

Figure 12. Slender Man cosplay at Chicago Comic and Entertainment Expo (C2E2) 2014. Photo: © GabboT (via Creative Commons).

Series 3, the Operator increasingly becomes little more than the quarry in a spooky game of *Where's Waldo*: the immediate danger and the real threat in *Marble Hornets* is technology itself. That the Operator corrupts digital video puts him in direct odds with the diegetic documentary mission that keeps the camera rolling. He stands in opposition to the camera's promise to capture the truth of the moment, an act its diegetic filmmakers have constructed as fundamental to their ability to understand the past.

While *Marble Hornets* concluded in 2014 and the pleasures the Slender Man mythology afforded broadly decreased due perhaps to its gruesome real-world association with the events in Wisconsin acting as an effective buzz-kill, in retrospect it is a revealing – almost prescient – moment in new media horror history. With so many of its audience unsure of its ontological status due to the low-key nature of its YouTube posts and the apparent validating association of Twitter, there is something of the spectre of the now oft-cited 'fake news' that hovers retrospectively around memories of *Marble Hornets*. That its primary antagonist is a nameless, faceless white man in a business suit makes that aspect today even more potent.

Acknowledgement

This section reworks ideas previously explored in two previous articles: 'Textures of Silence and Decay: *Marble Hornets* and the Haunted Archive', *Bright Lights Film Journal*, 15 May 2014 <http://brightlightsfilm.com/found-footage-2-textures-silence-decay-marble-hornets-haunted-archive/> and 'In Defence of Slender Man', *Overland Literary Journal*, 13 June 2015 <https://overland.org.au/2014/06/in-defence-of-slender-man/>.

Part III
Categories of Contemporary Horror

Steve Jones

Spierig Brothers' *Jigsaw* (2017)

After a seven-year hiatus, 'just when you thought it was safe to go back to the cinema for Halloween' (Croot 2017), the *Saw* franchise returned. Critics overwhelmingly disapproved of the franchise's reinvigoration, and much of that dissention centred on a label that is synonymous with *Saw*: 'torture porn'. Numerous critics pegged the original *Saw* (Wan, 2004) as torture porn's prototype (see Lidz 2009, *Canberra Times* 2008). Accordingly, critics such as Lee (2017) characterized *Jigsaw*'s release as heralding an unwelcome 'torture porn comeback'. This chapter will investigate the legitimacy of this concern in order to determine what 'torture porn' is and means in the *Jigsaw* era.

'Torture porn' originates in press discourse. The term was coined by David Edelstein (2006), but its implied meanings were entrenched by its proliferation within journalistic film criticism (for a detailed discussion of the label's development and its implied meanings, see Jones 2013). On examining the films brought together within the press discourse, it becomes apparent that 'torture porn' is applied to narratives made after 2003 that centralize abduction, imprisonment, and torture. These films focus on protagonists' fear and/or pain, encoding the latter in a manner that seeks to 'inspire trepidation, tension, or revulsion for the audience' (Jones 2013: 8).

The press discourse was not principally designed to delineate a sub-genre, however. Rather, it allowed critics to disparage popular horror movies. Torture porn films – according to their detractors – are comprised of violence without sufficient narrative or character development (see McCartney 2007, Slotek 2009). The label allowed critics to posit that various horror films adhered to a shared set of values and a narrative formula. Indeed, critics typically presented individual films and filmmakers as a collective, as if each were intending to 'outdo' another by intensifying the amount of gory violence displayed within each film (see Johnson 2007, Puig 2009), and by aiming to shock audiences who allegedly treat cinema-going as a masochistic endurance test (see Billson 2008, Hare 2010, Hill 2007). Torture porn films have been presented as 'shoddy … lazy' examples of filmmaking (Nelson 2010; see also Tookey 2007). Even more damningly, torture porn films have been deemed altogether 'pointless' (Cumming 2010, Muir 2010) and 'meritless' (Ordona 2010) by some critics.

These attacks illustrate that critics were affronted by torture porn, or (more precisely) by its presence in the mainstream multiplex context. It appears that critics were intentionally aiming to drive torture porn out of that context. Notably, the films described (and decried) as torture porn were distributed theatrically (Jones 2013: 14). Few critics expressed concerns about the availability of torture porn on DVD, or the continued release of direct-to-VOD torture porn films. This is unsurprising given that press critics typically focus on cinematic releases rather than the home-viewing context. By pushing torture porn out of the multiplex, critics would no longer have to review films that they (evidently) found distasteful. That agenda is evident in recent responses to torture porn, including Smith's admission that enduring 'the extremes of *Hostel* and *Saw*' was 'the most challenging part of [her] otherwise rewarding job as a film critic' (Smith 2017), and Lee's disgruntlement that 'the hardest' horror is usually relegated to 'the periphery', but was 'on wide release' in the *Saw* franchise's hey-day. Lee's explicit denouncement of *Jigsaw* as a return 'of ultra-violence that's long been pushed back to the realm of the video nasty' (2017) demonstrates his support for the critic's ostensible role as guardian of mainstream cultural sensibilities.

Having supposedly defeated torture porn once before by seeing off the *Saw* franchise in 2010, critics such as Lee seek to hinder a resurgence of multiplex torture porn before it recurs. Indeed, Lee's article used *Jigsaw* as an excuse to describe 'why the horror genre doesn't need a torture porn comeback', prior to *Jigsaw*'s release. This prejudicial assessment of *Jigsaw* exemplifies a problem with torture porn discourse more broadly; torture porn's detractors routinely ignore filmic content in favour of ill-evidenced, hyperbolic claims. To illustrate, numerous commentators exaggeratedly posited that torture porn was a transient fad (see Kenny in Johnson 2007, Monahan 2010), suggesting that torture porn was always-already 'over' (see Barnes 2009, Safire 2007, Mundell 2008). *Saw*'s return threatens to dispel that story, even if some critics strive to maintain that notion in their responses to *Jigsaw*; *The New Zealand Herald* (2017) claims that *Jigsaw* is unnecessary because 'horror has evolved beyond torture porn', for instance. Moreover, torture porn did not decline to such an extent that a 'comeback' would be necessary. Although torture porn may have been less visible in the multiplex since 2010, it certainly has not vanished from press discourse or the filmic landscape. In 2017 alone, numerous theatrical releases have been referred to as torture porn in press reviews, including *Detroit* (see Semley 2017), *Eyes of My Mother* (see Potton 2017a), *Killing Ground* (see O'Sullivan 2017, Jaworowski 2017), and *mother!* (see Nashawaty 2017). Indeed, contrary to long-standing journalistic claims that torture porn has been 'over' since 2007, press use of the term in major English-language world publications peaked in 2009, but has not dipped below 100 uses per year since the term was instituted in late 2006 (see Figure 13).

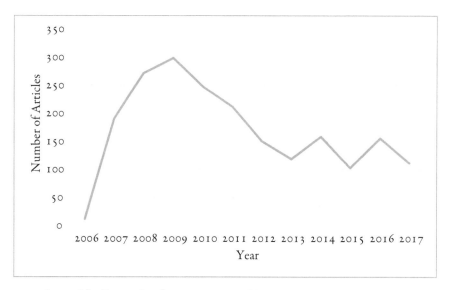

Figure 13. 'Torture Porn' use in major world English-language publications (data source: Nexis UK).

This data only accounts for cases in which the label itself is used. Since torture porn is a pejorative discourse, it is only applied to films that critics seek to disparage. Thus, films that fit into the category, but which do not affront critics are described using alternative terms. Occasionally, there is slippage; films such as *Hounds of Love* (Young, 2016) have been valorized for not being torture porn (Stratton 2017). Yet it is unclear why *Hounds of Love* – in which a young woman is abducted, spends most of the film tied to a bed, and is sexually abused by her male captor – does not match the prevailing (mis)assessment that torture porn is 'a cinematic genre in which women are bound, gagged, [and] raped' (Kingston 2007, see also Orange 2009).

Jigsaw certainly fulfils the essential criteria journalists used to categorize torture porn movies. Protagonists are abducted, chained up, and told to 'confess their sins' under physical duress. In that sense, the sustained ordeal they face could be termed torture. The film follows those protagonists, centralizing their fear and emotional reactions. Since *Jigsaw* is a horror film, the situation is encoded with the apparent intention of leveraging protagonists' emotional responses to generate related emotive reactions in its audience (see Figure 14). The latter is associated with salacious gratuity ('porn') in torture porn discourse (see Jones 2013: 78–80, 129).

Figure 14. *Jigsaw* focuses on chained protagonists' emotive responses. *Jigsaw*, dir. Michael Spierig and Peter Spierig (Twisted Pictures, 2017).

Although *Jigsaw* broadly fits the torture porn mould, it deviates from the series' established characteristics in numerous ways. The series has traditionally played with narrative space and time (Jones 2010). While *Jigsaw*'s twist relies on a temporal sleight-of-hand (revealing that the main game occurred ten years prior to the narrative present), the individual game-stages are not marked by the countdown timers that are among the series' core leitmotifs. The industrial settings synonymous with John Kramer's traps are also absent, having been replaced with an agricultural backdrop. Although these shifts are explained via the plot-twist – the main games are Kramer's first-run, so he has not yet established his modus operandi – the shift also changes the series' established aesthetic. The exaggerated primary-hued lighting that graced the series' shadowy industrial buildings is replaced by a well-lit, neutral palette. The rapid editing that conveyed protagonists' panic in prior episodes is absent from *Jigsaw*. These differences are arguably intended to help relaunch the series anew (see the directors' comments in Quinn 2017). Regardless, they are indicative of discrepancies between *Jigsaw* and the franchise's earlier chapters, rather than a shift away from torture porn's tropes.

Many critics ignore these modifications in favour of erroneous presumptions about the series, however. Disregarding the overt alterations delineated above, Lazic (2017) posits that *Jigsaw* 'seems to consciously adopt a retro, mid-noughties horror movie aesthetic' (Lazic 2017), for example. Gleiberman's claim that *Jigsaw* 'opens, as any *Saw* movie must, in an intensely art-directed enclosed space, with its human guinea pigs trapped, shackled, and terrified' (2017) is patently untrue; *Jigsaw* opens with a police chase across a city, making it the only *Saw* film apart from *Saw IV* (which opens with Kramer's autopsy) not to open with distressed protagonists in an enclosed environment (see Figure 15). Rather than demonstrating that *Jigsaw* is a 'Facile Reboot of a Gruesome, Facile Franchise' (Yoshida 2017), such comments suggest that the critical discourse itself is a lazy re-tread of the accusations allayed at the franchise's previous episodes.[2] Indeed, many critics rehash previous complaints that torture porn exists (as most films do) to turn a profit (see Lacey 2009, Fern 2008, Collins in Di Fonzo 2007), suggesting that 'sheer cash-grab cynicism' is the sole explanation for *Saw*'s reinvigoration (Clarke 2017, see also Scheck, 2017).

---

2   *Saw*'s critics routinely recycle their complaints. Notably, the *Daily Record*'s review of *Saw VI* (Greutert, 2009) purloins their *Saw V* (Hackl, 2009) review, superficially restructuring verbatim self-plagiarized phrases, while simultaneously accusing the series of 'diminishing returns'.

Figure 15. Edgar is chased by police in the atypical outdoor opening sequence of *Jigsaw*. *Jigsaw*, dir. Michael Spierig and Peter Spierig (Twisted Pictures, 2017).

Where critics notice how *Jigsaw* has changed over time, they focus on what was presumed to be torture porn's defining characteristic: gory violence. However, the responses are intriguing. Clarke bemoans that *Jigsaw* offers 'no shock, no horror' resulting in a 'tame' (Clarke 2017) film; Lui terms *Jigsaw* 'more teen-friendly' than its predecessors, and is disappointed because he 'enjoy[s] a good squirm' (Lui 2017). These criticisms suggest not only that the reviewers expected shocking gore (based on prior critical assessments of *Saw* and torture porn), but also that they were aggrieved by its absence. That is, the very trait reviewers previously objected to is now longed for. When Potton declares that this new *Saw* film is 'really not very scary this time' (Potton 2017b), it seems to be a half-hearted admittance that the previous entries' directors – who stood accused of relying on violence and failing to scare (see Robey 2007) – knew what they were doing after all. Either way, it appears as if *Jigsaw*'s creators were doomed to critical failure because it was destined to be measured against 'torture porn', a label generated and imposed by the critical press in the first instance. Thus, *Jigsaw* was *a priori* damned for supposedly adhering to torture porn's facets and condemned for deviating from that established paradigm.

Whether such denouncing will make much difference to the ostensibly entwined fates of the *Saw* franchise and torture porn is another matter. Although critics present their views as representing and speaking to most cinema-goers, *Jigsaw* – the eighth part of an established series – was unlikely to appeal that widely; rather it was likely to attract a core fan base. The latter is mischaracterized in reviews of *Jigsaw* (and in responses to torture porn more broadly). Various critics proclaim that torture porn's 'violent set-pieces' are sufficient to attract fans (Yoshida 2017, see also Scheck 2017), 'who've come to regard empathy as a snowflake emotion' (Gleiberman 2017), and who seek to slake their 'thirst for blood' by watching such films (Lazic 2017). These insults illustrate two pernicious aspects of 'torture porn' discourse. First, fans are disparaged along with the films, suggesting that anyone who enjoys a supposedly 'bad' film is also a 'bad' person (for more detail, see Jones 2013: 46–8). Second, critics' condemnation of alleged fan responses is meant to signal the gulf between the two perspectives, with fan responses being found inadequate. However, that strategy also underscores that critics do not understand why fans find these films appealing (thereby undermining the claims made about what fans think).[3]

The *Saw* series did decline in profitability between 2004 and 2010, but to suggest that 'the series lost its appeal' because '[e]ach film would need to be crueler than the last ... and eventually this became tiresome' (Lee 2017) is to misrepresent the series' narrative progression. The ongoing story was pitched towards a core fan base rather than a crossover audience. For example, Leigh Whannell declares that he wrote *Saw III* 'for the fans', refusing to 'pander to ... people who haven't seen the previous' episodes, even if it meant the latter 'have a lot of trouble following' the sequels or even find them 'completely mystifying' (Whannell 2008). Up until *Jigsaw*,[4] the sequels excluded casual viewers, including those critics who were not sufficiently versed in the ongoing narrative (Jones 2010: 225). Resultantly, it is unsurprising that the franchise declined in profitability over time; if one missed *Saw III*, one was unlikely to return for *Saw IV* (or, being baffled by its story, would be less likely to return for *Saw V*). This also helps to explain why critics perceived the *Saw* series as emphasizing 'gory' over 'story': critics may have been tasked with reviewing one sequel in isolation, and so may not have been able to follow its plot.

---

3   Fan responses are more articulate about *Jigsaw*'s failings; see, for example, Adlakha 2017.
4   *Jigsaw*'s separation from the series' prior events is its central weakness. This deviation may alienate the core fan base. Although its title masks *Jigsaw*'s status as a seventh sequel, a remake of the original would be more likely to reach a crossover demographic.

Moreover then, the fan base predominantly drove Lionsgate's decisions about whether to produce more sequels; while critics pass judgement in words, fans vote with cash. The insults aimed at fans in reviews speak to this underlying reality. Each *Saw* sequel was condemned in the press (see *Canberra Times* 2008; Anderson 2009; Croot 2017), yet the series accrued over $980m (unadjusted, worldwide) in return for an estimated $75m combined production budget (*The Numbers* 2017). *Saw*'s future is based on whether *Jigsaw* turns a sufficient profit, not critics' opinions. *Saw*'s success thus underlines the futility of reviewers' proclamations more generally.

If *Jigsaw* leads to a wider reinvigoration of torture porn in the multiplex setting, horror fans could take the opportunity to embrace 'torture porn', thereby debunking notions that horror films are 'brainless' (Mumford 2017) or 'concocted by and for people with a teenage boy's grasp of morality and human nature' (Yoshida 2017). By replicating 'torture porn's' pejorative connotations, horror fans reproduce a discourse that was founded on disparaging the genre and those who find it appealing. Buying cinema tickets to see torture porn films flags that critics' insults are impotent. Co-opting 'torture porn' as an acceptable subgenre label would be a powerful additional step towards legitimating horror despite those derogatory voices.

Elizabeth Parker

Alex Garland's *Annihilation* (2018)

In its simplest sense, the term 'eco-horror' refers to any work of fiction that reflects and expresses our fears of the nonhuman natural world – as well as our increasingly troubled relationship to this world. The idea that nature is somehow frightening is of course not new, but as a 'subgenre' of horror, eco-horror is a comparatively recent phenomenon. Eco-horror originated with the emergence of the atomic era (Beal 2002, Heumann and Murray 2016, Tidwell 2018) with such classic texts as *Godzilla* (Honda, 1954), had its heyday in the flurry of 1970s 'creature features' such as *Jaws* (Spielberg, 1975), and has endured ever since, varyingly dramatizing our environmental anxieties. Over the last few decades, it has seen numerous progressions and is an area that continues – especially in the current climate of environmental crisis – to evolve and thrive.

'Eco-horror' has typically been conceived as a collective term for texts in which nature, in one form or another (be it oversized insects, killer sharks, or insanity-inducing pollen), attacks humankind in retribution for their mistreatment of nature, and for texts which somehow promote some degree of ecological awareness (Foy 2010). These elements are what we might call the two traditional 'requisites' of eco-horror. The former, that of nature's revenge, is easily the most common 'type' of eco-horror, reflecting the genre's origins in fears concerning humanity's increasingly harmful presence in this world. This 'nature-strikes-back' narrative reached its zenith in the 1970s, with countless eco-horror titles released in this decade, owing in large part to the popularization of environmental awareness in the 1960s (e.g. Carson's 1962 *Silent Spring*, the 1964 Wilderness Act, and the formation of the Environmental Protection Agency). Such titles reflect back to us what Simon C. Estok has famously called 'ecophobia': humankind's longstanding 'contempt' for and 'fear' of the natural world (2009). Moreover, they violently undermine the common tendency to view nature as a mere 'object' (Clark 2011: 57), 'passive resource' (Hall 2011: 4), or 'background' (Marder 2013: 3). They cast nature, instead, as an active, consuming threat – frighteningly reversing our consumption of nature – as it becomes either literally edacious or threatens to swallow civilization through its constant encroachment. The second 'requisite' of eco-horror, the elevation of the green agenda, suggests that eco-horror should be didactic: it should provide us with cautionary tales. These stories should awaken us from the widespread apathy and/or paralysis that accompanies environmental crisis. They should do so in part by transforming ecological issues so enormous and surreal as to be easily ignored into tangible fictionalizations. This is demonstrated, for example, in *Godzilla*, where the gargantuan lizard-like monster that terrorizes entire cities is strangely enough more palatable than the spectre of atomic dread for which it stands. Moreover, in encouraging ecological awareness, these texts provide us with more ecocentric (as opposed to anthropocentric) perspectives, thus destabilizing ideas of humankind's supremacy.

In recent years, there has been a significant shift in how eco-horror is defined and conceived. Explicit calls have been made for a 'more expansive definition of eco-horror' (Soles and Rust 2014: 509). The aforementioned 'requisites' of eco-horror remain dominant, but as a basis for wholly defining eco-horror, they are increasingly cited as too restrictive. For example, the 'nature-strikes-back' paradigm has been criticized for only *seeming* to give nature an ecocentric voice, whilst imbuing it with decidedly *human* motivations of revenge and domination (Keetley 2017). Examples in which nature is shown as truly alien are decidedly rarer. Similarly, the stipulation that eco-horror intentionally promotes eco-awareness is also in question, as this limits eco-horror to its most 'obvious' texts, excluding a wealth of narratives that may be valuably interpreted within an eco-horror framework. Indeed, this leads to the key idea that eco-horror, perhaps, should no longer be strictly delineated as a *genre*. As Christy Tidwell suggests, eco-horror is 'not just [...] a distinct subgenre of horror', but 'an effect that may surface within other horror narratives as well' (2018: 116).

Unsurprisingly, work in this field has recently flourished, inciting ever-more nuanced discussion and debate. This is due in part to the fact that the term 'Anthropocene'[1] is increasingly common. The growing awareness that we

---

1   This term was first suggested in 2000 as a title for our current geological age, beginning in the eighteenth century, in which human activity has been the dominant influence on climate and environment.

have detrimentally affected everything from the ozone layer down spills into our fictions: it is therefore more fitting, perhaps, to talk in terms of 'Anthropocene Horrors' than 'eco-horrors'. This takes for granted Lisa Garforth's argument that environmental disaster is now 'embedded in our social consciousness' (2005: 393) and allows for a wider discussion of all texts which tie in with what Tidwell calls eco-horror's 'broader functions' of 'blurring the lines between human and nonhuman' (2018: 116).

Alex Garland's 2018 film *Annihilation* is an interesting and innovative text to discuss in these contexts. Based on the first novel of author Jeff VanderMeer's *Southern Reach* trilogy (2014), though intended as a standalone piece as opposed to the foundation of a franchise, *Annihilation* is filled with various themes and tropes associated with eco-horror and provides an intriguing commentary on the term's evolutions. The film revolves around the mysterious existence of something known only as 'The Shimmer': an enclosed, but ever-expanding and dome-like space in which all living things mutate and transmogrify at unprecedented rates. It follows the expedition and fates of four scientists who enter The Shimmer, all seeking to discover its source at a lighthouse in the fictionalized Blackwater National Park on the East Coast of America. The events are relayed in a series of flashbacks, from the perspective of our protagonist, Lena (Natalie Portman). It transpires that since its appearance several expeditions have been sent into The Shimmer, but only one individual has returned: Lena's husband Kane (Oscar Isaac), who is dying from mysterious causes, thus prompting Lena to enter the alien landscape in order to understand and cure his sickness. We chart the progression of the scientists as one by one they fall victim to the dangers of this environment.

Annihilation plays with and problematizes the idea of the 'nature strikes back' narrative and whilst it contains elements that can be read as enticements to environmental awareness, these are not didactically explicit. Nature here is far from passive, and the nonhuman and human are increasingly imbricated. What is particularly interesting to observe in this film within the context of these ideas is the *ways* in which nature's threats progressively manifest, first through The Shimmer itself, and then through its various 'monsters'.

The physical appearance of The Shimmer, from both the outside and inside, is significant. Externally, it looks like a giant, multi-coloured bubble, its surface evocative of the effect achieved when petroleum is mixed with water (see Figure 16). The symbolic importance here is twofold. Firstly, it is likely no

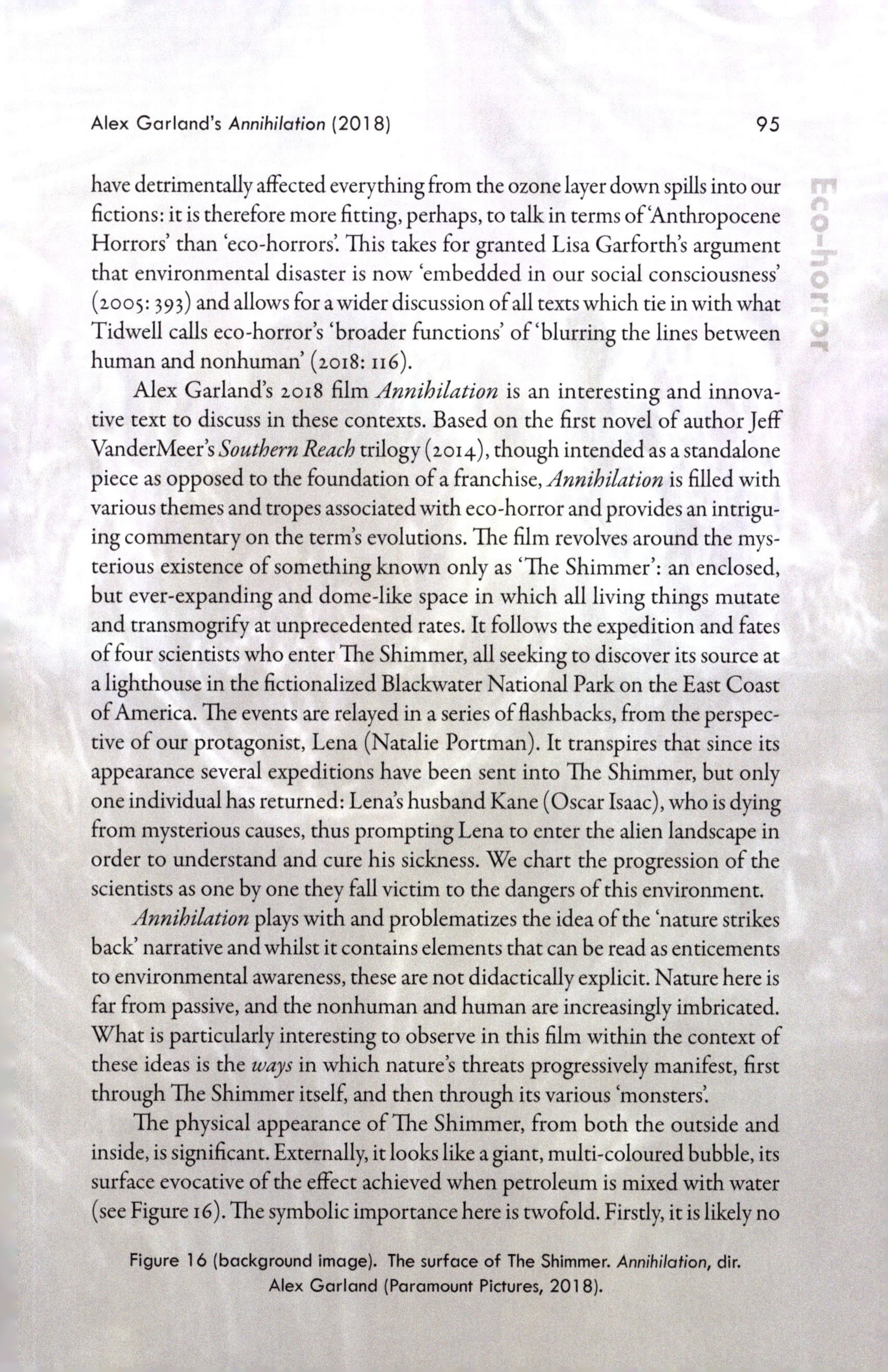

Figure 16 (background image). The surface of The Shimmer. *Annihilation*, dir. Alex Garland (Paramount Pictures, 2018).

coincidence that this 'bubble' forms over a national wildlife reserve, potentially providing a critique of the illusion that 'nature' can ever be neatly divided and sequestered from humankind. Secondly, its surface's likeness to petroleum hints at themes of human-caused pollution: an idea further emphasized by the fact that the reserve is called *Blackwater* National Park and by the lie – that there has been a 'chemical spill' – told to the public to keep them away. Inside, The Shimmer is wet, lush, and vibrantly green and seems at first Edenic. Indeed, Edenic themes are signalled from the outset in the opening lines as Lena is asked 'What did you eat? What do you know?', symbolically alluding to forbidden fruit and knowledge. However, unlike the myth of Eden, The Shimmer is decidedly *not* built for human habitation. It is likened recurrently to one of humankind's most feared enemies of the modern age, cancer, 'mutating' all in its path. At first, these mutations are subtler, observed only in plant life, as different species bleed fantastically into one another, but grow more extreme closer to the centre. The cancerous imagery is emphasized by the fact that The Shimmer is endlessly *spreading*: as it grows in size, forcing the need for evacuations in nearby areas, it provides us with the typical eco-horror image of nature *encroaching* on civilization. Human-made structures, and all humans for that matter, within its parameters are visibly *reclaimed* by the natural world. This exponential growth of The Shimmer demonstrates the consuming threat of nature so frequent in ecological horror, interestingly emphasized in one review of the film in which the alien phenomenon is described as 'the thing that is going to *eat* us all' (Jackson 2018). We have here a visual representation of civilizational extinction, as humankind's centuries-long efforts to 'tame' or 'order' the wilderness are strikingly destroyed.

Nature's threat also manifests in *Annihilation* through its various monstrous corporealizations. Essentially, the film features three main monsters which attack the scientists, the first two of which very directly draw on established eco-horror conventions. These two are twisted versions of real-life animals, harkening back to the infamous 'creature features'. The first of these monsters is what appears to be a crocodile with the teeth of a shark. The 'ingredients' for this amalgamation are significant in the context of eco-horror because both crocodiles and sharks are mainstays in eco-horror in films such as *Killer Crocodile* (De Angelis, 1989) and *Lake Placid* (Miner, 1999), or *Jaws* and *Deep Blue Sea* (Harlin, 1999). Moreover, the fact that

Alex Garland's *Annihilation* (2018)

Figure 17. A crocodile/shark. *Annihilation*, dir. Alex Garland (Paramount Pictures, 2018).

these two animals are merged is also indicative of the tendency in many eco-horror texts towards hybridizations, as in *The Fly* (Cronenberg, 1986) and *Cobragator* (Wynorski, 2017). As the scientists examine the animal, once it has been killed, their predominant focus – which is reflected in the camerawork – is its mouth, therein emphasizing the consuming threats of nature. We significantly have a shot from *inside* its mouth, providing us with a strikingly ecocentric perspective, viewing the humans from within the animal. The second animal adversary we encounter is a creature that has been rather wonderfully dubbed 'screambear' in various anonymous online forums. This creature is also hybridized, but this time is an amalgamation of bear *and human*. Again, the nonhuman animal element is a typical adversary of the 'creature features', whilst the human element makes this monster all the more terrifying, as the human and nonhuman are intermixed. Once more there is an emphasis on the creature's mouth, drawing attention to nature's voracity. We see 'screambear' twice: once when it attacks and takes one of the scientists, Cassie (Tuva Novotny), and later when it returns for the others. What is so effectively frightening in the latter scene is that its human element is not generic. As Cassie, or at least a part of her, is consumed by the bear when

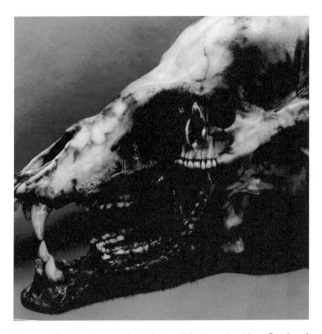

Figure 18. The 'screambear'. *Annihilation*, dir. Alex Garland (Paramount Pictures, 2018).

it first attacks, she specifically *becomes* it. Firstly, part of her skull is just visible on the side of the creature's mouth and some of her teeth can be inside its mouth – details which are much clearer in lit images of the bear's artistic design (see Figure 18).

What is most sinister, however, is the fact that her dying screams become the creature's roar, which are then used to lure prey. This beast is an unforgettable demonstration of ecophobic dread, as the illusion that humans and nature can remain wholly distinct is harshly contradicted. This idea ties in with recent ecocritical scholarship on 'trans-corporeality', which is essentially the argument that humans are *always* intermeshed with other parts of nature (see Alaimo 2010). The film provides a further exaggerated image of trans-corporeality, as seen in the plants that are discovered towards the centre of The Shimmer. These, we are told, have 'human hox genes', meaning they imitate human form (see Figure 19). One of the scientists, Josie (Tess Thompson), ultimately chooses

Figure 19. Plants taking on human shape. *Annihilation*, dir. Alex Garland (Paramount Pictures, 2018).

to become one of these, as she submits to merging with the natural world in a twisted – or at least, unexpected – version of what it means to become 'one with nature' (see Figure 20).

The last 'monster' in the film is what Lena finally finds in the lighthouse: a metallic, human-shaped, but alien form – literalizing the idea that nature is alien – which mirrors and imitates her every move. This is the most anthropomorphic manifestation of The Shimmer: a fact that is greatly significant in the context of eco-horror, as there is a growing trend in the Anthropocene to move away from representations of humans as the vulnerable species and cast *us* instead as the ultimate threat. Yet, the idea here is complicated as we are refused a human motivation behind this alien nature. In interview, when asked what it *wanted*, Lena replies 'I'm not sure it wanted anything ... it *mirrored* me [but] I'm not even sure it knew I was there'. Its 'motivation', if this word can even be used, has far more to do with its biological life cycle than it does with any sense of want or domination. In the end, as the alien morphs momentarily to look exactly like Lena, it seems that the 'real Lena' sets fire to

Figure 20. Alien nature. *Annihilation*, dir. Alex Garland (Paramount Pictures, 2018).

what has now become her clone and exits The Shimmer, leaving her ablaze reflection to ignite all in its reach. We are thus ostensibly left with a literalized image of self-destruction – or annihilation – which is emblematic of the important eco-horror sentiment that in destroying the nonhuman nature that surrounds us, we in fact only destroy ourselves. However, *Annihilation* does not unambiguously leave us with this message, but instead encourages us to doubt what we have seen and surmised. Though on the surface of it, it seems to some degree a tale of human conquest – Kane and Lena, ostensibly, both survive and escape The Shimmer – there are subtle implications which undermine this 'neater' reading. It is hinted, through visual clues such as close-up images of the characters' eyes, that in fact no human, or 'pure' human, *has* ever escaped The Shimmer. We are encouraged to at least wonder if both 'Kane' and 'Lena' at the end are in fact Shimmer versions, doubles, or hybridizations of their former selves. In this version of events, what we are left with is not a tale of human conquest, but of *nonhuman* conquest. We are presented with an alien parody of both traditional 'ends' and human 'beginnings': in the denouement, the alien versions of Kane and Lena on the one hand satirize our romantic 'happily ever afters' of the reunited couple, and on the other hand, offer us twisted revisions of Adam and Eve, as the first 'man' and 'woman' of an entirely new species.

Eco-horror is a multifarious, growing, and fascinating area of horror today. Thriving and evolving amidst cultural conversations centring on the

Anthropocene, it provides important commentaries on and representations of our complex relationship with and to the natural world. *Annihilation* serves as an interesting case study when it comes to the future of eco-horror and how we can define and conceive it: in this instance, what might formerly be sequestered as a science fiction narrative is opened up to an analysis of its more horrific depictions of nature, using 'eco-horror' less as a categorical signifier and more as a critical lens. It forces us – and this is the very essence of eco-horror I think – to ask the difficult questions as we consider our place, and if we even *should* have a place, in the natural world.

Thomas Fahy

The Duffer Brothers' *Stranger Things* (2016–present)

Horror and Nostalgia

The immense popularity of the television series *Stranger Things*, which premiered in the summer of 2016, surprised creators Matt and Ross Duffer. The twin brothers had been struggling filmmakers when Netflix decided to greenlight their show about a group of middle school friends battling supernatural forces and government conspiracies in the 1980s. They hoped this valentine to Stephen King and Stephen Spielberg would '[appeal] to people like us who [were] nostalgic for this style of storytelling' (Briger 2017), but it resonated with younger viewers as well.

In many ways, *Stranger Things* celebrates the important place of both horror and cinema in 1980s America. Joyce Byers (Winona Ryder), for example, surprises her youngest son with movie tickets to *Poltergeist* (1982). The close-knit protagonists dress as Ghostbusters for Halloween, walk along railroad tracks like the buddies in *Stand by Me* (1986), and escape government agents with the help of a telekinetic friend, reworking the iconic bike-flying sequence in *E. T.: The Extra-Terrestrial* (1982). The bullies in *Stranger Things* evoke the likes of Henry Bowers in *It* (1986) and, as a Cobra Kai costume suggests, the high school thugs of *The Karate Kid* (1984). Likewise, the scientific tests performed on Eleven (Millie Bobby Brown) resemble those in Stephen King's *Firestarter* (1980), and the Demogorgon, a predatory supernatural creature from the Upside Down, attempts to stretch through walls like Freddy Krueger hovering over Nancy's (Heather Langenkamp's) bed in *A Nightmare on Elm Street* (1984). This list only scratches the surface, for these types of cinematic and literary allusions shape every aspect of *Stranger Things*, including narrative, characterization, directorial choices, and themes. In the tradition of horror and science fiction, the Duffer brothers use these intertextualities to challenge nostalgic idealizations of the past and to comment on some of

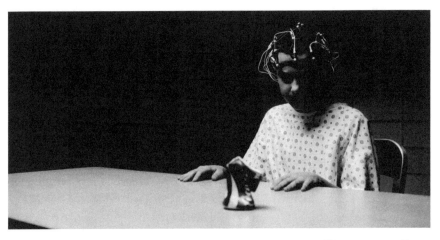

Figure 21. Eleven crushes a Coke can with her mind. *Stranger Things*, creators The Duffer Brothers (Netflix, 2016). Netflix/Photofest. © Netflix.

the darker aspects of human nature such as 'abuse, divorce, violence, cruelty, substance abuse, depression, death' (Miyamoto 2017; see Figure 21).

Before looking more closely at *Stranger Things*, we should not take this nostalgic appeal for granted. Critics continue to dismiss 1980s horror films as vapid, sensationalized, and redundant. This critical assessment raises some questions: is there anything redeeming about 1980s horror? Can these films help explain the popularity of *Stranger Things*? And can they enhance our understanding of the show's social commentary?

Many film critics consider 1980s horror, like Freddy Krueger himself, to be the bastard son of a hundred maniacs. It's a decade that lacked originality and good taste, producing countless sequels and B-movies such as *Splatter University* (1984), *Cannibal Hookers* (1987), *Cheerleader Camp* (originally titled *Bloody Pom Poms* (1988)), and *Las Vegas Bloodbath* (1989). It abandoned the gritty, countercultural sensibility of the previous decade, that contained films such as *The Texas Chainsaw Massacre* (1974) and *Halloween* (1978), for serial killers wielding knives and campy one-liners with equal ferocity. It privileged special effects over characterization, serving up a host of interchangeable victims that made audiences root for the likes of Freddy, Jason, Michael, and even a doll named Chucky. And its shift from remote, rural settings to a suburban landscape teeming with consumer products revealed a shameless attempt to capitalize on the teenage market. Coca-Cola even acquired Columbia Pictures in 1982 to secure more advertising in film, television, and cable (Prince 2000: 51). From this vantage point, it's not surprising that critics like Robin Wood find 'little to salvage' in 1980s horror (Wood 2003: 169).

These characteristics, however, need to be understood and evaluated in the context of 1980s culture – beginning with its predilection for sequels. 1989 marked a banner year for sequels, featuring the fifth instalments of *Halloween* (Othenin-Girard), *A Nightmare on Elm Street* (Hopkins), and *The Howling* (Sundstrom) as well as *Amityville 4: The Evil Escapes* (Stern), and *Friday the 13th Part VIII: Jason Takes Manhattan* (Heddon). Even technology, through the development of the videotape and videocassette recorder (VCR), fuelled repetition: 'Yearly sales of VCRs jumped from 802,000 in 1980 to 11–12 million per year during the second half of the decade', and over 200 million pre-recorded videocassettes were sold in 1989 alone (Prince 2000: 94). One could now record films on television, re-watch tapes at will, and copy videos for others. This proliferation of tapes and sequels embodied the orgiastic celebration of consumerism in the Reagan era. Watching another instalment of *Friday the 13th* or perusing the crammed shelves at Blockbuster, which first opened in 1985, promised more of a good thing in a culture that believed enough was never enough.

Special effects played an important role in many of these films as well. Vivid onscreen transformations – like those experienced by David (David Naughton) in *An American Werewolf in London* (Landis, 1981) and Seth (Jeff Goldblum) in *The Fly* (Cronenberg, 1986) – marvelled and horrified audiences. At the same time, this imagery played into the country's growing obsession with the body. The exercise craze, fad diets, and plastic surgery gave testament to America's self-punishing desire to rip away the old skin for something new. In many ways, 1980s horror presented the killer's violence as a metaphor for what many people were doing to themselves to be thin and 'beautiful'. All manner of tools – knives, axes, cleavers, drills, arrows, spears, chainsaws, ice pics – were used to shred the body in these films, and many Americans appeared hell-bent on doing the same. Not surprisingly, some filmmakers considered the gym a perfect setting for this self-destructive obsession. One trailer for *Killer Workout* (Prior, 1987) weaves images of weightlifting and aerobics with a description of failed dieting: 'You've tried Atkins, South Beach, and even the Cookie Diet. This October lose those extra pounds with *Killer Workout*'. The film itself features enough dance routines to rival a music video, and the killer eliminates clients with everything from a barbell to an enlarged safety pin.

This emphasis on bodies may explain another aspect of 1980s horror that is typically lambasted by critics – the limited characterization of its victims. In *Shock Value*, Jason Zinoman criticizes the 'flood of unnecessary sequels' for elevating the status of the monster at the expense of developing his victims into sympathetic figures: 'Just as the killers seemed increasingly ordinary in mainstream horror, the victims in the most popular horror movies became completely interchangeable, forgettable blank slates. This shifted the audience identification radically. People rooted for the killers and saw their victims as irrelevant casualties' (Zinoman 2012: 216). Yet one could argue that 1980s audiences identified with both killers and indistinguishable victims. Dieting to look more like Christie Brinkley and working out to achieve the muscle tone of Sylvester Stallone made physical appearance the marker for personal value. It suggested that everyone should look the same, and in a sense, it made millions of Americans feel like Victim Number Three. No novel critiqued this dynamic more savagely than Bret Easton Ellis's masterpiece *American Psycho* (1991). Protagonist Patrick Bateman views women as hardbodies and himself (as well as other men) in terms of ripped abdominals, body fat, fashion sense, and an encyclopaedic knowledge of skincare products. Everything in 1980s yuppie culture, according to Ellis, de-individualized people, and he reinforces this message by making all of the characters indistinguishable from one another. As the novel suggests, this context made it easy for people to identify with being nothing more than a body.

Lastly, horror films tended to migrate to the suburbs in this decade, and Carter Soles attributes this geographical shift to teen culture: 'For as teenagers (rather than whole families) became the sole focus of late 1970s and 1980s slashers, the sites of their encounters with killers migrated to suburban neighborhoods, summer camps, sorority houses, and the like' (Soles 2012: 247–8). Just as Soles argues that the 1970s cannibalistic hillbilly enabled (sub)urban viewers 'to project their fears of environmental collapse' (235), the violation of suburban spaces in 1980s horror speaks to similar concerns about the environmental costs of these communities. Whether through the destruction of marshes, swamps, forests, or rivers, suburbia devoured more than a million acres of land annually in the 1980s. *Poltergeist*, for example, critiques these excesses when the Freelings learn that Cuesta Verde was built on an old cemetery. Zombies, too, found themselves at home in the suburbs. The use of an unfinished housing development in *The Return of the Living Dead Part II* (Wiederhorm, 1988) challenges audiences to see beyond the veneer of tract housing, manicured lawns, and white picket fences to consider the environmental consequences of so much construction.

Unlike Robin Wood's assertion that 1980s horror essentially reinforces the dominant ideology, my reading of this period argues the opposite. All of the critical focus on slasher films, which has made figures like Freddy Krueger shorthand for the decade's horror, tends to overshadow the genre's diversity and its nuanced engagement with cultural issues. As Kendall R. Phillips has argued, horror films tend to project the nation's collective anxieties on the screen, and in doing so, they engage in 'the broader politics of their day' (Phillips 2005: 8). The preoccupation with fitness and fat bias in 1980s horror offers a powerful example of this. A great deal of these works explore concerns central to American life, and they do so in ways that remain provocative and socially relevant today. Placed in the context of 1980s America, they demonstrate a richness and versatility often overlooked by critics.

Stranger Things taps into this tradition through its characters' concerns about dieting, junk food, and environmental harm. Dustin (Gaten Matarazzo), for instance, has the eating habits typical of fat kids in 1980s films. Like the diets of Vern (Jerry O'Connell) in *Stand by Me* (Reiner, 1986), Chunk in *The Goonies* (Donner, 1985), and Chubby (Mark Holton) in *Teen Wolf* (Daniel, 1985), Dustin snacks on Pringles, Bazooka gum, Vanilla Wafers, and Smarties. In a moment reminiscent of Elliot (Henry Thomas) luring E. T. with Reese's Pieces, Dustin feeds 3 Musketeers candy to a Demogorgon. Yet he never gets called fat, chunky, or chubby. Instead, his lisp and absent collarbone (a result of the actor's cleidocranial dysplasia) becomes the focal point of school bullies. After writing this condition into his character, the Duffer brothers decided to abandon the 'fat friend' trope and shifted body weight anxieties onto Chief Hopper (David Harbour). In the first chapter of *Stranger Things 2*, for example, the police station secretary replaces his donut with an apple. He tells Eleven, 'I'm going to eat all this candy. I'm going to get fat. It's very unhealthy to leave me out here' ('Chapter Two: Trick or Treat, Freak'). And in the closing moments of season two, he claims to be on a diet. These details acknowledge the preoccupation with fatness at the time. Like Billy Halleck's failed diets in Stephen King's *Thinner* (1984) and the heavyset female victims trying to lose weight in Thomas Harris's *The Silence of the Lambs* (1988), the violence in *Stranger Things* serves, in part, as a metaphor for what many Americans were doing to themselves to be thin.

Junk food permeates the show's portrait of American life as well. The characters consume Kentucky Fried chicken, donuts, Jiffy Pop popcorn, soda, and syrup-soaked waffles. Eleven's first meal outside of the laboratory – French-fries, a hamburger, and ice cream – sets her on the path to becoming a junk food addict. At one point, the Chief jokes that her Eggo breakfast topped with syrup, whipped cream, and candy, 'is only 8,000 calories' ('Chapter Three: The Pollywog'), and *Stranger Things* clearly links these cravings for sugar, fat, and salt with the addictiveness of alcohol and cigarettes. Such connections appear throughout 1980s films. Whether through Grandpa's Oreos and root beer in *The Lost Boys* (Schumacher, 1987), Mark's (Jim Carrey's) ice cream truck in *Once Bitten* (Storm, 1985), the junk food in Dana's (Sigourney Weaver's) apartment in *Ghostbusters* (Reitman, 1984), the potato chips under Dana's (Dominique Dunne's) pillow in *Poltergeist* (Hooper, 1982), or the junk food consumed regularly by the Elm Street teens, 1980s horror, like *Stranger Things*, presents the processed food industry as a monster lurking in the open, but instead of wielding a knife, it kills slowly with every bite.

Lastly, fears about environmental devastation haunt both 1980s horror and *Stranger Things*. The Upside Down, a dark reflection of our world, is a place of death and decay. It exists without sunlight and vegetation, and in many ways, it offers an apocalyptic vision of humanity's potential to destroy the planet through nuclear technology, toxic waste, acid rain, and depleted ozone. The show points to consumer waste as one source of the problem. The friends take shelter in a field with abandoned buses and cars, and the Bryers's shed stores nothing but garbage. In addition to trash, the Demogorgon destroys the landscape itself, killing trees, grass, crops, and pumpkins. The show's environmental message becomes most pointed when Nancy (Natalia Dyer) and Jonathan (Charlie Heaton) use the threat of 'dangerous toxins, a leak from the lab' to create a media scandal that closes the laboratory – likening it to the nuclear coolant spill of Three Mile Island ('Chapter 5: Dig Dug'). This detail alludes to a common trope in 1980s horror in which government agencies or the military illegally dump toxic waste with deadly consequences. For instance, the Nuclear Regulatory Commission disposes radioactive materials beneath New York City, transforming a subterranean homeless community into cannibals in *C.H.U.D.* (Cheek, 1984), and a toxin created for the military reanimates the dead in both *The Return of the Living Dead* (O'Bannon, 1985) and *The Return of the Living Dead Part II*. Whether from chemical agents, nuclear waste, or car exhaust, *Stranger Things* draws on this tradition of exploring the apocalyptic consequences of such pollution, and it reminds viewers that the survival of humanity depends on the well-being of the planet.

In these ways, the show presents dieting, junk food, and environmental harm as strangely familiar sites of horror that continue to haunt and threaten American life. While nostalgia explains some of the appeal of *Stranger Things*, its exploration of these themes also accounts for part of the show's popularity today. Its messages about fatness and thinness, about excess and restraint, about the dangers of addiction, and about environmental responsibility are more pressing than ever. They demand attention and activism just as they did in the 1980s. Perhaps, when placed in dialogue with these works, contemporary horror like *Stranger Things* might be most frightening in its revelation about how little has changed or at least about how far we still need to go to combat issues such as fat bias, processed food addiction, and ecological harm.

Steffen Hantke

Alex Garland's *Ex Machina* (2014)

Across all their incarnations in twentieth-century popular culture, robots are commonly considered a staple of science fiction. Though the imagination that came up with the figure of the fabricated human coming to life is fed by premodern sources, reaching back to the Greek myth of Galatea or the Jewish myth of the Golem, its most popular cultural expression relevant to the twentieth century and beyond comes from Mary Shelley's *Frankenstein, or The Modern Prometheus* (1818). Conceived at the dawn of industrial modernity, Shelley's novel explores to full horrific effect of Freud's observation that 'waxwork figures, ingeniously constructed dolls and automata' evoke the uncanny when endowed with animation, as does, conversely, any phenomenon that triggers 'vague notions of automatic – mechanical – processes that may lie hidden behind the familiar image of a living person' (Freud 2003: 135). Shelley's novel wrapped these horrors at its mythological core with layers of significance more relevant than ever to contemporary scientific and technological rationality. Shelley's deployment of the rhetoric of science in the service of bringing to life the tragically misunderstood and abandoned wretch – paying tribute to the medical jargon of her time's fascination with electricity – placed this robotic creature firmly into the tradition of science fiction Shelley herself would help to shape. So successful would this placement turn out to be that, when it came to the robot, the other tradition Shelley's novel would help to shape would be relegated to the margins of popular awareness. Undoubtedly, *Frankenstein* is one of the greatest novels in the Gothic tradition, and thus, at the very least, a prototypical horror text. In that tradition, the novel's nameless wretch has registered not specifically as a robot, but more broadly as a monster. Its effect on others is an indication of his nature as is its body composed of rotting parts pilfered from the local graveyard in the middle of the proverbial 'dark and stormy' night. It may take later horror films in which artificial creation is achieved by biological rather than mechanical technology (*Species* (Donaldson, 1995), *Splice* (Natali, 2009), *Morgan* (Scott, 2016)) to remind us that Shelley's wretch – an artificial creature brought to life by a human creator – is not just, broadly speaking, a monster, but very specifically a robot.

With Shelley's novel standing at the crossroads of the two genres – science fiction branching off in one direction, horror in the other – the history of popular culture has seen to it that the robot has shed its generic impurity, at least in the popular imagination, in favour of science fiction. It is easy to be distracted from the deep unease that accompanies all representations of the robot by the countless kids' toys, the cute robots, the debased harmless versions of robots that circulate through popular culture. It is that deep unease, however – repressed or sublimated as it may very well be – that still gets centre stage whenever a film or television series permits the robot to return to its roots in Gothic horror. Among the recent films that stage such a return of the robot to the horror genre and do so with a full awareness of the intertextual richness of the figure (*The Machine* (James, 2013), *Automata* (Ibanez, 2014), *Chappie* (Blomkamp, 2015), *Ghost in the Shell* (Sanders, 2017), and *Blade Runner 2049* (Scott, 2017), as well as television series like *Real Humans* (2012–16) and *Westworld* (2016–)), is *Ex Machina*. Reading this film as a horror film and reading the history of films about robots as engaging with the horror genre throughout, will be the goal of this discussion.

Ex Machina tells the story of Caleb (Domhnall Gleeson), a lowly coder in a global digital corporation, being invited to a remote wilderness retreat by the company head, Nathan (Oscar Isaac), to serve as the human component in conducting a Turing test on Nathan's top-secret robot Ava (Alicia Vikander). As Caleb's paranoia about Nathan's objectives increases in the course of his interactions with both of them, Ava's endearing desire to become more human grows, in turn sinister and then violent, culminating in her killing her creator Nathan and imprisoning Caleb, outwitting both as she makes a successful escape into the wider world.

As much as the film's cast is stripped down to these three major players – with another female robot named Kyoko (Sonoya Mizuno) added along the way – its choice of Nathan's remote wilderness mansion as its claustrophobic major location as well as its basic plot line, is lean and austere and yet, simultaneously, richly resonant with added intertextual layers. Many of these layers reach back to the point of origin of the robot as a figure of Gothic horror, *Frankenstein*. From the robot's desire to win approval from its creator and then, rejected and abandoned, turning with murderous violence against him, to the whisking away to a remote location of a guileless innocent by the story's overpowering, sinister Byronic hero, *Ex Machina* follows the Gothic script. By the end of the twentieth century, however, that script already includes a number of gender reversals that had, at their inception, turned eighteenth-century values on their head, but had become a standard variant of the familiar story (see Creed 1993). Caleb, the innocent implicated into a plot beyond his comprehension, plays the role of the Gothic heroine, as much as Ava takes over the role of Shelley's menacingly hyper-masculine wretch.

Though topical and often satiric, science fiction has often played the gender reversal of the Gothic monster from male to female for laughs (*Weird Science* (Hughes, 1985), *Making Mr Right* (Seidelman, 1987)). *Ex Machina*, meanwhile, taps into a rich vein of techno-horror in which the robot's femininity draws more vitally from film noir's femme fatales (*Eve of Destruction* (Gibbon, 1991), *Terminator 3* (Mostow, 2003)). Thus, it is hardly surprising that, in her final act of violence against Nathan, Ava gets to wield a phallic knife, leaving the hapless Caleb imprisoned in Nathan's secure wilderness fortress like a fairy-tale princess in her father's accursed castle. Like all the other robots rising up against their creators, Ava is dangerous, a force to be reckoned with (see Figure 22).

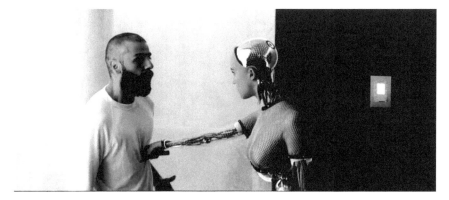

Figure 22. Ava kills Nathen. *Ex Machina*, dir. Alex Garland (Universal Pictures, 2014).

Reading *Ex Machina* as a horror film, viewers will pay attention not only to Ava's monstrous actions but also, and more importantly, to her robotic body. As Julia Kristeva's introduction of abjection into the discussion of horror (*Powers of Horror* 1980) continues to remind us, it is the body in its disturbing mortality – put on display by the horror film through the barely tolerable yet endlessly fascinating display of surface penetrated, of warm and wet and squishy insides erupting, of blood and guts and gore-spilling and contaminating – that often helps to draw the line between science fiction and horror. Science fiction often lands on the side of bodily transcendence, or even the bodily sublime, when imagining the robot. It often keeps abjection at bay by favouring the mechanical over the biological when it comes to granting us a glimpse of the robot body's insides. At first glance, *Ex Machina*'s visual imagination casts Ava as a classic science fiction robot, her body not only vaguely mechanical and digital with its transparent abdominal section where something is always humming and blinking just below the viewer's perceptual threshold. But, as with its gendering, Ava's body bears the mark of an intertextual lineage richer than this simple dichotomy between biological and mechanical (see Figure 23).

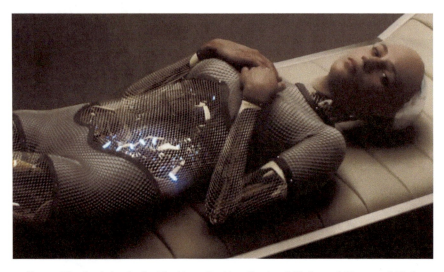

Figure 23. Ava's body. *Ex Machina*, dir. Alex Garland (Universal Pictures, 2014).

For one, there is the rich generic hybrid of techno-horror, the overlap between horror and science fiction that has, ever since *Alien* (Scott, 1979), worked hard at blurring the boundary between the two conceptual categories. In *Alien*, a robot is spectacularly torn apart and opened up to the viewer's gaze: in Ridley Scott's original, this is Ashe (Ian Holm), whose insides turn out to be filled with a slimy, milky liquid, spurting and oozing throughout a tangle of vaguely organic tubes and bubbles, giving off the occasional muted electric spark as his system is shutting down. Scott's visuals replay Kristevan abjection in every register, mixing connotations of seminal fluid with those of blood and shit. This robot's insides are both wet and sticky, much like a human body, and yet vaguely mechanical and digital, like a machine. Kristeva would applaud the mixing of categories, the collapse of meaning, and the unspeakable yet fascinating spectacle of human mortality.

Ava's insides failing to look anything like Ashe's do not make *Ex Machina* pure science fiction. Conscious of the visual tradition initiated by *Alien*'s ingenious abject imagery, *Ex Machina* self-consciously positions Ava within a different strand of horror's iconographic genealogy, this one plotted against *Alien*'s explicitly abject imagery. In fact, Ava fits into a tradition that displaces abjection from the body of the monster to its surrounding space or objects or other bodies within its reach (Hantke 2003). This tradition gained traction with the rise of psychological horror in the early 1960s and became a dominant trope during the 1990s serial killer cycle, all of which posited monsters whose outsides were conspicuously lacking the abject markers that had been horror's stock in trade for the visualization of otherness. From the displacement of monstrosity from Norman Bates's body to that of the rotting corpse of his late mother (*Psycho*, Hitchcock: 1960), to the blood spattering emanating from his butchered victims' bodies covering Patrick Bateman's body like a mask (*American Psycho*, Harron, 2000), to the signs of insanity inscribed upon the pages of John Doe's notebooks (*Se7en*, Fincher, 1995) and the walls of Buffalo Bill's underground lair (*Silence of the Lambs*, Demme, 1991), abjection travels in search of a space where it can manifest itself. *Ex Machina* plays that same game. While Ava's body is disarmingly transparent, revealing nothing but comforting mechanical dryness, her creator's body is a site of abjection throughout. Sweating and panting prodigiously during his workout sessions or spilling out of his gym shorts in drunken torpor, Nathan provides a perpetually

Figure 24. Nathan's body. *Ex Machina*, dir. Alex Garland (Universal Pictures, 2014).

uncomfortable spectacle of the body in its struggle against, and embodiment of, abjection (see Figure 24).

It is all too fitting that his body should be the one into which Ava plunges the phallic knife in the end. What is more, the disavowal of abjection is not only ensured by Nathan's demise. During Ava's escape from captivity, the earlier robotic model, Kyoko (Sonoya Mizuno), is also mangled and ripped. Unlike Ava, who is unique, Kyoko is merely an iteration in a series. As such, she exists in a state of being disembodied by being endlessly repeatable, her essence dispersed along a developmental series of earlier models. Unlike Ava, whose female sexuality ultimately remains opaque to the same degree to which it is identified with her pragmatic strategizing to escape imprisonment, Kyoko's body is explicitly linked to sexuality. Taking its cue from Kristeva and positing female sexuality as abject, the film displaces sexuality from Ava's disarmingly transparent body to that of Kyoko. Consequently, it is Kyoko's face, not Ava's, from which the deceptively human surface is peeled off to reveal the metallic substratum of the robotic self underneath – an iconic moment of robot films, replayed endlessly in films from *Westworld* (Crichton, 1973) to *Terminator* (Cameron, 1984).

As a monster from whose body abjection is strategically displaced, Ava stands in a long tradition that recognizes its disavowal as a dehumanizing condition imposed upon the body by industrial and post-industrial modernity. In this tradition, *Ex Machina* links Ava to robots that have a far more complex relationship to their bodies: the HAL 9000 in *2001* (Kubrick, 1968), Proteus in *Demon Seed* (Cammell, 1977), or 'Mother' in *Alien*. Kubrick's *2001* (1968) goes furthest in imagining HAL either as a completely disembodied voice and all-seeing red camera eye, or imagining the entire space ship Discovery as HAL's body. As the controlling consciousness animating this body, HAL sanitizes itself by delivering the humans inhabiting it like infectious organisms unto their silent, antiseptic, and conspicuously bloodless deaths. Scott's production design for *Alien* disambiguates Kubrick's complexity by liberating abjection from its representational – and ideological – constraints; the vaguely biological interiors of the Nostromo are simultaneously Mother's digestive and her reproductive organs, mixing birth and excretion in a fantasy that recuperates the full impact of abjection.

A whiff of HAL's red-eyed paranoia surrounding fully technological environments controlled by disembodied robot intelligences still hangs around *Ex Machina* but is attenuated by our gradual acceptance of digitally responsive environments as a matter of daily life. But as *Ex Machina* ties the robot into a framework of contemporary anxieties around surveillance and the loss of privacy, the film's carefully thought-out production design presents viewers with a space that, though ostensibly the Gothic workshop of horror's mad scientist, is more intimate and familiar. Despite its high-tech bells and whistles, Nathan's wilderness retreat is a version of the suburban home, one of the horror film's most cherished settings. Since the spread of suburbanization in 1950s America, Freudian family dramas unfold in these spaces, with Nathan as the patriarch violently trying to control the Oedipal narrative emerging from the romantic ties between Ava and Caleb. As horrors do not intrude from without but emerge from within this space and the social institutions it houses, *Ex Machina* harks back to the tradition of critical self-examination Robin Wood emphasized in the best of post-classical horror (Wood 2003).

At first glance, reading *Ex Machina* as a horror film seems to produce little of genuine novelty in regard to the robot as an iconic monster. If anything, the film's accomplishment consists primarily of the clever ways in which it selectively mobilizes its intertextual genealogy and connects it to urgent issues of its time. Paranoid anxieties around responsive technology reach back as far as *2001*, even though *Ex Machina* reframes them specifically as a threat emanating from social media owned by digital global corporations. Gender politics in *Ex Machina* follow a similar pattern. Watching Ava stage a successful uprising against her sexist male creator and, in turn, this creator's well-intentioned male enabler, viewers encounter a feminist message in tune with horror's gender politics in the wake of 1970s 'final girls' (Clover 1992). But then *Ex Machina* delivers this gesture in a cinematic vernacular that still casts the female robot Kyoko as an object within the male gaze – ostensibly that of Nathan and Caleb, but effectively that of an implied viewer construed as male. Again, the film is not breaking new ground with its sexual politics, as much as Nathan's unapologetic sexism is tempered by Caleb's guilt-ridden liberal complicity (and to the extent that Kyoko is the suitable sexual object for Nathan's gaze, just as Ava is for Caleb's – and both are for ours). Nonetheless, *Ex Machina* captures with uncanny prescience a sense of an ongoing cultural dynamic that tries to balance itself between the neoliberal permissiveness in matters of social policy on the one hand and the stubborn persistence of neoconservative sexism within the culture on the other. Years before the 2016 presidential election and its outcome and aftermath, *Ex Machina* demonstrates that the most *recent* popular model in life-like robotics may not always be the most *advanced* model. With robots as with the horror film, the more things change, the more they stay the same.

Stacey Abbott

James DeMonaco's *The Purge: Anarchy* (2014)

Claims of the death of the horror genre seem to recur with every decade but, like any great movie monster, when audiences and critics start pronouncing its demise, the genre defies expectation and returns with a vengeance. Such a pattern categorizes the horror genre in the twenty-first century. In the early years of the millennium, according to Steffan Hantke, horror criticism was characterized by a 'rhetoric of crisis', in which many critics, taking 'a pessimist's point of view', tended to dismiss contemporary developments in the genre, arguing that the focus on remakes, sequels, and pastiches served to empty the genre of meaning and reduce it to a commercially driven formula (Hantke 2010: viii).[1] Reynold Humphries concluded his discussion of *The American Horror Film* with the statement: 'The state of things is not conducive to optimism, let alone enthusiasm: with the exception of Shayamalan, no major talent has emerged in the last decade and the occasional important film ... seems to be an isolated phenomenon leading nowhere' (2002: 189).[2]

In contrast in 2017, films such as *Get Out* (Peele, 2017) and *IT: Chapter One* (Muschietti, 2017) have courted positive critical responses from mainstream and genre critics, with *Sight and Sound* reviewer Trevor Johnson praising *Get Out* for being 'grounded in the troubled realities of today's America, evidently born of an African American consciousness racked with fear and anger' (2017) while Mark Kermode revelled in *IT*'s coming of age, *Goonies*-inflected style, as an 'energetic romp with crowd-pleasing appeal that isn't afraid to bare its gory teeth' (2017). Horror was even recognized by the 2018 Academic Awards, with

---

1 See Laura Mee (2019) for a counter reading of Horror Remakes in this period.
2 David Church (2006) makes similar claims about the decline of the genre.

Get Out winning the Oscar for Best Original Screenplay, and self-proclaimed horror aficionado Guillermo Del Toro winning Best Director for his modern monster-movie, *The Shape of Water* (2017), which also won Best Film. In 2018, critic Graeme Virtue noted that the contemporary landscape is marked by 'a legion of smart, subversive and downright scary horror movies [that] have been packing them in' (Virtue 2018). It seems the horror genre has never been more popular.

In between its presumed death and this perceived resurgence, however, the genre has been marked by incredible productivity, heightened visibility and increasing globalization. This period has witnessed the global reimagining of the vampire and zombie genres, exploring questions surrounding identity, religion, and gender, alongside anxieties around global pandemics and terrorism in films such as *Let the Right One In* (Alfredson, 2008), *Thirst* (Park, 2009), *Byzantium* (Jordan, 2012), *Transfiguration* (O'Shea, 2016), *28 Days Later* (Boyle, 2002), *Shaun of the Dead* (Wright, 2004), *Dead Snow* (Wirkola, 2009), and *Train to Busan* (Yeon, 2016; see Abbott 2016); the rise of torture horror with extended franchises such as *Saw* (Wan, 2004) and *Hostel* (Roth, 2005) that, according to Isabel C. Pinedo, expresses a post-9/11 'fear of terrorism and ... of our own ambivalence about torture and invasive government surveillance' (Pinedo 2017: 345); and the proliferation of found footage horror responding to changing technologies, including digital video, mobile phones, and screencast, as utilized in films such as *Diary of the Dead* (Romero, 2007), *[REC]* (Balaguéro & Plaza, 2007), *Unfriended* (Gabriadze, 2014) and *Cold Ground* (Delage, 2017; see Blake and Aldana Reyes 2015). While always international in scope, the increasingly globalized film industry alongside international DVD, Blu-ray and streaming markets have allowed horror to circulate across borders with increasing ease. As such, internationally recognized horror films from the USA circulate alongside product from Australia (*Wolf Creek* 2005), Canada (*Ponytpool* 2008), France (*Martyrs* 2008), Iran (*Under the Shadow* 2016), Japan (*Dark Water* 2002), Norway (*Troll Hunter* 2010) South Korea (*The Wailing* 2016), Spain (*The Orphanage* 2007) and the UK (*Eden Lake* 2008; see Hudson 2017; Siddique and Raphael 2016).

While horror has often featured work produced by women directors the new millennium has seen an increase in the number of women directors working within the genre from across the globe, revisiting and revisioning Barbara

Creed's notion of 'the monstrous feminine' by producing thought provoking and women-centred explorations of sexuality, desire, grief, the body and motherhood examined through the lens of horror (Creed 1993; see also Short 2006). Notable examples include Ana Lily Amirpour (*A Girl Walks Home Alone At Night* 2014), Marina De Van (*Dans Ma Peau/In My Skin* 2002), Julia Ducournau (*Raw* 2017), Jennifer Kent (*The Babadook* 2014), Karyn Kusama (*The Invitation* 2015), Alice Lowe (*Prevenge* 2017), and Jen and Sylvia Soska (*American Mary* 2012), among others.

Alongside this exciting array of independent global horror cinema, the American horror genre has also become invested in a new selection of franchises such as *Paranormal Activity* (2007–15), *The Conjuring* (2013–16), *Insidious* (2010–18) and *The Purge* (2013–18). Many of these have emerged from Blumhouse productions, a leading producer of twenty-first-century horror, alongside Glass Eye Pix and A24. Glass Eye Pix produces ultra-low budget productions such as *Stakeland* (Mickle, 2010) and *The Innkeepers* (West, 2011) and A24 specializes in art-house horror such as *The Witch* (Eggers, 2015), *It Comes at Night* (Shults, 2017) and *Hereditary* (Aster, 2018). The Blumhouse franchises highlight a conscious marketing of horror toward large mainstream, multi-generational, audiences, producing the films independently and then distributing them via larger studios such as Universal. *The Purge: Anarchy* is a model Blumhouse production that demonstrates the complexity of the mainstream horror market and counters the perception that sequels and franchises represent the dumbing down of horror.

The Purge franchise is comprised, to date, of four films (*The Purge* (DeMonaco, 2013), *The Purge: Anarchy*, *The Purge: Election Year* (DeMonaco, 2016) and *The First Purge* (McMurray, 2018)), plus a television series (DeMonaco 2018–). It is set in a not-too-distant future in which a right-wing party has entered the White House and in order to combat rising crime and unemployment alongside a plummeting economy, they establish an annual event – The Purge – in which for a period of twelve hours all crime is legal. Each film in the series takes place during the Purge and follows a group of people as they attempt to survive the night. While the original film is a variation on the home invasion narrative, where a wealthy patriarch attempts to protect his family and home from a group of Purgers, the first sequel – *Purge: Anarchy* – takes the audience out onto the urban streets. While the first film was an attack on the nuclear family and upper-middle-class privilege, the second is an exposé of the hardships facing the socially and economically disenfranchised. It follows five characters – a working-class African American mother and daughter (Eva and Cali), a Caucasian middle-class husband and wife (Shane and Liz), and a lone white male (Sergeant) – who all end up outside on Purge night. Working together, and under the protection of the heavily armed Sergeant, the group make their way across the city to safety. Along the way they fight off attacks from masked juvenile bikers, a lone rooftop shooter, government funded military operatives using Purge Night to thin out the working-class, multi-ethnic population, and finally a group of the wealthy elite, who pay the less privileged to round up victims for them to hunt safari-style with their high-powered assault weapons. The film is an ideal example of the twenty-first-century American horror film on a number of fronts.

Purge: Anarchy is one of Blumhouse's model micro-budget films, made for $9 million but bringing in a global box office of over $111 million – a model that is proving extremely lucrative for the company. Largely shot at night and on the streets of Los Angeles, it features a small cast, contains no-major stars, and is slickly produced with polished visual imagery and dynamic action set-pieces. *Anarchy*, builds upon the success of twenty-first-century slasher film variations such as *Final Destination* (2000–11) and *Saw* (2004–17), which Ian Conrich describes as representing a hybrid genre, merging the slasher with action and disaster film set pieces (Conrich 2015: 114). Like other examples of twenty-first-century horror such as *The Shape of Water*'s horror/romance (del Toro, 2017) and *Life*'s horror/science fiction (Espinosa, 2017), *Anarchy* is generically hybrid. *Anarchy* positions its protagonists in a form of survivalist horror, drawing upon conventions of the videogame, in which they must move through the city confronted by a series of escalating encounters. These set pieces oscillate between high octane fight and chase scenes to more intimate and suspenseful confrontations. The high speed energy of the scene where the group are chased by motorcycle-riding Purgers racing through the subway system, hunting for the homeless – the most vulnerable on Purge night – stands in contrast with the suspenseful standoff when the group get caught in the crossfire of a domestic dispute when Eva's friend Tanya is shot by her sister as revenge for having slept with her husband.

Alongside the conventions of the action film are moments of unsettling surreal horror. In the opening scenes as sundown approaches and the city prepares for the Purge, Shane and Liz are accosted by a hooded skateboarder with his face painted white who then skates away to re-join his biker-friends, gathered on the horizon, reminiscent of the recent British trend toward 'hoodie horror' in films such as *Eden Lake* and *F* (Roberts, 2010; see Walker 2016: 86).

In slow motion one of the biker's pumps his chest and lets out a primal scream while the others look on. A montage of faces reveal that they are all wearing grotesque masks and face paint evoking the masked killers of the slasher film. These masks, utilized in all the *Purge* films, position the franchise within a lineage running from Leatherface in *Texas Chainsaw Massacre* (Hooper, 1974) to the home invaders in *The Strangers* (Bertino, 2008) and *Hush* (Flanagan, 2016). These masks are designed not to conceal but to terrorize with their distorted visages. For instance, as Shane and Liz prepare to drive away their eyes lock onto one Purger with a chalk-white baby face mask, with rosy cheeks and the word God scrawled on the forehead (see Figures 25 and 26).

This surreal imagery is later juxtaposed with more familiar images of mayhem and violence in a montage of Purgers taking to the streets, accompanied by the sound of the siren announcing Commencement. These images include shots of a lone white gunman carrying a high powered rifle and a six pack of beer as he walks out onto a rooftop; a masked axe-wielding executioner with the word 'PIG' scrawled on his bare chest; a group of armed men with dogs, rifles, machetes and flamethrowers stalking the urban streets; a school bus filled with tattooed gang members aiming their rifles and machine guns through the bus windows as they chant and cheer; and a black truck careening over the horizon and opening up to reveal a white man with a semi-automatic machine gun who shoots everyone in his field of vision. The slow motion and night time cinematography offer a nightmare tinge to the scenes of pending violence that seem all too familiar within contemporary society, embodying the duality of realism and surrealism that recurs throughout the genre.

In this manner, the film also signals a political edge that is increasingly prevalent across numerous other twenty-first-century horror films such as the revisionist representation of gender in *The Love Witch* (Biller, 2016) and *The Witch*; the racial politics of *Get Out* and *Green Room* (Saulnier, 2015); and the near apocalyptic depiction of post-recession Detroit in *Only Lovers*

Figure 25. Hoodie Horror. *The Purge: Anarchy*, dir. James DeMonaco (Blumhouse Productions, 2014).

Figure 26. The surrealism of the horror mask. *The Purge: Anarchy*, dir. James DeMonaco (Blumhouse Productions, 2014).

Left Alive (Jarmusch, 2013), *It Follows* (Mitchell, 2014) and *Don't Breathe* (Alvarez, 2016). The *Purge* films demonstrate that rather than seeing sequels and franchises as representing an emptying of meaning, thought provoking and politicized readings are equally possible. In fact, *The Purge: Anarchy*, alongside the other films in the series, wears its politics openly through the depiction of the Purge in which race and class privilege promise safety and prosperity, while the poor and disenfranchised are most at risk of injury and death. The image of a poor African American man surrounded by a white upper-class

Figure 27. The horror of race privilege. *The Purge: Anarchy*, dir. James DeMonaco (Blumhouse Productions, 2014).

family holding machetes, having sold himself to provide for his daughter and granddaughter, effectively communicates the horror of class privilege and the racial tensions that fuelled the #blacklivesmatter campaign, while the sequel *Election Year* takes the political divide between the political right and the left to nightmarish extremes (see Figure 27).

Yet while the series offers an intellectual social commentary on contemporary society, it also embodies, through its action film aesthetic, the visceral thrill of contemporary horror that enables it to spread beyond the screen through transmedia platforms and immersive experiences. In 2014, Blumhouse toured *Purge: Breakout* across numerous cities of the USA to promote the release of *Anarchy*, fusing the narrative of the *Purge* films with the growing popularity of Escape Room Immersive Experiences, in which participants are told that they are being held prisoner before Commencement and must solve a series of puzzles to escape. *The Purge* also features in Universal Studios' annual Halloween Nights in which the theme park is transformed into a series of haunted house mazes and scare zones drawn from classic and contemporary horror cinema including *Nightmare on Elm Street* (Craven, 1984), *Child's Play* (Holland, 1988), *Saw, Insidious*, and *Happy Death Day* (Landon, 2017). In the *Purge*-zone, masked Purgers stalk the streets, teasing, tormenting and scaring park participants. These live events exist alongside other transmedia horror experiences and texts such as the *28 Days Later* Secret Cinema (UK 2016), *Friday 13th* videogame (Illfonic 2017), *Tales from*

Beyond the Pale audio dramas (Glass Eye Pix), *Saw: Rebirth* digital comic book (IDW Publishing 2005), *Saw: The Video Game* (Zombie Studios 2009), and the growing number of television adaptations of popular horror films including *From Dusk Till Dawn: The Series* (Rodriguez, 2014–16), *Ash Vs Evil Dead* (Raimi, 2015–18), *The Exorcist* (Slater, 2016–18), and *The Purge*. Instead of emptying the genre of meaning, emotional affect and visceral impact, the increasing transmedial nature of horror franchises showcases the genre's expansion, inviting diverse forms of audience interaction and engagement.

As this overview demonstrates, rather than suffering a slow decline as had been prematurely predicted in the early years of the new millennium, the horror genre in cinema has thrived, responding to industrial, technological and cultural factors that have rendered the genre one of the most significant on display within twenty-first-century cinema. *The Purge: Anarchy* is but one film of many that embodies the many facets of horror – entertaining, affective, meaningful, political – and signals the genre's place within an increasingly transmedial film industry in which horror is not perceived as niche but as a lucrative and popular genre that has become ubiquitous across culture.

Stephanie A. Graves

Jordan Peele's *Get Out* (2017)

As audiences, we are always looking to justify our desires, to cloak those things we enjoy in a mantle of respectability. As such, when Jordan Peele's *Get Out* became a surprise critical and box office hit in 2017, the rhetoric surrounding the film from pre- to post-release press experienced a notable shift. Upon becoming a critical darling, it was set apart by an attempt at generic distinction, no longer merely a *horror film*, but instead referred to – along with such films as *The Babadook* (Kent, 2014), *It Follows* (Mitchell, 2014), *The Witch* (Eggers, 2016), and *Split* (Shyamalan, 2016) – as 'smart horror' or 'elevated horror'. When *Get Out* was later nominated for several Oscars, including Best Picture, it was then categorized even by Peele himself as a 'social thriller'. This categorical slippage comes as little surprise to avowed horror fans; after all, it is not a new phenomenon, and this trend of critically acclaimed horror films being rhetorically or generically distanced from the often-denigrated horror genre is well established. Successful films like *Silence of the Lambs* (Demme, 1991) and *The Sixth Sense* (Shyamalan, 1999) are both inextricably steeped in horror subjects, tropes, and tone, yet – as 'serious', critically acclaimed Oscar nominees – are described instead as 'psychological thrillers'. Within independent film (itself a frustrated categorization at best), this discursive distancing from the generic stain of 'horror' is more evident. As Jamie Sexton notes, 'horror films have been a frequent staple of independent film production within the United States, yet since the 1980s they have been marginalized from discourses relating to American independent cinema' (Sexton 2012: 67). However, influenced no doubt by the emergence and increasing acceptance of the category of 'smart cinema', the designation of 'smart' or 'elevated horror' arose as a shorthand to describe this recent spate of horror films exemplified by *Get Out* – box office high performers that have been lauded by critics for their cerebral narratives and pointed social criticisms.

Not specifically a genre but rather a kind of tonal designation, 'smart cinema' refers loosely to films that exhibit what Jeffrey Sconce identifies as 'a predilection for irony, black humour, fatalism, relativism, and, yes, even nihilism' (Sconce 2002: 350). *Smart cinema* became a way to describe films within the changing landscape of independent versus mainstream creative endeavours; building off Sconce's work, Claire Perkins notes that the term arose from the late twentieth-century concern over the erosion of 'independent cinema', a category that, as it gained more widespread success, became part of the large media conglomerates to which it had once stood in opposition (Perkins 2012: 2). As 'independent' lost its significance as a meaningful designator, *smart cinema* sought to fill this lacuna, applied to the work of directors such as Todd Haynes, Paul Thomas Anderson, Todd Solondz, Sofia Coppola, Ang Lee, Kelly Reichardt, Tamara Jenkins, Michel Gondry, and Wes Anderson. Rather than exhibiting tight generic markers, the work of these filmmakers instead shares an ironic sensibility and conscious distancing from mainstream fare; Sconce argues that smart cinema is 'almost invariably placed by marketers, critics and audiences in symbolic opposition to the imaginary mass-cult monster of mainstream, commercial, Hollywood' (Sconce 2002: 351). Although Perkins acknowledges that 'the designation "smart" can never be exact', as a classification, smart film exhibits a stylistic fondness for irony, parody, and blankness (Perkins 2012: 16). While the adolescent pathos of Solondz's *Welcome to the Dollhouse* (1995), the cynical surrealism of Jonze's *Being John Malkovitch* (1999), and the whimsical phantasmagoria of Gondry's *Science of Sleep* (2006) have little in common in terms of plot or style, nonetheless, they all exhibit the same ironically disaffected tonality; more so, they all stand in stark contrast to their Hollywood blockbuster contemporaries. However, although *smart cinema* is used to differentiate these films from the masses, there is nonetheless an attendant concern embodied in the genre over the high/low cultural divide. 'Smart' film teeters precariously between the lofty designation of 'art film' and the intertextually postmodern 'indie' that revels in pop culture references (Perkins 2012: 8; Brereton, 2012: 1).

Overlap between discourses of smart cinema and smart/ elevated horror were perhaps inevitable given that the horror genre – as disparate and complex as such a designation may be – similarly bridges the uneasy high/low divide with which smart cinema engages. Adding to this tension between art and commerce, economic concerns have recently demanded that studio executives take notice of the horror genre when the returns on big-budget, glossy, over-hyped movies were outperformed by the steady release of modestly budgeted horror films. Consider four films from the mid-2010s as a kind of case study: Michael Bay's *Transformers: Age of Extinction* (2014), David Ayer's *Suicide Squad* (2016), David Robert Mitchell's *It Follows* (2014), and James DeMonaco's *The Purge: Anarchy* (2014). *Transformers* cost $210 million to make, and in the US, it only saw a $245 million return on that investment. Similarly, *Suicide Squad*, part of the DC Universe film franchise, had a budget of $175 million, and only grossed $325 million. *It Follows*, however, was filmed for an estimated $1 million, yet it grossed $15 million domestically; *The Purge: Anarchy* had a budget of $9 million and grossed $72 million domestically (IMDBPro.com 2018). For studios, it seems clear that horror constitutes less of a financial risk with a higher yield – yet in spite of this, there is an observable tendency of studios to exploit the horror genre while attempting to reframe the work as something *other* than horror. When the horror film in question transcends its genre audience and garners both critical acclaim and mainstream box office success, there is often an attendant distancing from horror as a genre, and descriptors such as *thriller*, *suspense*, *mystery*, or *psychological drama* are embraced instead (M. Night Shyamalan's surprise 2016 hit *Split*, for instance, is alternately attributed to drama, horror, mystery, or suspense). Film critic Nicholas Barber notes this tension, arguing that 'what it articulates is the film industry's perennial ambivalence towards horror – the genre it can't live with, but can't live without' (Barber 2018).

It might be more useful to conceive of horror that breaks through to wider cultural appeal in terms of *film cycles* (see Klein 2011). The 1970s largely featured horror located within a threat to authority (*The Exorcist* (Friedkin, 1973) and *Jaws* (Spielberg, 1975)), the 1980s saw the reign of the self-aware slasher (the *Friday the 13th* and *Nightmare on Elm Street* franchises), the 1990s were marked by the runaway success of the parodic postmodern horror film (*Wes Craven's New Nightmare* (Craven, 1994) and *Scream* (Craven, 1996)), and the 2000s were largely distinguished by the widespread popularity of both spectacle horror (*House of 1000 Corpses* (Zombie, 2003), *Saw* (Wan, 2004), and *Hostel* (Roth, 2005)) and new storytelling technologies (*Paranormal Activity* (Peli, 2007), *[REC]* (Balagueró and Plaza, 2007), and *Cloverfield* (Reeves, 2008).

Yet these are not clean-cut designations – *Halloween* (Carpenter), the prototypical slasher, premiered in 1979, and *The Last House on the Left* (Craven), an early example of spectacle horror (or, as it is often denigratingly called, 'torture porn') was released in 1972; this 'unruliness' foregrounds how such a taxonomic project based in genre is problematic. Rather than obsessively attempting to identify sub-genre designations within horror, considering these trends in terms of *cycles* is a more useful endeavour – especially in considering how the term 'smart' or 'elevated horror' has been applied to those horror films that have spilled over into mainstream success since roughly 2012.

Klein defines the film cycle as a 'pragmatic' designation, largely 'dependent on audience desires' and 'subject to defined time restraints': 'while film genres are primarily defined by the repetition of key images (their semantics) and themes (their syntax)', she argues, 'film cycles are primarily defined by how they are used, … a direct result of their immediate financial viability as well as the public discourses circulating around them' (Klein 2011: 4). Horror releases that have gained widespread success – particularly those from Blumhouse Productions and A24, both independent production companies – have been rhetorically positioned (by both critics and studios) as *smart horror* or *elevated horror*. Blumhouse's *Get Out*, along with other critically acclaimed releases including *It Comes at Night* (Shultz, 2017), *A Quiet Place* (Krasinski, 2018), and *Hereditary* (Aster, 2018), benefit from this heightened discourse. There is an inherent alignment of the term 'smart horror' with the arthouse cinematic tradition – as is the case with smart cinema. A survey of recent headlines illustrates this trend: 'Why smart horror is putting the fear into sequel-addicted Hollywood' (*The Guardian*, 12 April 2018); 'Can horror movies be prestigious?' (*TheRinger.com*, 15 June 2018); 'Why horror is having its moment' (*The Hollywood Reporter*, 28 August 2018). In the *Hollywood Reporter* article, screenwriter David Kajganich, who penned the 2018 remake of horror classic *Suspiria*, suggests that 'Maybe we've been riding a wave of lazy, cynical horror films in the last decade … so that anything with a few more IQ points stands out much more than they should' (Aquilina 2018: n.p.). Like smart cinema, 'smart horror' is principally defined in *opposition to* mainstream Hollywood – or, as the case may be, in opposition to the genre of horror itself.

While the appellation of 'social thriller' may indeed apply to *Get Out*, it is still undoubtedly a horror film. Its categorization as 'smart horror' seems like an attempt to describe the film's visual distancing from the slasher, splatter, or spectacle film; Peele slowly builds an atmosphere of menace rather than relying on shadowy spectres or jump scares. Stylistically, *Get Out* does share an aesthetic with films commonly referred to as smart cinema – Peele makes liberal use both of the 'long-shot' and 'static composition' that Sconce identifies as typical framing devices of smart cinema (Sconce 2002: 359). In terms of pacing, *Get Out* feels different than the typical Hollywood 'action thriller', a mode that emphasizes the frenetic cutting associated with the dominant visual mode of intensified continuity; Peele's use of longer shot lengths and increased distance between the camera and the subject increase the sense of blankness and ironic detachment that mark smart cinema. The Armitage house is often filmed at an exaggerated distance, reduced to an impression of suburban whiteness – the details are of no real consequence, because the impression of affluent, banal *sameness* is part of the point (see Figure 28).

Visually, there are strong similarities between the *mise-en-scène* of *Get Out* and that of Todd Haynes' *Safe* (1995), which Sconce explicitly references as an exemplar of smart cinema's blank style (Sconce 2002: 359). Although Peele's film is somewhat more naturalistic, both films often strand the main character in the frame, placing them in static positions that underscore the ways they are trapped – both physically and metaphorically. Chris (Daniel Kaluuya) is usually centred in the frame, but is caged in within the frame,

Figure 28. The Armitage home is repeatedly depicted in long-shot. *Get Out*, dir. Jordan Peele (Blumhouse, 2017).

Figure 29. Chris (Daniel Kaluuya) restrained – both physically and metaphorically – in the Armitage basement. *Get Out*, dir. Jordan Peele (Blumhouse, 2017).

rendered immobile – whether by the set, the façade of politeness, or by the empty void of the Sunken Place (see Figure 29).

When he is bound in the basement of the Armitage house, the physical restraints around his wrists and ankles are metaphorically reinforced by the tall pedestals and lamps that flank him in both the front and reverse shot, as well as by the repetition of vertical seams in the wooden panelling that evoke the bars of a cell (see Figure 30).

A common stylistic attribute in smart cinema, there is a particularly antiseptic quality to the production design – especially to the Armitage house – that is epitomized in this shot. The sparseness of the subterranean space reiterates the film's themes precisely *because* it is so empty – the basement has a surgical quality (albeit a nightmarish, 1970s suburban-style surgical quality) that is doubled by Rose's (Allison Williams) disaffected, clinical internet search for her next victim. After Chris is subdued, the façade is no longer required; her demeanour, hairstyle, and costuming all shift, conveying a cold, starched severity that starkly contrasts the persona she crafted to seduce Chris. As such, Peele's overt use of the tropes of smart cinema makes its classification as 'smart, elevated horror' no surprise.

Yet herein lies the problem with the designation of 'smart horror' – it creates a false, binary divide between these films and those that must, then, be 'dumb' – the very kind of high/low art divide that films designated as 'smart' routinely problematize. Sconce acknowledges this predicament: 'for "smart"

Figure 30. Chris Washington (Daniel Kaluuya) trapped within the Sunken Place. *Get Out*, dir. Jordan Peele (Blumhouse, 2017).

cinema to exist, after all, someone or something must be perceived and portrayed as "stupid", a demarcation that can understandably lead to conflict' (Sconce 2002: 353). When it comes to the moniker of 'smart horror', there is implicit in the descriptor a denigration of the genre itself. Horror films lumped under the category of 'torture porn' perhaps receive the brunt of these blows – which fundamentally discounts the biting social critique inherent in the sub-genre. But the wider field of horror is also inherently disparaged by the designation of 'smart' or 'elevated' horror – to label *Get Out* smart horror suggests that other horror is *dumb*, an undeserved and inaccurate critical opprobrium of a complex, innovative genre. Film critic (and horror fan) April Wolfe notes in the *Washington Post* that '*Get Out* earned its "elevated" moniker when critics realized the film was full of frights, as well as cutting social critiques on race and liberalism' (Wolfe 2018).

Get Out is undoubtedly a well-crafted, intelligent indictment of the myth of post-racial America and the insidious nature of white hegemonic privilege in the twenty-first century. But it is *also* a horror film. So while 'smart horror', aligned as it is with the problematic designation of smart cinema, is one way of considering Peele's work, it might also – more usefully – be contextualized as part of either a film cycle consisting of the recent spate of African American narratives such as *The Butler* (Daniels, 2013), *Fruitvale Station* (Coogler, 2013), *12 Years a Slave* (McQueen, 2013), *Dear White People* (Simien, 2014), and *Moonlight* (Jenkins, 2016), or as part of the underdeveloped yet extant sub-genre of horror films that foreground racial issues, including *Night of the Living Dead* (Romero, 1968), *Blackula* (Crain, 1972), *Ganja & Hess* (Gunn, 1973), *The People Under the Stairs* (Craven, 1991), *Candyman* (Rose, 1992), and *Tales from the Hood* (Cundieff, 1995). Pragmatically, either approach better contextualizes *Get Out* without devaluing the genre to which it belongs.

Part IV

National and Cross-Cultural Horror in the Twenty-First Century

Tracy Fahey

Jeremy Dyson, Mark Gatiss, Steve Pemberton and Reece Shearsmith's *The League of Gentlemen* (1999–2017)

In his 2017 article 'Folk horror, a history: from the Wicker Man to the League of Gentlemen', Ben Myers reflects on the persistence of the genre of folk horror in contemporary British culture noting 'Folk horror has gained greater traction in a new century defined by financial crises, terrorist attacks and digital threats. It offers a double dose of nostalgia' (Myers 2017, n.p.). This contemporary resurrection he identifies with the popularity of the seminal comedy horror of *The League of Gentlemen*. Created originally as a radio series in 1997 by Jeremy Dyson, Mark Gatiss, Steve Pemberton and Reece Shearsmith, *The League of Gentlemen* spawned three series which aired from 1999 to 2002, a 2002 Christmas special, *The League of Gentlemen Apocalypse* film if 2005, and a three-episode special released in December 2017.

In 2010 in his BBC4 series *A History of Horror*, Mark Gatiss, co-creator of *The League of Gentlemen*, paid tribute to the genre Pier Haggard had dubbed 'folk horror' in 2003 in a discussion of *The Blood on Satan's Claw* which he directed in 1971. Gatiss defined as folk horror those films which 'shared a common obsession with the British landscape, folklore and superstition' (Gatiss 2010). In *A History of Horror* he identifies three films as being pivotal to this genre; Michael Reeves' *Witchfinder General* (1968), Piers Haggard's *The Blood on Satan's Claw* (1971) and Robin Hardy's *The Wicker Man* (1973). These films which are referred to as 'the unholy trinity of Folk Horror cinema' (Beem and Paciorek 2015: 9), have differing settings but all share similar characteristics and explore common tropes of the folk horror genre as defined by James Gent:

Hermetically sealed (usually rural) communities; imagery of agriculture, fertility and the soil; modern man standing on the precipice of deeper, hidden, horrors and the friction that arises; a haunting of the present by the past; and the arrival of an innocent outsider drawn into this hinterland. (Gent 2017: n.p.)

These films listed by Gatiss represent a significant part of the British folk horror genre, but other seminal works worthy of consideration include the writing of M. R. James, Susan Cooper and the BBC adaptations of Alan Garner's *The Owl Service* (1969–70) and David Rudkin's *Penda's Fen* (1974–84). So how does *The League of Gentlemen* connect with this genre? From the first episode of Series 1 'Welcome to Royston Vasey', *The League of Gentlemen* openly references the folk horror tradition it derives from. The protagonist of the series, Benjamin Denton, is the 'innocent outsider' referred to by Gent. He arrives in the village separately to his friend, Martin Lee, who meets an untimely end at the hands of Edward and Tubbs Tattysyrup, the sinister proprietors of the local shop. This triggers a police investigation, akin to that conducted in Hardy's *The Wicker Man*, which concludes with Tubbs' outburst of 'We didn't burn him!' The scene cuts neatly to a shot of the policeman's helmet being thrown on the fire, another knowing tribute to the burning of Sergeant Howie in the final, climatic scene of *The Wicker Man*. The first series is rich in such folk horror allusions; with another explicit reference in 'The Beast of Royston Vasey' (Series 1, Episode 4). In this episode the central premise is the unearthing of a hideous beast in the bowels of the new road, an obvious nod to *The Blood On Satan's Claw*. The scene featuring uncovering of the beast offers a visual parallel with the appearance of the fiend in the furrows in Haggard's film; the Devil who emerges from the earth. According to Leon Hunt it is precisely the League of Gentlemen's mix of 'gothic qualities and film-buff referentiality' (Hunt 2008: 78) that explains this liberal and knowing use folk horror allusions.

The spirit of what Scovell (2017) calls 'occultivation' haunts *The League of Gentlemen*; the waves of dystopian violence that break over the village when the sanctum of Royston Vasey is threatened by progress in the shape of a new road that will link the village more directly with the rest of the world. As Edward darkly says; 'This is a community. We don't bother the outside world. We don't want it bothering us.' Robert Mcfarlane, in his article 'The eeriness of the English countryside,' remarks on the attachment of the indigenous genre of contemporary folk horror to the idea of a darkness that lies at the heart of rural Britain:

> A loose but substantial body of work is emerging that explores the English landscape in terms of its anomalies rather than its continuities, that is sceptical of comfortable notions of 'dwelling' and 'belonging' and of the packaging of the past as 'heritage'. (McFarlane 2015: n.p.)

It is precisely this mix of unease and parody that underpins the *The League of Gentlemen*. In folk horror, the past is never really over. The uncanny recurrence of old fears informs the closed and secretive microcosm of Royston Vasey, its mysterious rituals, and its violent opposition to change. As Myers puts it: 'Folk horror represents a fear of being governed by outside forces' (Myers 2017). The unfolding story of Edward and Tubbs Tattysyrup is perhaps the most fruitful to analyse in terms of this cultural xenophobia. The couple, who are both husband and wife and brother and sister, represent the consequences of inbreeding and the forces of conservatism in the village. As Edward remarks to Tubbs in 'A Plague on Royston Vasey' (Series 1, Episode 3); 'Our mother was lucky. She had us to carry on the line.' In 'The Beast of Royston Vasey' (Series 1, Episode 2), Edward wishes upon a shooting star: 'I wish; I wish for an end to this plague of strangers. For our future to stay local.' The duo actively try to preserve their village from the outside world, represented by the construction workers that they dub 'roadmen', through the performance of intimidating rituals that reference the dance sequences in *The Wicker Man* and *The Blood on Satan's Claw*. Finally, in 'Escape from Royston Vasey' (Series 1, Episode 6), to their horror, their son David is revealed as the head of the road construction crew. Tubbs is seduced into contemplating escape to live life with her son in London before the final reveal of the episode; David's corruption by his father Edward. 'I want,' says a glassy-eyed David, 'to live ... locally.' Throughout Series 2, David transmutes into a howling and seldom glimpsed beast who Edward and Tubbs endeavour to mate with a local woman, or, as they put it in 'Death in Royston Vasey', a 'local no-tail.' The urgency of fathering a future generation is tied to the idea of heritage and primogeniture; the need to populate Royston Vasey with a new generation to ensure its continuity as a boundaried and closed space.

In the first episode of Series 2, 'Destination Royston Vasey,' Edward and Tubbs' worst fears are realized by the arrival of the sublimely sinister Papa

Lazarou. The circus master Lazarou is one of *The League of Gentlemen*'s most controversial characters; he initially appears to be wearing blackface and speaks a gibberish language (Gippog), both markers of a peculiar colonial attitude seen in racist portrayals of the exotic Other. The racial intolerance that Lazarou confronts is also experienced by the recurrent non-British characters of the malign landlord Pop and especially that of the grotesque Herr Lipp who is presented as both a German paedophile and possible vampire. Lazarou, Pop and Lipp are all bizarre and exaggerated caricatures that spell out the cultural unease of the villagers and their resistance to cultural Otherness. Lazarou's carnival comes to Royston Vasey and the circus master begins his reign of terror, forcing his way into village homes, and collecting wives. This he does by dint of verbal intimidation until the terrified women are bullied into handing over their wedding rings. Papa Lazarou then renames all of the women 'Dave' and enters them into his Book of Wives. However, in spite of Lazarou's grotesque behaviour, 'Destination Royston Vasey' concludes with the circus master and his retinue fleeing from the village; a response to their fear of what they term the innate 'freakishness' of the villagers. However, the most significant episode in the Lazarou saga is 'How The Elephant Got It's Trunk' (Series 3, Episode 6). In this episode, which contains nods to *The Exorcist*, *Don't Look Now* and *The Elephant Man*, Lazarou successfully masquerades as actor and charity shop worker, Keith Drop. To affect his disguise, he paints a flesh tone over his (natural) blackface, and assumes more conventional attire. This deception strikes at the heart of the conservative anxieties of *The League of Gentlemen*, the idea that a threatening outsider can successfully pass as one of their own. The finale of the episode descends into surreal madness that references another seminal horror movie, *The Island of Doctor Moreau*, when the circus animals are revealed to contain the tortured bodies of kidnapped villagers.

With its unapologetic darkness, its obstinate cleaving to the past, and the representation of the cultural cul-de-sac of Royston Vasey, the first three seasons of *The League of Gentlemen* (1999–2002) seem grimly prescient. Edward's battle cry of 'This is a local shop for local people!' finds an echo in the complex and often xenophobic political debates current in Brexit Britain. Myers persists in seeing the contemporary turn to folk horror as optimistic, arguing '[I]f folk horror playfully revels in all things rural/local, it is by definition the enemy of globalisation and capitalism' (Myers 2017). Indeed, Myers views the genre as essentially nostalgic, yearning to escape from the harsh realities of twenty-first-century life in order to return to a simpler, pastoral national identity. Does this ring true of *The League of Gentlemen*? There is little gentle nostalgia to be found in the grotesque scenarios enacted in the fictitious Royston Vasey. Instead the scriptwriters glory in the savage black comedy occasioned by the peculiarities of the villagers; the tyranny of monstrous social worker Pauline, the bitterness of Bernice the vicar's sermons, the horrifying voyeurism of the landlord Pop, and the 'secret stuff' sold by butcher Hilary Briss that causes an outbreak of plague. For all their natural affection for the tradition of folk horror, Dyson, Gatiss, Pemberton and Shearsmith are keenly aware of the sinister nature of the genre they reference. This is most acutely sensed in the 2017 specials which betray a critical awareness of the national context of post-Brexit cultural division in which they are framed. These episodes are deeply concerned with the overwhelming importance of boundaries and borders to the protagonists of the series. This disquiet is most vividly represented by the characters of Edward and Tubbs who take hostages in an abandoned London apartment block in order to stage a national protest that will ensure that the boundary changes to Royston Vasey are not implemented. In a twist, the series later reveals that Royston Vasey has already been sold for fracking by Bernice the vicar to the nightmare character of Papa Lazarou. Lazarou, the ultimate sinister outsider in *The League of Gentlemen*, now owns all of Royston Vasey and its female inhabitants. Papa Lazarou collects his final wife, the xenophobic Tubbs, and speaks the final words of the last episode; a declaration that the village is now completely colonized and subverted. As the camera pans over a cellar of incarcerated and terrified female villagers, Shearsmith's rasping tones declaim 'It's a wife mine now.' Here the fears of Edward and Tubbs are fully realized; outside forces have now taken over Royston Vasey, and the assertion of the strength of the closed community, so familiar from the final scenes of the original folk horror triad of films, crumbles in the face of the inexorable invasion of the present and the consequent obliteration of tradition.

For all its loving references to the original British films of the late 1960s and early 1970s, *The League of Gentlemen* presents a reinvention of the folk horror genre. It represents not just a continuation of a tradition, but a fresh perspective and interpretation of the classic tropes it represents; the closed community, the uncovering of secret cultish rituals, human sacrifice and the fraught existence of ill-fated outsiders. Although the first series offers many knowing nods to classic folk horror films, as the series goes on, the writing finds its own voice, offering a comedic but insightful take on the cultural xenophobia that led to Britain voting to leave the European Union in 2016. Like other outstanding manifestations of contemporary folk horror, Ben Wheatley's films *A Field in England* (2013) and *Kill List* (2011), the music of Ghost Box, and the Scarfolk mythos created by writer Richard Littler, *The League of Gentlemen* goes beyond the limits of the genre to speak directly to the concerns and anxieties of contemporary Britain.

Ian Olney

Julia Ducournau's *Raw* (2016)

Western Europe boasts a long and rich tradition of horror cinema, especially on the Continent, where the genre was arguably born and still flourishes in the twenty-first century. Unique in its storytelling and style, Continental horror is in many ways quite distinct from the Anglo-American brand of cinematic terror that tends to dominate discussions about the genre. This chapter briefly surveys the history of Western European horror cinema and touches on several of its key characteristics before turning to an analysis of a representative contemporary Continental horror film: Julia Ducournau's *Grave* [*Raw*] (2016).

Although some scholars maintain that 'the horror film' did not exist as such until Hollywood studios like Universal established the genre in the 1930s (see Hutchings 2004 and Benshoff 2014), others like Casper Tybjerg (2004) insist on the importance of earlier developments in Western Europe to the evolution of horror cinema. Indeed, it is difficult to imagine the genre existing at all without the pioneering work done by filmmakers on the Continent during the silent era. Shortly after the invention of motion pictures, directors like Georges Méliès and Segundo de Chomón introduced elements of the fantastic, the uncanny and the supernatural into the cinema with their 'trick films'. Germany produced the first feature-length horror movie, *Der Student von Prag* [*The Student of Prague*] (Wegener and Rye, 1913). And the visual grammar of horror was cemented by German Expressionist pictures like *Das Cabinet des Dr Caligari* [*The Cabinet of Dr Caligari*] (Wiene, 1920) and *Nosferatu* (Murnau, 1922), which employed distorted sets, dramatic lighting and eerie makeup effects to tell chilling tales of madness, murder and monstrosity. At the very least, early horror films from Western Europe set the template for the genre that would take root in the United States with the coming of sound.

The production of horror cinema slowed considerably in Western Europe in the years leading up to the Second World War, but the genre enjoyed a golden age on the Continent in the post-war era. The decline of the Hollywood studio system, an increase in transcontinental co-productions, and the relaxation of film censorship across Europe led to a boom in the production of horror movies during this period. Although many of them initially fell into the Gothic tradition of horror favoured in America and England, more exotic genre variants soon emerged: *giallo* [murder-mystery] films from Italy, 'blind dead' movies from Spain, lesbian vampire pictures from France and *krimi* [crime] thrillers from Germany, for example. These films minted a new generation of European horror auteurs, among them Mario Bava, Dario Argento, Jesús Franco and Jean Rollin. And a number are now regarded as genre classics, including *La maschera del demonio* [*Black Sunday*] (Bava, 1960), *Les yeux sans visage* [*Eyes without a Face*] (Franju, 1960), *Les lèvres rouges* [*Daughters of Darkness*] (Kümel, 1971) and *Suspiria* (Argento, 1977; see Figure 31). Dwindling film audiences in Europe and the rise of Hollywood blockbuster cinema ended the golden age of Continental horror in the 1980s, but the arrival of home video ensured the continued circulation of these movies and garnered them a cult following among genre aficionados (see Hawkins 2000 and Olney 2013).

Figure 31. Suzy Bannion (Jessica Harper) in *Suspiria*, a film from the golden age of Continental horror now regarded as a genre classic. *Suspiria*, dir. Dario Argento (Seda Spettacoli, 1977).

The twenty-first century has seen a new flowering of horror cinema in Western Europe. Since the turn of the millennium, another generation of Continental horror directors has emerged, fuelled by the digital revolution in filmmaking; the advent of novel distribution platforms like DVD, Blu-ray and video-on-demand; and the explosive growth of the internet, which has enabled genre fans around the world to seek out and celebrate alternatives to Hollywood horror online. Spain and France, in particular, have been hotbeds of activity. In Spain, many horror films, beginning with *Los otros* [*The Others*] (Amenábar, 2001), have returned to the genre's gothic roots with great success (see Willis 2004); others, such as the found-footage zombie movie *[REC]* (Balagueró and Plaza, 2007) and its sequels, have struck a chord with audiences by updating the genre for the postmodern era. Meanwhile, a number of French horror films, including *Haute tension* [*High Tension, aka. Switchblade Romance*] (Aja, 2003) and *À l'intérieur* [*Inside*] (Bustillo and Maury, 2007), have drawn much attention for their embrace of a 'new extremity' in cinematic depictions of sex and violence (see West 2016). Although it is perhaps too soon to declare the current renaissance in Continental horror a second golden age, it certainly ranks among the most exciting recent developments in the genre.

As this brief history suggests, Western European horror cinema is exceptionally diverse, spanning a range of different narrative forms, stylistic modes, periods, countries and languages. It is possible, however, to identify several shared characteristics that set Continental horror movies apart from the Anglo-American films that tend to dominate discussions about the genre. One is their distinctive treatment of sex and violence, which is typically more explicit and provocative than in horror films from England or the United States. Since the 1960s and 1970s, especially, Continental horror movies have been infamous for staging scenes of shocking brutality, from the flesh-eating in *Cannibal Holocaust* (Deodato, 1980) to the flesh-peeling in *Martyrs* (Laugier, 2008). They have also been notorious for their graphic depictions of sex, which veer into hard-core pornography in films such as *Die Marquise von Sade* (Franco, 1976) and *Baise-moi* (Despentes and Coralie, 2000). Furthermore, Continental horror movies made since the genre's golden age in Western Europe blur the boundary between sex and violence in unique and frequently disturbing ways (see Tohill and Tombs 1995). Featuring taboo-shattering scenes of rape, sado-masochism and necrophilia, films from *La frusta e il corpo* [*The Whip and the*

Body] (Bava, 1963) to *Nekromantik* (Buttgereit, 1987) offer an unsettling blend of terror and eroticism rare in the genre.

Continental horror also blurs the boundary between art and exploitation in a distinctive fashion. Purveying violent shocks and erotic spectacle in the pursuit of profit, it resembles other forms of 'Eurotrash' and exploitation cinema (see Mathijs and Mendik 2004). At the same time, it shares key features with European art cinema, including a penchant for stories exploring trauma and transgression, and a style defined by dreamlike discontinuity and painterly compositions. This is largely a reflection of the porous border between 'high' and 'low' film cultures in Western Europe. Acclaimed auteurs like Federico Fellini and Werner Herzog dabbled in horror during the heyday of arthouse cinema in the 1960s and 1970s – and continue to draw inspiration from the genre today, as the 'extreme' art films of Claire Denis, Lars von Trier and others demonstrate (see Horeck and Kendall 2011). Conversely, cult horror directors have often taken their cue from art cinema, as evidenced by the Surrealist touches in Jean Rollin's vampire films and Lucio Fulci's zombie pictures or the Expressionist aesthetic of Jesús Franco's mad scientist movies and Alfred Vohrer's *krimi* thrillers. The cross-fertilization of art and horror on the Continent has even involved cases of direct homage like Dario Argento's adaptation of *Blowup* (1966) in *Profondo rosso* [*Deep Red*] (1975) and Pedro Almodóvar's reworking of *Eyes without a Face* in *La piel que habito* [*The Skin I Live In*] (2011).

A final defining characteristic of Western European horror cinema is its unconventional treatment of women and female sexuality. Although femininity is routinely linked with otherness and monstrosity in Continental horror movies, as it is in Anglo-American horror films, it is also frequently framed as a source of supernatural power and the bane of the patriarchal order. A vivid example of this can be found in the Gothic chillers that starred 'queen of horror' Barbara Steele in the 1960s. In films like *Black Sunday* and *Amanti d'oltretomba* [*Nightmare Castle*] (Caiano, 1965), Steele plays spectres of female rage who return from the grave to exact revenge on the men who murdered them (see Jenks 1992; see Figure 32). Femininity is also unconventionally framed in the lesbian vampire films that enjoyed a vogue during the genre's golden age on the Continent (see Baker 2012). Movies like *Daughters of Darkness* and *La novia ensangrentada* [*The Blood Spattered Bride*] (Aranda, 1972) present

Figure 32. The 'queen of horror' Barbara Steele in *Black Sunday*, framing femininity as a source of supernatural power. *Black Sunday*, dir. Mario Bava (Galatea Film and Jolly Film, Film still).

vampirism as a queerly alluring alternative to the heteronormative status quo for women. Although it is perhaps going too far to call these films 'feminist', they open a rare space in the genre for the exploration of female experience – a space that has expanded with the recent emergence of women horror directors like Marina de Van, Lucile Hadžihalilović and Julia Ducournau in Western Europe.

Julia Ducournau's debut feature film *Raw* (2016) is a fascinating example of contemporary Continental horror cinema. A French-Belgian-Italian co-production, *Raw* premiered at the Cannes Film Festival, where it won an International Federation of Film Critics (FIPRESCI) Award. It tells the story of Justine (Garance Marillier), a teenage girl who enrols at the veterinary school which her parents attended and where her older sister, Alex (Ella Rumpf), is currently a student. Shortly after she arrives, Justine, a strict vegetarian, is forced by Alex and the other upperclassmen to eat a rabbit kidney as part of a hazing ritual. Following a violent allergic reaction to the raw meat, she develops an insatiable appetite for human flesh. We learn that Alex shares these cannibalistic urges and has been satisfying them by feeding on the victims of car accidents she causes. Justine, however, tries to resist temptation, even when her bloodlust is aroused by her gay roommate, Adrien (Rabah Nait Oufella). Ultimately, Adrien is devoured by Alex, who is caught and imprisoned. In a final twist, Justine discovers that she and Alex inherited their cannibalistic proclivities from their mother (Joana Preiss), who has tried to shield them from their true nature since birth (see Figure 33).

Figure 33. Cannibalistic heroine Justine (Garance Marillier). *Raw*, dir. Julia Ducournau (Petit Film, 2016).

Raw exhibits all the major hallmarks of Western European horror cinema. In the first place, its representation of sex and violence is characteristically disturbing and explicit. The film features graphic scenes of cannibalism, including one in which Justine gnaws on her sister's severed finger and another in which Alex feeds from the head of a car crash victim. Gory and sickeningly realistic, these scenes have a visceral impact uncommon in Anglo-American horror. Indeed, they reportedly caused faintings when the film was screened at the Toronto International Film Festival. *Raw* also gives its violence an erotic dimension rare in horror movies made in England and the United States. Justine's acts of cannibalism carry a sexual charge; her bloodlust is frequently indistinguishable from carnal longing. When she and a male classmate, both covered in body paint, passionately kiss at a party, she bites off part of his lower lip. And when she seduces her roommate Adrien, she repeatedly snaps at him during sex and sinks her teeth into her own wrist upon orgasming. Yoking desires of the flesh with the desire for flesh in an unsettling fashion, the film constructs a uniquely Continental erotics of cannibalism.

Raw also blurs the boundary between art and exploitation in a manner typical of Western European horror cinema. Like lowbrow 'Eurotrash' movies, it exploits the shock value of the abject and the taboo. Its focus on cannibalism ties it to a long tradition of *cinéma vomitif* (Brottman 1997) on the Continent. And the film is full of images designed to scandalize the audience, among them

Justine gagging as she pulls clots of half-swallowed hair from her throat in the lavatory and Alex with her arm inserted up to the shoulder in a cow's rectum during a livestock exam. At the same time, *Raw* draws from the highbrow tradition of European art cinema. It deals with such serious philosophical themes as the opposition of ethical behaviour and animal impulse. As Ducournau has remarked, in tracking Justine's battle against her cannibalistic urges, the film 'shows the birth of a moral entity' (Sélavy 2017: 53). Moreover, it is a formally ambitious work. Eschewing the seamless illusionism of commercial cinema, it alternates between hard-edged realism and hallucinatory surrealism in its use of colour, lighting, editing and music. Simultaneously poetic and provocative, *Raw*, like other Continental horror movies, emerges as an amalgam of art and exploitation.

Finally, *Raw* resembles other examples of Western European horror in its treatment of women and female sexuality. Although it links femininity with monstrosity in imagining a form of cannibalism passed matrilineally from mother to daughter, it also makes monstrosity a source of empowerment for its female protagonist. Timid and unsure of herself at the outset of the film, Justine grows stronger and more confident as her cannibalism manifests itself; she also demonstrates a newfound maturity in ultimately overcoming her appetite for human flesh. In addition, her monstrosity is favourably contrasted with that of the veterinary school she and Alex attend, a quasi-fascist institution ruled by toxic masculinity. Ducournau has said that she intended Justine's cannibalism to be 'a punk gesture against this patriarchy' (Rapold 2017: 45). *Raw* routinely privileges a female gaze, especially in scenes where Justine surveys the (frequently male) objects of her cannibalistic lust. And it delves into distinctively female realms of experience, from the bonds and travails of sisterhood to the pitfalls associated with bikini waxing and losing one's virginity (see Figure 34). In a fashion familiar to fans of Continental horror, the film upends the gender norms of the genre, giving it a feminist spin.

Figure 34. The sisterly solidarity of Alex (Ella Rumpf) and Justine. *Raw*, dir. Julia Ducournau (Petit Film, 2016).

It is worth noting, as well, that *Raw* announces its kinship with Western European horror through a host of specific cinematic references. Its teenage heroine, sinister school setting and bold use of colour and music recall Dario Argento's landmark occult thriller *Suspiria*. Its focus on female cannibalism and sisterly solidarity brings to mind Jean Rollin's funereal zombie film *La morte vivante* [*The Living Dead Girl*] (1982). And its exploration of the fine line between lovemaking and flesh-eating evokes Claire Denis's art-horror hybrid *Trouble Every Day* (2001). Such references demonstrate Ducournau's awareness that *Raw* belongs to a rich heritage of horror cinema on the Continent. Her movie reminds us that this heritage stretches back for many decades, forming one of the genre's major wellsprings; at the same time, it testifies to the continued vitality of Western European horror in the twenty-first century.

Katarzyna Ancuta

Sadako Yamamura and the *Ring* Cycle (1991–present)

Asian horror is an extremely versatile label applied to such diverse cases as Japanese big monster *kaiju* movies, Korean serial killer thrillers, Southeast Asian ghost comedies, Hong Kong category III cannibal crime dramas, Chinese supernatural romances, and Bollywood horror musicals. It is filled with iconic portrayals of vengeful spirits, chainsaw-wielding schoolgirls, devious witches, and Taoist exorcists *kung-fu*-fighting hopping vampires. Despite its rich history, the promotion of Asian Horror as a single marketable category arguably began at the turn of the millennium with the release of Hideo Nakata's *Ring* (1998) and *Ring* 2 (1999), introduced to the world through the festival circuit. The long-haired vengeful spirit of Sadako Yamamura was hailed a 'new' figure of evil, critics welcomed the emergence of 'J-horror', and film distributors rushed to cash in on the growing appetite for Asian ghosts and monsters. Originating in the novels of Koji Suzuki, Sadako is a character bound in a cycle of repetitions, appearing in five novels and seven movies to date in Japan (not counting manga and television series), spawning one Korean and three American remakes, and present as an instantly recognizable pop-cultural reference in countless other productions. This brief discussion of Asian Horror will therefore focus on the novels and films of the *Ring* cycle and examine the evolution of Sadako as a representative 'face' of Asian horror.

The films consistently portray Sadako as a contemporary version of the *onryō*, often described in Japanese folklore as a vengeful spirit of a wronged woman. The visual depiction of such spirits crystallized in the Edo period (1603–1868) thanks to popular Kabuki performances that featured female ghosts with 'long black hair, and pallid, staring visages' (McRoy 2015: 199) dressed in 'funeral white attire' (199). The disfigured ghost of Lady Oiwa from *Ghost Story of Yotsuya* (Tsuruya Nanboku IV, 1825), seeking vengeance on her deceitful husband and his lover, is often seen as a prototype of this look. Thrown into a well, where she died a slow painful death entombed alive, Sadako fits the profile of a 'wronged woman' whose grudge turns her into a vengeful spirit. However, unlike the grudge-bearing spirits of the past that demanded karmic justice and were appeased with offerings, this modern ghost is more indiscriminate in her hatred 'challenging one and all' (Gerow 2002: 20). Her method of haunting has also been appropriately modernized. Sadako exploits the reproductive properties of analogue (VHS), digital, and networked technologies (CD/DVD and the internet) and broadcasts herself into the world as an audio-visual message (and more recently as html code).

Figure 35. Sadako crawling out of the TV set. *Ring*, dir. Hideo Nakata (Toho, 1998).

While the films simplify Sadako to a tech-savvy *onryō* (see Figure 35), this does not do this complicated character justice. Sadako is notoriously difficult to define, her complexity and liminality growing exponentially throughout Suzuki's five novels and the films. In the first book of the cycle, *Ring* (1991), a bio-technological horror novel that predates the publication of perhaps the most famous example of the genre, Hideaki Sena's *Parasite Eve* (1995), Sadako's ghost is described as a telepathic transmission of the real Sadako's DNA sequence blended with a smallpox virus, broadcasted as a television signal, and then recorded on a VHS tape: 'This video hadn't been recorded by a machine. A human being's eyes, ears, nose, tongue, skin – all five senses had been used to make this video' (Suzuki 2004: 146).

The second novel, *Spiral* (1995) identifies Sadako's DNA-carrying ring-like virus. 'Some specimens were twisted and some were unshaped, but most of them looked like a slightly distorted ring, the kind one wears on a finger. ... There was even a protrusion at one point that resembled nothing so much as a stone on a setting' (Suzuki 2005: 325). The ring virus infects the people who watch the tape through their retinas and modifies their cells, growing tumours in their coronary arteries and effectively causing a heart attack in one week. The nature of the virus demands reproduction (hence the idea that the curse can be averted when the video is copied) but with each copy of Sadako's code the virus mutates, and its new form is capable of inducing pregnancy in women who happen to be ovulating while watching the recording. The virus then grows a foetus-clone of Sadako inside them which is born after a week of gestation and quickly matures into an adult version of Sadako. The reborn Sadako is described as 'a complete hermaphrodite' (429) capable of asexual reproduction: 'A child born without input from a male and a female would have the same genes as its single parent. In other words, Sadako would give birth to another Sadako' (430). In a metanarrative gesture, Suzuki reveals Sadako's plans to repopulate the planet with her clones as the mutated virus spreads through the *Ring* novel, soon to be adapted into film. The reader is left with a promise that 'All the diversity of human DNA would converge with a single DNA pattern that was Sadako' (454).

The third novel, *Loop* (1998) reconceptualizes Sadako even further by introducing a parallel universe kick-started by a computer simulation program known as the Loop. It is within the Loop universe that Sadako's story supposedly takes place and her rebirth and subsequent reproduction in that world manifests itself as a viral meta-cancer that infects the world outside the Loop:

> *Ring* was published. Soon nearly twenty thousand of its female readers were pregnant. They all gave birth to Sadako ... What life gained in exchange for its diversity was immortality: driven to the brink of chaos, it achieved absolute stability. ... The denizens of the Loop thenceforc lived repetitive, unchanging, boring lives. They stoped evolving. They had become cancer. (Suzuki 2006: 188–9)

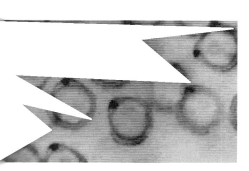

Figure 36. The ring virus. *Spiral*, dir. Jōji Iida (Toho, 1998).

The Sadako-virus from Suzuki's novels had to undergo massive simplification to appear as the long-haired vengeful spirit known from the films. In fact, only two lesser known films, Jōji Iida's adaptation of the second novel, *Spiral* (1998) and the Korean remake, *The Ring Virus* (Dong-bin Kim, 1999), mention the virus at all (see Figure 36). Most films refer to Sadako as a 'curse' instead, because curses, like viruses, depend upon reproduction.

Before Sadako became a virus, curse, or a vengeful spirit, she was a daughter of Shizuko Yamamura, a psychic from Izu Oshima Island whose ESP abilities were occasionally described as 'otherwordly'. Nakata's films go as far as to suggest that Sadako may have been conceived with a water god/demon. *Ring 2* maintains that Sadako managed to stay alive for thirty years in the well because of her demonic ancestry. The supernatural parentage of Sadako informs Norio Tsuruta's *Ring 0: Birthday* (2000), losely based on Suzuki's *Birthday* (1999) which comprises three narratives centred on the heroines of the trilogy, Sadako from *Ring*, Mai Takano from *Spiral*, and Reiko Sugiura from *Loop*, representing three different timelines: before the virus, during its mutation, and in the aftermath of the outbreak. But while Suzuki focuses on Sadako's theatrical debut and the first manifestation of her uncanny powers, killing her troupe members through a psychic impression on an audio tape, the film also introduces a new thread which sees Sadako split into two independent beings – one innocent, taking after her mother and one evil, taking after her demonic father (see Figure 37).

The novels identify Sadako's father as Heihachiro Ikuma, a psychiatrist who became romantically entangled with Shizuko while researching her powers. Sadako inherited Shizuko's psychic abilities but having seen her humiliated by scientists and driven to suicide, hoped to hide her own powers. In the films, Sadako's rage makes her kill a journalist present at Shizuko's presentation simply by willing him dead. This ability is later used to explain Sadako's curse in the films, which do not follow Suzuki's bio-medical reasoning. Tsuruta describes the persecution of the innocent Sadako for the actions of her evil twin. The two Sadakos eventually merge into one and her subsequent murder by Ikuma is presented as stage one of *oyako shinju* or parent-child suicide often seen as an expression of responsibility in Japan. Interestingly, Sadako dies wearing her stage costume of a ghost. She therefore falls into the well already looking like an *onryō* (see Figure 38).

Much of Sadako's complex bio-psychological make-up is absent in the films. In Suzuki's novels, Sadako was born with a rare medical condition known as testicular feminization syndrome, which gave her a female body while being chromosomically male, complete with male and female genitals, and no uterus. Unable to bear children, Sadako learnt to transmit her genetic material telepathically. Ultimately, Suzuki concludes, it was Sadako's inability to reproduce as a

Sadako Yamamura and the *Ring* Cycle (1991–present)

Figure 37. Two Sadakos merging. *Ring 0: Birthday*, dir. Norio Tsuruta (Toho, 2000).

Figure 38. Sadako in her stage *onryō* costume. *Ring 0: Birthday*, dir. Norio Tsuruta (Toho, 2000).

woman that motivated her to reproduce as a virus and a curse. Sadako's hermaphroditism is mentioned in only one film, *The Ring Virus*, which repeats Suzuki's depiction of Sadako's murder as a punishment for her condition exacted by her enraged rapist. Additionally, the fact that Sadako did not use her formidable powers to punish her murderer also suggests that to a certain extent she wished herself dead: 'Sadako didn't want to be raped. Of course she didn't. … It was only after it had happened that the thought of dying occurred to her, and without even considering it she guided Nagao in that direction' (Suzuki 2004: 233).

With the first book published in 1991, Sadako has been haunting us for nearly thirty years. Over the years she has undergone several transformations to the point that her literary and cinematic representations do not seem to have much in common any longer. Beginning with *Spiral*, the novels shift focus from Sadako to Ryuchi Takayama, a genius physicist who dies in the first novel, only to be reborn through Sadako in the second. *Loop* focuses on the years between Takayama's death and rebirth during which he is born into the world outside the Loop and then scanned back into it. The next two books present two alternative versions of his later life. In *Birthday* he heals the world by infecting Sadakos with a virus speeding up their metabolism to make them die faster. In *S* (2012) he is wrongly accused of abducting and murdering Sadako copies and ends up executed. During his execution he transfers himself into the two-dimensional digital space within the internet to contact the last living Sadako – Akane. A biological daughter of Takayama and Masako – another asexually produced Sadako's clone – Akane is Sadako's wish come true – 'a perfect woman' (Suzuki 2017: 224). The novel predictably ends with Akane being pregnant.

Tsunomu Hanabusa's *Sadako 3D* (2012) and *Sadako 2 3D* (2013) reference Suzuki's *S* through characters' names and Akane's teaching profession but the similarity ends here. Most importantly they rewrite Sadako's character transforming her from the menacing *onryō* into an insect-like monster with blue skin, long grasshopper legs, and sharp teeth capable of ripping her victims' throats open. Instead of one Sadako, the screen is flooded with dozens of them swarming around like locusts (see Figure 39). In *Sadako vs. Kayako* (2016), Kôji Shiraishi stages the battle of the spirits between Sadako and her rival in fame, Kayako, a vengeful ghost of a battered housewife from *Ju-on* films, as they fight over two teenagers exposed to a double curse. Despite the assumption that the two curses are going to balance themselves out, the film

Figure 39. Akane swarmed by the insectoid Sadakos. *Sadako 3D*, dir. Tsunomu Hanabusa (Kadokawa Pictures, 2012).

ends with Sadako and Kayako merging to become a double-charged monstrosity and the next level in the character's evolution.

Discarding the bio-medical themes of the novels, all the films are preoccupied with Sadako's ability to infiltrate analogue, and later digital and networked media. *Sadako 3D* replaces the VHS tape with a viral video on the internet, while *Sadako 2 3D* disposes of the video altogether making Sadako rewrite the html code of a shopping website or scramble a phone conversation. In *Sadako vs. Kayako* the original VHS recording is digitized, saved to a CD, and uploaded to the internet. The transition to digital media enables Sadako to kill instantly rather than wait a week like her analogue predecessor. Networked media allow her to appear on several devices at once, to take over large public screens, or to reach people through mobile phones. Digitized Sadako is no longer limited to a home entertainment system and the modern world's addiction to screens makes her omnipresent and impossible to eradicate. While the literary Sadako played into the millennial fears of the apocalypse brought about by a viral outbreak, the cinematic Sadako exposes our ambivalent attitude to advanced telecommunication and surveillance technologies that dominate every aspect of our life.

Since Suzuki's novels were translated after the release of Nakata's film, to the world Sadako is predominantly a cinematic heroine. Academic discussions explore this character as a means to engage with wider socio-cultural fears ranging 'from trepidation over the impact of emerging technologies … to apprehension stemming from transformation in gender codes and their impacts upon the structure and function of families in contemporary Japan' (McRoy 2015: 211). Sadako's endless returns evoke what Aaron Gerow calls 'images of circularity, of a movement proceeding away and then returning, of endless repetition' (Gerrow 2002: 19), which he sees as a recurrent theme in Japanese millennial horror. Ramie Tateishi connects the films with the tension between cultural nostalgia as the attempt to re-experience the past and modernization that asks for its destruction instead, resulting in the fear that 'the remnants of yesterday may turn vengeful' (Tateishi 2003: 296), whilst Colette Balmain links the emergence of the monstrous past to 'the demise of the family' and the 'system of obligations that dictate wider relationships with the community' (Balmain 2008: 174). Sadako's presence has also been read in terms of a chaotic element seen as a threat to order and harmony, which rank high among Japanese cultural values (Ancuta 2008: 92). A character with nearly thirty years of history, Sadako continues to haunt, fascinate and confuse us. Trapped in the endless cycle of reproduction, mutation, and repetition she remains always ready to redefine herself for a new decade and leaves trails of Asian horror heroines moulded in her image behind.

Cristina Santos

Mariana Enríquez's *Things We Lost in the Fire* (2009/2017)

Mariana Enríquez (Buenos Aires, 1973–) is a journalist and writer who, in her horror fiction, combines the reality of Argentine history with elements of the 'Gothic horror' style while maintaining a sharp focus on social criticism. Her writing brings to life the terrible elements of a not-so-distant Argentine past marked by its last dictatorship (1976–83), clandestine torture centres, *desaparecidos*[1] and children taken from their mothers while they were political prisoners to be adopted out to 'good' (military) families. Horror is real and the real is horror in Enríquez's *Things We Lost in the Fire: Stories* – a collection of stories characterized by elements of the supernatural that delve into the dark history and realities of Buenos Aires from a past scarred by dictatorship to contemporary issues surrounding the femicides, poverty, misogyny, and corruption.

Enríquez's version of the horror genre in *The Things We Lost in the Fire* (2017)[2] includes an exploration not only of the macabre and the supernatural but also an examination of the real dreadfulness of living through socio-political injustices of Argentina's past and present. Her style of writing horror has been defined as an Argentine 'cocktail of politics and cult horror' (Bett 2017: n.p.) that exists in the blurred space between fiction and historical reality. It is a horror genre that reclaims, reminds, and memorializes a shameful national history as well as an ignored contemporary reality of poverty, corruption, and social inequality. Horror is not always about situational violence but rather a

---

1 'Disappeared' are defined as 'someone alive yet missing ... into someone dead yet unaccounted for' (Robben 2007: 131).
2 Original Spanish title *Las cosas que perdimos en el fuego* (2016); this is Enríquez's first book to be translated into English.

style of writing that allows Enríquez to trigger her reader's imagination with superstitious repertoires as well as a touch of discomfort because of its level of verisimilitude with everyday life (Orosz 2009: n.p.).

Heraldo Alfredo Pastor positions Enríquez's writing as part of 'Nueva Narrativa Argentina' [New Argentine Narrative] that emerged after the last military dictatorship in Argentina and as a literature that *participates* in the horror genre because:

> Argentina has not been able to remove itself from the political factor in the configuration of its literature; and it seems to have adopted discursive conventions associated with the horror genre, and its antecedent, gothic literature, understood as appropriate in order to represent a horror of a political nature. (Pastor 2012: 68)³

Enríquez was born in December 1973 and was 2 years old when the dictatorship began and she was 8–9 years old when news of the atrocities committed by the armed forces began to be revealed to the public. She has also stated that, unlike many other Argentineans, she grew up in a household well aware of what was happening in the political arena of the dictatorship. Enríquez goes on to say that writing about the ghosts of events that form part of Argentine history seemed like her way of contributing to the discussion to the happenings of this era (Orosz 2009: n.p.) but which also became her way of relieving herself of these 'nightmares' (Enríquez 2017: n.p.). In the end: 'I [Enríquez] love the country [Argentina], but I think that's why I'm harsh with it … I'm harsh because I care about it and I want it to change' (Bett 2017: n.p.).

In order to comprehend the reality of Enríquez's 'fictional' Argentine terror one needs to understand the way in which the last dictatorship devised and used horror as a psychological weapon against its opponents. Part of this history includes the tragic figure of the *desaparecido* onto which Enríquez builds a spectral quality in 'The Inn' by extrapolating the historical unaccountability of the *desaparecido* (see Figure 40).

---

3   My translation. '… la Argentina no ha podido abstraerse del factor político en la configuración de su literatura; y pareciera haberse valido de las convenciones discursivas del terror como género y de su antecedente, el gótico, percibidas como apropiadas para representar un terror de naturaleza política' (Pastor 2012: 68).

Figure 40. Parque de la memoria [Park of Memory], Buenos Aires. One of the walls with over 30,000 name plates of *desaparecidos*. © Photo courtesy of Cristina Santos.

That is, the haunting of the Inn stands in for the personal and psychological haunting the last dictatorship has left on generations of Argentinians. The sense of fear in the short story represents this intrinsic political awareness and underlines the effects of an intergenerational socio-political trauma characterized by an inherited trauma of a collective cultural space.

Enríquez states the following when asked about the political subtext of her writing Enríquez states:

> The sheer terror of the institutional violence and the dictatorships in South America has always verged on something that is beyond just a government's mechanical repressions – there was and is, when it surfaces, something more essentially evil about it. ... I care about politics and I'm interested in history, so it shows up in my work. The fact that I choose a genre that doesn't usually deal with this is more important, although I think that contemporary genre fiction approaches these issues more and more often now. But to me it's just a circumstance of my writing. (Wallace 2018: n.p.)

The short story begins with a reference to the province of La Rioja[4] – known for having clandestine detention centres (such as military and police buildings, houses and hospitals, to name but a few) to torture political prisoners, especially after the coup d'état on 24 March 1976.[5] However, it is Rocío's father who has the courage to mention the Inn's history as a police academy thirty years prior to being transformed into a hotel (Enríquez 2017: 41). This acknowledgement of a dark piece of town history is not accepted by his employer and ultimately leads to his dismissal as the town's tour guide since relating the Inn's past as a police academy links it to the history of clandestine detention and torture centres: 'it was a police academy during the dictatorship. You remember the stuff we studied in school?' (Enríquez 2017: 42). This is a recognition of a past the Inn owner wishes to ignore because of its negative impact on her business, yet the tourists express an interest in wanting to know more 'about disappearances, torture, whatever' (Enríquez 2017: 42).

'The Inn' is a horror ghost story that not only mixes Argentine history with the supernatural, but also includes, as Enríquez seems to imply, postmodern elements of the contemporary horror film as defined by Isabel Pinedo: (1) there is a violent disruption of the everyday world; (2) there is a transgression and violation of boundaries; (3) the validity of rationality is thrown into question; (4) there is no narrative closure; and (5) the film produces a bounded experience of fear (Pinedo 1996: 20). Pinedo's features of the horror film are further highlighted in the short story by Eníquez's refusal of a narrative closure, thereby blurring the lines between the real and spectral space to underline the representation of an unstable, paranoid universe where familiar categories collapse and where the human body is the site of this collapse (Pinedo 1996, 20). Like postmodern horror films, Enríquez's short story remembers 'ordinary people's ineffectual attempts to resist a violent monster' (Pinedo 1996: 19) – though the monster in this story is of a socio-political nature. The author writes horror not only in the liminal spaces of the public and political but also in the haunted minds and memories of the protagonists as they engage with hostile historical spectral spaces of violence, torture, and death.

---

4   According to local records more than 1,500 people from La Rioja were imprisoned during the last dictatorship (Carreño 2018: n.p.).
5   See Carreño 2018; and 'Señalizan' 2018.

The dead do talk – and sometimes as a cacophony of urgency and desperation to be remembered.

While the protagonists, Florencia and Rocío, catch up over a 2 litre bottle of Coca-Cola there is a strong sense of them being under surveillance by a group of women gathered to pray the rosary under the flickering light of candles. Rocío, as the local, warns Florencia (who is just visiting) that 'Back at the kiosk it was no good, they might have been listening to us' (Enríquez 2017: 43) – a cautioning that disrupts the normality of their meeting by a foreboding danger of something concealed. This fear of surveillance by the ghostly figures of the praying women recalls an Argentine past of kidnappings and disappearances of suspected political subversives. Enríquez emphasizes the political undertones of the meeting by describing Florencia's first impression of the cured meats in Rocío's back pack looking: 'like the meat was a dead animal, a piece of human body, something macabre' (Enríquez 2017: 44). The fact that Florencia automatically assumes it could be a 'piece of human body' highlights the idea that what is horror and unbelievable for some is, for others, part of a reality lived in which the dreadful is not unexpected. After all, Florencia previously referred to the Gypsy's Skirt as 'that part of the hill that looked like the stain from a now-dry waterfall of blood' (Enríquez 2017: 38) another reference to historical occurrences of mass executions by those in power.

Upon their night time arrival at the Inn Florencia remarks that '[t]he Inn's shape was odd – it really was a lot like a barracks' (that is, a policy academy housing disguising a clandestine detention centre; Enríquez 2017: 45) – and with this short observation the reader is transposed back to buildings's police academy days but also to a medial space that transgresses the real with horror and the supernatural. The girls begin their sabotage plan of hiding cured meats in cuts made into the mattresses of various rooms with the idea that 'the smell of decomposing meat would be unbearable, and with luck, it would take them a long time to find the source of the stench' (Enríquez 2017: 45). Considering the underlying historical narrative, the hidden 'decomposing meat' can be read as the missing bodies of the *desaparecidos* executed and secretly disposed of in the Atlantic Ocean, in the Río Plata or in mass graves.[6]

---

6   See Timerman 2002; CONADEP 1984.

Nevertheless, 'the stench' of these missing body's reveals what history cannot hide since these ghosts make their presence felt despite an institutionalized denial of the events.

The Inn is a space marked by a blurring of boundaries not only between what is real and what is imagined but it is also a space that questions 'the validity of rationality' (Pinedo 1996: 20) in making sense of the haunting by the ghosts of victims of the buildings disturbing past. The girls' experience is one of supernatural horror – the Inn is a haunted site of memorialization as a former clandestine place of detention operating as a torture centre but not necessarily known as such by those living in the area. It becomes a spectral space that breaks away from the rational and highlights the denial of the population of what was truly happening inside the police academy – like in many other similar sites across the country.

At the moment that the girls are about to lay down beside each other on one of the beds the supernatural interference escalates to the point that the girls cower in fear from the noises that seem unnatural and impossible to be real. Sounds of car engines, scrambling feet, and shouting men is overlaid with the pounding of windows and shutters creating an atmosphere of confusion, fear, and imminent life-threatening danger – so frightening that Florencia loses control of her bladder and wets herself. It is a basic bodily reaction to distress of a supernatural witnessing of something horrific that also reinforces the reality of night kidnappings of political prisoners the girls learned about in the classroom.

The acknowledgement of the historical past of the Inn and the girls' psychological break reflects a destabilized emotional state that makes them question their supernatural experience. When interviewed by *La voz* Enríquez admitted that: 'The best way I have found to narrate madness in a horror story is to locate it in that borderland zone between the external threat and the distorted interpretation of reality – which must be absolutely hopeless' (Orosz 2009: n.p.).[7] The level of distress is such that even Florencia's mother finds it difficult to be angry with her daughter after seeing how traumatized the

---

7   My translation. 'La mejor manera que encontré de contar la locura en un relato de terror es en esa zona fronteriza entre la amenaza externa y la interpretación distorisionada de la realidad, que debe ser absolutamente desesperante' (Orosz 2009: n.p.).

young girl is. In essence, the mother is more concerned that something terrifying really did happen to the girls, thereby extending the girl's fear also to those around them. Unfortunately, it is a terror that follows the girls back home – a haunting caused by the dread that the ghosts will return – of ghosts moving in the hallways of their own homes. It represents an anxiety of history repeating itself because of its denial – the parents not believing their story and dismissing their experience by questioning the girl's possible lesbian inclinations.

The dark abandoned space of the Inn reflects the tortured process of memorialization of a troubling period of Argentine history haunted by horrific acts against human rights by those in political power. The Inn becomes a site of convergence of a spectral past, a dark history written onto the walls of the Inn – a historical reality that cannot be removed nor denied no matter how much one hopes to discount it as a mere 'ghost story' made up to destroy the property as a business. It is a reminder that no matter how much there is a desire to erase or deny history, the 'stench' of the rotting 'meat' will denounce the atrocities of the past and render the disembodied *desaparecidos* onto official history.

'The Inn' is a fictional exploration of both the horror and the traumatic legacy of Argentina's history. The characters in Enríquez's short story suffer an experience that is a reflection in itself of the dehumanization of the *desaparecidos* that still haunt Argentina's present.[8] Enríquez's horror fiction does what testimonial literature has done in the past: it unites the political and the social with the literary as a method of not forgetting the atrocities of the past so that they may not be repeated in either the present or future.

---

8   See Angulo and Stemberger 2017: 317.

Gina Wisker

Tananarive Due's *Ghost Summer: Stories* (2015)

Space, place, homes and bodies are the living locations for the horrors of repressed, silenced histories in African American horror. In the literally ground-breaking *Beloved* (1987), Toni Morrison disinters the hidden past, opens the poorly closed wound at the heart of African American history. The novel is mostly set at the official end of slavery in the Northern states in the US, and Morrison reveals how ordinary families try to live while the haunting presence of a very recent brutal history dominates everything they think and do. Thirty years after Morrison's novel, in Tananarive Due's African American horror short story collection *Ghost Summer* (2015), set in the twenty-first century, the terrible past is just as restless and unquiet.

Gothic horror narratives act to disturb complacencies and trouble the silenced into being heard, in order to make new sense, rewriting the past, and in much African American Gothic horror, as it intersects with Afrofuturism, writing potential futures.[1] This is a politicized act. Michael J. Sandel reminds us of the importance of community, the political and social justice orientation of narrative, noting: 'Political community depends on the narratives by which people make sense of their condition and interpret the common life they share'

---

[1] The recent *Get Out* (Peele: 2017) reflects such complacencies, initially envisioning a version of ostensibly enlightened racial pluralism amongst a rich, white neighbourhood, the darkly comic horror narrative soon exposes the hypocrisy of such pretences while maintaining blatant white privilege. It then becomes much more more worrying and destructive since this entitled white enclave have stolen, mind warped and enslaved African Americans, turning them into forms of house-partner and golfing buddy zombies. Chris the protagonist is both taken in by his rich white college girlfriend then lined up to be taken over as the new victim manages to be a comic and horror lead, and to expose this dangerously destructive sham.

(Sandel 1998: 350). Commenting on loss and rediscovery, central to Gothic horror, Abraham and Torok note 'What haunts us are not the dead, but the gaps left within us by the secrets of others' (Abraham and Torok 1994: 171).

Stories are passed on by storytellers, from the relics and bodies of the past, haunting spaces places and bodies, and read through the eyes of the living. In *Beloved*, Grandma, Baby Suggs the healer remarks 'Not a house in the country but is packed to its rafters with some dead Negro's grief' (Morrison 1987: 5). In Tananarive Due's short story collection *Ghost Summer*, historical evils are disinterred along with bodies that were never laid to rest. Another Grandma comments: 'I wasn't gonna say anything to you kids – but there's bodies buried over on that land across the street, out beyond Tobacco Road' (Due 2015: 67–8).

Tobacco Road recalls slave plantation brutality. The unceremoniously unshriven bones belong to the unnamed dead and the partially repressed memories of a poorly buried history. In Due's collection Grandmas pass on the stories to the new generation to expose the secrets, embody the legacy, sometimes take the evil within them, to be lived with or move the town on into a more aware future, revealing the histories and embracing the other within their midst.

African American horror upsets any sense of settled history, of shared reality, and exposes deeply disturbing psychological insecurity in all that seems safely real. Some of this intersects with Afrofuturism (Hopkinson 2005), where history is reconceptualized, destroyed and rewritten from a positive African American perspective incorporating features of fantasy and science fiction. For Nalo Hopkinson, an Afro-Caribbean Canadian Gothic horror and Afrofuturist writer, this sees the actual historical horrors of slaves being thrown overboard on the transatlantic slave crossing being rewritten as them deliberately jumping into the sea to escape. The slaves, now free agents, become mer-people, living happily on Dolorosse, an island where magic reacts to diminish environmental disasters (Hopkinson 2007).

African American horror is based historically and psychologically in the utter dehumanization and erasure of all that everyone and anyone holds dear, enacted initially through slavery, and through the racism and Otherizing that both fuelled, and followed it. Narratives such as *Beloved* and *Ghost Summer* help to re-write and re-balance such history. These texts expose a festering, rotting wound at the heart of not just America but wherever genocidal histories erase and bury the despicable, dehumanizing, Otherizing of humans. African American horror reveals the warped theorizing underpinning the erasure of others whilst offering ways into understanding and arguing against the destruction of difference, as noted by Audre Lorde, 'In our work and in our living, we must recognize that difference is a reason for celebration and growth, rather than a reason for destruction' (Lorde 1983: 100).

Beloved (1987) is a powerful example of African American Horror. Based on the true story of Margaret Garner (Sethe in the novel), an escaped slave who in 1854 tried to rescue her children from the horror of slavery by killing them, *Beloved* focuses on Sethe's haunted family in Cincinnati, the first state in the free North, where the angry ghost of her displaced baby acts as a disruptive poltergeist. The ghost hides food and crockery, shaking and disturbing everything, removing the small family from the community. Then as Sethe starts a new relationship with Paul D, one of the other survivors from the ironically named plantation, 'Sweet Home', Beloved returns as a full-grown ghost, a woman who has to re-learn movement, speech and engagement with humans. Morrison emphasizes the invasiveness and ever-present overwhelming drain of the hidden, silenced, abusive past. The longed-for but invasive, debilitating presence of this horror of the past, embodied in Beloved, dramatizes ways in which this little family, as one of many, must not be eaten up by its haunted history. The ghost is eventually exorcized by the humming of the community so that Sethe and her family can settle, having acknowledged their history and its effect on the present, without forgetting.

Some of Morrison's (1987) and Due's work (1997, 2001, 2006, 2008, 2011) goes beyond terrifying revelations to a form of recovery. This involves living with and beyond the horror, utilizing a psychoanalytic turn, recognizing that the construction of the Other springs from the self. The notion of abjection is useful in considering how colonial and African American people have been considered as 'Other', as Stuart Hall comments the 'Other' is 'constructed as the absolute opposite, the negation of everything the West stood for' (Hall 1992: 314). Julia Kristeva (1982 and 1988) builds on Lacan's engagements with Freud, in which it can be seen that the Other (traditionally the mother/women) is considered as abject and then rejected. Kristeva points out that this abject constructs the Other as a projection from the self. If women, and those of ethnicities (because of African origin) other than the dominant European originated white are considered as Other, a projection based on the basic need to recognize the separate self during the childhood years, then it should be logical and straightforward to unpick this construction, expose it, move beyond it. Difference would not be a reason or argument for destruction. In these terms, communities could also recognize they produce the outsider, the Other.

In *Ghost Summer* (2015), Tananarive Due takes the full range of horror figures further. The tales' trouble any securities about space, place and bodies, with both the revelations of violent hidden histories and of current predatory behaviour. In some of the tales, the silenced histories of Otherized people are recovered while further tales, from the perspective of the predator, provide insights into the motivations and dark energies behind evil acts. The town in which these stories are set, Gracetown in Florida, hides terrible secrets of violence accompanying slavery, abuse and murder. The dead will not remain buried and their corpses are disentombed accidentally during new building or clearance; they rise from the swamp at certain times of the night or year, and infiltrate the consciousness of seers, calling out to be found. But it is not just the slave dead who affect the lives of the sensitives. Babies and young children spending summers round the lake are possessed by demons, with leeches entering through windows, and causing them to be preternaturally well behaved and precocious learners. These changelings are preferable to the other real, bad tempered and wilful children and accepted by parents who want obedience and respect, and are impressed by the speech, the learning abilities of their 'new' child. The changeling children behave in unexpected ways. They come to the lake for the summer to be with grandparents, but for each it is both dangerous and a rite of passage as they will meet the dead and become something else. In these stories it is both ostensibly just exciting, a summer escapade, and actually terribly disturbing to reveal such horrors just beneath the everyday. But this revelation also begins to address the wrongs of history.

Space, place and bodies are central to these tales. The lake is at the heart of Gracetown and in 'The Lake' it is a location for a tale of shapeshifting. As a new teacher relocates into a lakeside house. She and all the locals know that no one should ever swim in that lake. But the threat of the lake is minor compared to the threat she embodies with her sexually aggressive behaviour towards the (in her view) many handsome, available young men in her class, whom she invites to come and fix up her lake house during the summer. Her own (sexual) predatory nature is revealed in her gradual shifting into a water creature, webbed feet, gills, with the instincts of an alligator or a shark: 'That was the first moment Abbie felt a surge of fear, because she finally understood what she'd been up to ... Her feet betrayed her, their webs giving her speed as she propelled towards her giant meal [a student]. Water slid across her scales' (Due 2015: 27). Her transformation completes as she attacks.

Metamorphosis and shape shifting represent a very real threat to two runaway slave lovers in 'Free Jim's Mine'. Jim tells his niece and her Cherokee partner 'you've got to sell your heart for freedom' (139) when they seek safety in his house, in 1838, whilst fleeing the slave catchers. Jim's extraordinary rise to wealth is explained in his family by luck, by his 'mojo', 'you won't both survive the night' (140), he warns. Others sheltering have died there, but any threat or attack is preferable to beating, recapture and probable death. At night, sheltering in the foul smelling, damp mine, the noise terrifies the two of them. In the event, the main threat comes from a mine creature which could be Walasi, a giant frog. Jim sells his heart or soul to a devilish force to remain free. This is both characteristic of the lack of any real choice under such bondage, and a revelation of the unacceptable price to be paid for the opportunity to live a free, if hideously curtailed, life. Slavery and its violence warp people into predatory animals. Jim survived by becoming the frog creature.

Davie visits his grandparents for the summer with his little sister Neema. As he is now 12, he knows this is his last chance to see the ghosts in Gracetown, as they only reveal themselves to children before puberty. Grandma lets him know the bodies found at McCormack's, a local landowner, were not from a cemetery, but Grandpa underscores the worthlessness of African American bodies and lives when he says, 'If it was Indians, see, there's special laws about that. It's a burial ground so it's sacred. But not for *us*. Nothing that's got to do with *us* is sacred' (67). Davie reminds readers of *Ghostbusters* because he's been collecting gear related to his hobby of hunting ghosts: night vision video camera, mini cassette recorder, and a lantern type of flashlight. Seeking out the ghosts that only the young can perceive is initially both fun and a way of bringing his sister into the insider group, initiating her into the patience, speed, fearlessness of ghost discovery and watching. However, given the terrible secrets of this town they are destined to find their escapade more dangerous than just a night's fun. Davie and Neema both hear the barking tracker dogs seeking the escaped Timmons boys, and are caught up in the fast-flowing water which almost drowns them. The bodies are discovered as the sensitivity of the ghost-tracing children lead the adults straight to the deep gully in which they lie. But there is no real sense of justice in finding the boys who clearly fell in the gully during the chase and could not be heard, or rescued, but were not killed by the slave catchers or the plantation and property owners. The terror is immersive and real. The story is finally told and Davie's achievement is being able to enable them to momentarily be alive again, and to understand them and their story.

In another tale, werewolf Kenya tries to hide her nature, but her Gramps tells her about the importance of Moon nights, preparation, the onset of menstruation, the attempt to hide changes, here all defined as werewolf inheritance. Her grandfather knows the power of fear within this 'curse' and when Kenya says, 'Monsters don't create anything', he replies 'What's wrong with you, girl? Of course, they do. They create fear, and there ain't nothing more powerful on this planet Earth' (179).

This highlights the power of horror, creating fear and unease, disturbing, challenging, revealing, and showing that we, ourselves create the other to reject them. The lessons between the generations and the revelations and settling of painful memories lie at the heart of the short stories. Due's town is a liminal space, seemingly ordinary, replete with shapeshifters, undead, seers, at least one werewolf, hiding in plain sight in the seemingly ordinary town where the Summer is a gap in time, and the lake a place of danger in which no one swims. Everyone is hiding something, and the town is hiding its history of abuse, performance, and cover-up. In this bordered space with fences separating white plantation owners and their descendants and the established or newer homes of descendants of their slaves, crossroads of time and place allow leakage of moments in history buried or drowned, in the swamp, in a hole, in a fire, in memories.

African American horror has a more obviously positive mission than the Gothic horror of deeply disturbing revelation. Revealed through the trajectories of horror narratives, this is an active denial and destruction so fundamental as to leave readers gasping and incredulous when we find out the terrible, still barely buried details. This is the legacy of slavery and dehumanization embodied in Otherizing people different from whoever, whatever 'you' happen to be, and believe is superior, chosen, right – the complete denial of rights, values and lives, which is so shocking and at the root of African American Horror. Summer in Gracetown is both a fissure into other modes of being, undiscovered dead, repressed identities as shapeshifters, were-creatures, and the swamp which hides the unburied slaves while the uncovering of mass graves in McCormack's land disturbs the periods of silence as it enables the uncovering and settling of the restless dead. The disinterred bodies at the centre of Due's *Ghost Summer* are reminscent of horror's insistence of the need to rediscover, rewrite, revalue; it uses the power of fear, terror, defamiliarization, discord, to engage readers to focus on such change. The links are with slavery, and the civil rights movements, the learning widespread.

There is an inescapable haunting of space, place, memory, and people. When African American Horror is coupled with Afrofuturist intent and practices as in the work of Nalo Hopkinson, Tananarive Due and others, it also embodies other ways forward. It does not leave you in the charnel house of the monstrous history nor with the resentment at the impossibility of righting the wrongs it dramatizes – instead, African American Horror enables a speculating forward to new ways of understanding the hidden histories, telling the stories, and imagining a more powerful future.

Gail de Vos and Kayla Lar-Son

Cowboy Smithx's *The Candy Meister* (2014)

In America and Europe most horror movies tell the story of the extermination of evil spirits. Japanese horror movies end with a suggestion that the spirit still remains at large. That is because the Japanese do not regard spirits only as enemies, but as beings that co-exist with this world of ours. As noted by Suzuki (2005), as quoted by Colette Balmain: 'Japanese horror films are defined by the centrality of isolation, alienation and emptiness' (Balmain 2008: ix). These elements are also embraced by the emerging sub-genre of Indigenous horror films. Balmain identifies the Buddhist and Shinto beliefs in the supernatural and their rich backgrounds in cultural mythology as highly influential for Japanese horror films (Balmain 2008: 7). In the same way Indigenous belief systems and their enduring timeless tradition of storytelling have influenced the development of Indigenous horror films.

Genre fiction, and especially horror fiction involving Indigenous plotlines, is often built out of colonial tropes such as the Indian Burial Ground, which is 'fueled by the imagining of a disturbed bed of Indigenous spirits that take their vengeance on settlers who build their homes in sacred places' (McCall 2017: 325). For many Indigenous writers and filmmakers, genre is fluid and secondary to the transmission of knowledge by telling a good story well (McCall 2017: 326). Historically the horror genre has left out Indigenous voices, portraying Indigenous peoples as the savages that induce fear and suffering on the central or lead characters in films. Indigenous peoples typically were, and are arguably still, misrepresented, exploited, and Indigenous knowledges and stories are misinterpreted by mainstream cinema and screenwriters. However, Indigenous filmmakers have recently been able to enter the world of horror films, in a way that is more inclusionary and understanding predominantly through the use of indie films. Indigenous filmmakers, while they honour their traditions, are not bound to reflect only Indigenous tales, but to present universal stories through an Indigenous lens.

In this light, we are discussing the short film *The Candy Meister* which won a best director award for Cowboy Smithx in the 2014 Phrike Filmfest 72 Hour Competition. Smithx is the force behind Noirfoot Narrative Labs,[1] a Blackfoot, *Niitsitapi*,[2] style of collaborative filmmaker's society dedicated to strengthening the skills and talents of Indigenous filmmakers. In a recent interview Smithx discussed how film, especially DVD's, influenced him as he grew up in physical and media isolation on his reserve in southern Alberta. He would rent movies based on their cover art and was drawn, as a result, from an early age to horror films (Alberta Filmmakers Podcast).

In the film, four Indigenous women enter a radio contest on Halloween to determine who can stay overnight at the most haunted location, an empty Residential School with a violent history. They borrow the Candy Meister food truck from Hans, their employer, to earn more points in the contest. Horrific repercussions ensue from this purportedly light-hearted legend-tripping event, a reliable component of many contemporary horror films – legend tripping is an organized (although sometimes spontaneous) journey to an isolated area to test the bravery of the group when faced with supernatural phenomena. Usual sites for this include cemeteries, tunnels, deserted and 'haunted' houses, and remote lanes and bridges and the peak time is summer and early fall, especially around Halloween (de Vos 1996: 56).

Almost all legend trips have a fixed three-part structure: introduction, enactment (what happens at the site) and retrospective personal narratives (de Vos 1996: 64). The introduction sets the scene for the trippers before they arrive at the site and includes telling legends about supernatural activities at the location. In this instance, the ghostly and horrific stories of the former residential school are widely known and acknowledged by the characters.

---

1   Noirfoot is a playful spin on words and ideas: Canadian bilingualism, the Noir genre, and the tribal name of the Blackfoot.
2   The Blackfoot Confederacy, Niitsitapi or Siksikaitsitapi (ᒧᐟᒧᐟ, meaning 'the people' or 'Blackfoot-speaking real people') is a historic collective name for the four bands that make up the Blackfoot or Blackfeet people: three First Nation band governments in the provinces of Saskatchewan, Alberta, and British Columbia.

Perhaps due to the time factor in this short film or due to previously shared narratives regarding Residential Schools in Canada the introduction element of the legend trip structure is contracted and amalgamated with the cinematic anticipation of a shared experience for viewers. The enactment fills most of the screen time of the film, from the arrival on the site, to the separation of one of the characters from the group, a familiar factor of horror films, and the addition of comedic relief with a male character joining the remaining trio as they move through the dark and spooky corridors of the deserted school. The films viewers' watch as one of the evil characters is identified as the human Hans, offering some comfort before being frightened by the appearance of the malevolent ghost nun. The demonic nun, Sister Lacombe, may refer to Father Lacombe, one of the Oblate missionaries who aided in converting Indigenous peoples in Canada to Christianity and Catholicism. Father Lacombe did a lot of missionary work with the Blackfoot peoples where Cowboy Smithx is a member of the nation. Along with the inclusion of the demonic nun, Smithx introduces the audience to Nomakks the trickster. Nomakks is described by Smithx in another play *Napi and the Prettiest Girl in the Village* as being a forgotten Blackfoot trickster who is vengeful against Napi and other Blackfoot gods (Smithx). Four of the legend trippers and the human slasher die at the scene while the fifth makes her way safely to the protective shell of the Candy Meister truck and away from the tragic scene. The third element, retrospective narratives of the legend trip, must be supplied, in this instance, by the viewers of the movie as there is no tidy ending provided by the characters or film. Ironically, the iconic food truck has not made an appearance on Vancouver streets since 2014.

'The function of horror ... to scare, shock, revolt or otherwise horrify the viewer – also means that filmmakers are constantly pushing at the boundaries in order to invent new ways of arousing these emotions in audiences' (Cherry 2009: 4). With the appearance of the malevolent nun the tone of the traditional horror tale changes to reflect the past horrors of the Residential School in Canada. It is important to contextualize the time in which the film was written and produced. Between 1831 and 1996, Residential Schools operated in Canada through arrangements between the Government of Canada and the church. Although deemed to be institutions in which Indigenous children were to gain a European education, viable employment skills, and to be indoctrinated into the Christian religion, one common objective defined this period – the assimilation of Aboriginal children (*Where are the Children* 2018). During this era, more than 150,000 First Nations, Métis, and Inuit children were taken, often against their parents' wishes, and placed in these schools. Many were forbidden to speak their language and practice their own culture, and in some cases both violent and sexual acts were imposed upon them. While there are an estimated 80,000 former students living today, the ongoing impact of Residential Schools has been felt throughout the generations (*Truth and Reconciliation Commission of Canada* 2018). Although not taking place in a time when Residential Schools existed, the legacy of the trauma that took place within the schools at the time of operation and the legacy of trauma that exists for intergenerational trauma survivors today, is still reflected within the film.

The film is located within Vancouver, British Columbia, Canada and references made to areas of the city such as East Van and the Candy Meister truck. Interestingly within the film the location for the 'freak show competition' is shown as being the Sacred Heart Residential School. However, the Sacred Heart school operated with Fort Providence, NWT, but was nowhere near the location chosen for the film. An estimated 12,000 children from all over the North went through the school, and the legacy of the trauma that was created from the school is still being felt within the community (*CBC* 2018). Maseda (2014) indicates that many scholars in the field of Trauma studies have theorized that it is important to accurately portray or represent traumatic situations and that there is also a need to maintain dignity and an ability to continue mourning for those involved. Horror films, never shying away from the reproduction of trauma, can still be respectful in how that trauma and space is visualized as is seen in the case of *The Candy Meister*. The film is still able to give mention to a very real place of trauma, but change the locale, so as to keep in mind those who might have been affected by Indian Residential Schools in British Columbia, or those who may have been affected by the traumas of the real Sacred Heart Residential School. By doing this there is an understanding that we still need to be cognizant of how spaces are represented within films, and how those spaces can have an effect on the audience, and even those who are working on the film. An important comment is made in this regard by Elle Jae in the film 'our ancestors would not approve of this'. This is said as they are entering into the space where so much pain and trauma had previously happened. Whereas Elle Jae acknowledges the elders and respects their legacy, Shar in turn does not and counters with 'who cares what our ancestors think.' This is indicative of the dichotomy of Indigenous youth in the twenty-first century, where some are connected to community and culture and yet some are not. Technology becomes more important in this case than respecting one's ancestors.

Indigenous women are a key focus of the film, and with a cast of almost all Indigenous females as primary lead characters, the film makes for a unique contribution to Canadian cinema. Indigenous women are beginning to gain and see more representation and these characters are reflections of the strong, independent, resiliency of Indigenous women in Canada (Anderson, Campbell, and Bellcourt 2018; National Inquiry into Missing and Murdered Indigenous Women 2018; Amnesty International 2009; Hargreaves 2017). However, there are nods within the film to the very serious realities, and societal problems that Indigenous women face within a Canadian and a North American context. Although there is no obvious indication of why Hans was preying on the women, there is a truth to the dynamic between both Hans and the treatment of Indigenous women to this day. Violence towards Indigenous women is a reality within Canada. Not only do Indigenous women face more frequent incidences of violence, the violence is also much more severe. Violence affects Indigenous women and girls in their own families and communities, as well as in predominantly non-Indigenous communities, and threatens Indigenous women and girls from all walks of life. This violence against Indigenous women and girls has deep roots in racism, marginalization and poverty (*Amnesty International 2014*).

Indigenous filmmaking is growing by leaps and bounds within Canada. These stories are being told in different formats, from short films to fiction features and virtual reality, and in a variety of languages and genres, including horror (Smith 2014). Jesse Wente, an indigenous activist and film critic, notes that 'it is not just traditional community-based, issues-driven stories being created' and has predicted that there will be 'lots of folks that could be directing a horror movie in the next 10 years from our community' (*CBC* 2017), allowing for Indigenous peoples to actively participate in a genre that they were widely excluded from. In a later article, Wente, now the director of

Canada's new Indigenous Screen Office, spoke of the importance of owning one's own stories and stated: 'We know what it is to lose our stories to other people, and the harm that can do. I always relate narrative sovereignty with physical and political power' (Mitchell 2018). We look forward to the ongoing blossoming of Indigenous films that address contemporary issues as well as pay homage to ancient and resilient storytelling traditions.

Meheli Sen

Prosit Roy's *Pari* (2018)

'Not a Fairy Tale' proclaims the recently released *Pari* (Roy, 2018) in its subtitle. However, the word *pari*, in fact, signifies a fairy – an enchanting female creature in Hindi-Urdu folklore. Thus, from the very outset, the film announces its status as an aberration from what is known and expected, and gestures towards the constitutive duality of its central character. Hindi cinema has historically shared a fraught, if fascinating, relationship with the horror genre. Bollywood's typical attractions – songs and dances, melodrama, etc. – have long embraced the supernatural, but horror *per se*, at least in the western conceptualization of the genre, has often proved to be an uneasy alliance (Sen 2017). This essay explores as evidence of a new trend in the Hindi horror film, one that embraces the local but does so in a way that enables it to fit somewhat more snugly within global genre conventions; for example, the film does not include any lip-synched song sequences. The braiding of a specific kind of spatial imagination with a certain kind of gendered narrative enables this negotiation between the local and the global to unfold. *Pari*, like many other horror films, was made on a modest budget,[1] but remarkably, Anushka Sharma, a major Bollywood star, chose to co-produce the film while starring in the lead role. The film is largely shot in the Eastern city of Kolkata, and includes Parambrata Chattopadhyay as the other main lead, exemplifying contemporary collaborations between distinct industrial formations – especially those between Bollywood and the Bengali-language film industry.

---

[1] The film was made on a budget of Rupee 18 crores (approx. $2.6 million) and earned 43 crores (approx. $6.2 million) at the Box Office, according to imdb.com.

Briefly, *Pari* is about a mild-mannered young man, Arnab (Chattopadhyay), who shelters a young woman, Ruksana (Sharma), after the latter's mother dies in an accident involving his family's car. A police inquiry reveals that the mother-daughter duo lived completely alone in the woods, with only wild dogs for company. Equally feral, Ruksana has no experience of modern metropolitan existence, but Arnab eventually develops a deep affection for her. However, Professor Quasim (Rajat Kapoor) informs him that Ruksana is in fact the daughter of *ifrit*, the devil, who remains invisible, and that her sole purpose is to seduce him to procreate. A series of unsettling events confirms this story, and a panicked Arnab abandons a pregnant Ruksana to be tortured and killed by Quasim, the leader of a shadowy organization hell-bent on eliminating the spawn of the devil. A month later – the typical gestation period for the unholy foetus – Ruksana kills Quasim and escapes to attack Arnab's fiancée, Piyali (Ritabhari), only to go into labour in her home. A nurse by profession and someone who has endured a traumatic abortion, Piyali helps Ruksana give birth, but the latter escapes, leaving the baby soon after. When a remorseful Arnab finally tracks her down in the forest, Ruksana ingests her own venom and dies, claiming her child is human and not evil, born of love not hate. Arnab's closing voice-over confirms the fact of their child's essential humanity.

This skeletal plot summary does some disservice to the complexity of *Pari*, because much of its power derives from the film's richly evocative treatment of the city and its variegated spaces. Bollywood horror has often relied on interiors of apartments and mansions, or rustic and non-metropolitan locations to generate dread (Gopal 2011, Ghosh 2014, Sen 2017). Apart from Ram Gopal Verma's films like *Bhoot* (2003), the city – as a particular, unique, recognizable terrain – has seldom congealed in such a sustained manner. *Pari* is a notable exception in this regard: the city of Kolkata – capital of British India until 1911 – is not only the setting, but the film exploits its gothic cartography in a way that imbues even quotidian spaces and objects with unease and anxiety. Bollywood cinema typically imagines Kolkata as a space that is foundationally out of time, where familiar coordinates are either monumental, feudal or colonial: the Howrah Bridge, the crumbling North-Kolkata feudal mansion, stately and iconic Victoria Memorial, the bustle of Esplanade which was the erstwhile 'white town' during the Raj, etc.² *Pari* moves between Kolkata, Bangladesh, and a densely forested, desolate stretch between Kolkata and Barrackpore where Rukhsana lives with her mother, Rabia. What is extraordinary in the treatment of all these spaces is the way in which Jishnu Bhattacharjee's moody cinematography creates the atmospherics of fear and sinister portent. Shot primarily in a low-key style, the colour palette of *Pari* is a dejected amalgam of blues, greys and greens; the lush landscape of monsoon-Bengal is leached of colour and radiance.³ Additionally, it rains endlessly in the film, the sound of falling or running water often dominating its sonic texture;⁴ indeed, the sun never seems to shine in *Pari*, gesturing toward a darkness that is both real and metaphorical. In a potentially romantic scene as Arnab and Piyali share confidences on a park bench in Kolkata's familiar and expansive green space, the Maidan, the spectacular skyline featuring the imposing edifice of the Victoria Memorial is soon shrouded in pouring rain. Arnab sidles a little closer to Piyali, to seek refuge under her lone umbrella, but we *know* that this moment of intimacy will be fleeting at best. Similarly, in another tender moment, as Arnab teaches Ruksana to dunk a biscuit in tea near a window, the Howrah Bridge is visible as a smudge on the horizon, but just barely; Kolkata's most iconic modern landmark soon disappears in the haze. *Pari* systematically blocks our view of the monumental metropolis, frustrating audience expectations of a familiar cinematic city; the camerawork generates an oppressive, dreadful melancholy, defamiliarizing spaces and structures almost beyond recognition. Everyday objects – buckets of water, drying laundry, tubes of the antiseptic ointment, Boroline,⁵ incense sticks, nail-clippers and drawing books – are similarly pregnant with terrifying potentialities. The interiors – the grimy hospital and

---

2 For example, *Parineeta* (Sarkar, 2005), *Barfi* (Basu, 2012), *Piku* (Sircar, 2015), all of which were produced by major Bollywood studios, repeatedly return to these monuments and locations in order to concretize Kolkata as space.
3 The monsoons in Bengal are a beloved – if cliched – trope in literature, painting, music and the cinema. In this sense, too, *Pari*'s treatment of monsoon-Kolkata remains unusual.
4 *Pari* is reminiscent of *The Skeleton Key* (Softley, 2005), in which the tropical fetidness of New Orleans is evocatively signaled through a surfeit of rain and moisture.
5 A popular brand of antiseptic ointment in Bengal, Boroline.

Figure 41. Arnab and Piyali shrouded in rain. *Pari*, dir. Prosit Roy (Pooja Entertainment, 2018).

morgue, Ruksana's dismal hut, and finally Arnab's cramped, neon-lit apartment – are likewise dark and dank. *Pari* is a remarkably humid and sodden film, and its insistence on wetness and decrepitude extend to the bodies of characters as well (see Figure 41).[6]

The anxiety at the heart of *Pari*, of course, involves the monstrous fecundity of the female body. While this remains a common preoccupation for the horror genre, what is unusual is the manner in which Ruksana's face/body is used in the film.[7] Sharma wears shabby clothes, tinted blue contact-lenses, dishevelled hair, and a face full of freckles[8]; Ruksana is alternately feral and innocent, terrifying and childlike, wily and completely guileless, deserving of empathy, and striking fear into our hearts. Unlike the scores of Bollywood horror films that have come before, *Pari* steadfastly refuses to sexualize Ruksana in any way whatsoever; in other words, her monstrosity is a matter of ontology,

---

6   The insistence on wetness is particularly emphasized via shots of pregnant women being tortured by Doctor Quasim in giant bathtubs full of water, blood, and bodily fluids. In this sense, *Pari*'s insistence on rain as a motif constantly recalls the maternal body and amniotic fluids.
7   See Creed 1993.
8   These are unusual choices for an A-list Bollywood star to acquiesce to which demands that she relinquish the vanity/glamour that usually scaffolds female stardom in Bollywood.

Figure 42. Ruksana giving birth. *Pari*, dir. Prosit Roy (Pooja Entertainment, 2018).

not sexual deviance.[9] In the scene where she seduces a stunned Arnab, she awkwardly mouths 'I love you too,' in English, an utterance she has memorized from Bollywood potboilers on television, and their sexual encounter is discreetly screened from us behind a drying bed-sheet.

Following Julia Kristeva's ground-breaking work (1982), Barbara Creed has argued that the maternal body is a prime locus for abjection in the horror film (Creed, 1993). In its insistence on the 'poison' – a thinly veiled allusion to menstrual blood – that Ruksana must 'purge' by killing once a month, on corpses that litter the film, on blood, vomit, semen and parturition, *Pari* is effectively an ode to abjection (see Figure 42). In showing us or alluding to the unspeakable grotesqueness of the female body, the film forces us to confront an array of cultural taboos. The abject becomes *productive* in this sense, generating a series of images that force a reckoning of sorts with everything that remains obscured in mainstream culture (Fisher 1992).

---

9   Bollywood horror – from the 1970s onwards – has regularly relied on the hypersexual female monster to both titillate and horrify audiences, for example in the Ramsays' *Veerana* (1988). While Ruksana's satanic blood propels her into seducing Arnab, the film stresses her status as a victim as well. This is indeed a remarkably complex figuration of female malevolence for Bollywood.

But *Pari*'s inscription of gender and sexuality is even more audacious when it comes to masculinity. Arnab's gauche clumsiness is emphasized in the film from the very beginning, as he awkwardly bumbles through a conversation with Piyali. While she confesses to at least one serious relationship, he nervously remains silent; on another occasion we learn that he was a painfully shy child who hid under the bed when encountering adults, and that he still clings to his childhood toys. Ruksana, too, seeks refuge under the bed when threatened or terrified. Thus, *Pari* constantly draws parallels between Arnab and Ruksana, suggesting that they are drawn towards one another as social and sexual misfits, both childlike freaks, in a manner of speaking (see Figures 43 and 44).[10] Weeks after he has abandoned Ruksana to a violent death, and wracked by his own craven irresponsibility, Arnab plaintively asks Piyali, 'tell me, who is the real demon here?' a question that is also, of course, a confession.[11]

Arnab's phallic counterpart is the incense, whip, and Quran-wielding Quasim, the film's grim demon-hunter. Despite his power/knowledge, however, he remains a figure of maimed masculinity, a man with one eye, who was wounded and disfigured by Ruksana's mother as she escaped his torture-chamber. The film does not endorse his rage or his joyless religiosity; if anything, his appetite for violence and torture – and some of the most disturbing sequences revolve around the relish with which he forcibly aborts foetuses from wombs – aligns him squarely with the demonic energies he is ostensibly trying to destroy (Mubarki 2016). Solidly corporeal – with one grisly scene

---

10   For example, in two consecutive and identical top-angle shots, show a chained Ruksana is being tortured by Quasim followed by a scene of Arnab writhing in guilt on the bathroom floor, both curled up in similar fetal positions.
11   Actor Parambrata Chattopadhyay described the complexities of all three characters in *Pari* thus: 'When I heard the screenplay, there was one thing that really caught my attention – I wasn't able to understand if that is a hubris with the film [*sic*] or a virtue – it's one of those very rare films where the hero and the villain are the same person … Ruksana is the heroine, the one you want the audience to empathize with, but unwittingly and perhaps unwillingly, she's the dark force as well … In that respect Quasim is the good guy actually, but he looks like the bad guy … we don't see this duality very often, this shady grey area … this I found quite interesting, but it also scared me. How Many people will understand this? In the subcontinent we receive films in a very black-and-white way, that's what we are used to.' Personal interview with the author, June 2018.

Figures 43 and 44. Parallel, consecutive scenes of Ruksana and Arnab curled in the same positions. *Pari*, dir. Prosit Roy (Pooja Entertainment, 2018).

presenting his glass eye swimming in fluids while he dabs at the bloody socket with medicine – the murderous Quasim is as much an adversary as the vaporous *ifrit*. Unsurprisingly, Ruksana's most stunning act of vengeance is reserved for him: wearing a pair of headphones to block his holy incantations, she deftly wrings his neck 180 degrees.

In another noteworthy departure from more traditional Bollywood horror films, *Pari* does not affirm the heterosexual couple, romantic love, or the family at conclusion, a political gesture of considerable significance (Gopal 2011, Ghosh 2014, Sen 2017). Perhaps Arnab and Piyali do adopt the baby to become a family unit, but we do not know this for sure. The film leaves us with a top-angle shot of Arnab wailing over Ruksana's corpse, yet another image of loss and devastation.

Pari subtly, but unmistakably, recalls the illegal Bangladeshi immigrant. Irrespective of whether the narrative is based on real events, Rabia and Ruksana's flight from brutalization and certain death concatenates easily with narratives of violence and precarity that dominate news about Bangladeshis in India: unwelcome intruders, condemned to a shadowy, perilous existence on the absolute margins of Indian society.[12] It is no accident that Quasim's notorious crusade evokes multiple episodes of violence and warfare that the people of Bangladesh have historically endured, beginning with the Partition, continuing through the struggle of independence against Pakistan in 1971, and to the present day. In each of these cataclysmic events, rape was/is routinely used as a weapon of war; the film recalls this bloody history without relying on any one episode. Predictably, *Pari* was banned in Pakistan for 'promoting black magic, some non-Islamic values and anti-Muslim sentiments' (Lodhi 2018).

However, despite its reliance on a specifically Islamic discourse – *ifrits*, *djinns*, incantations from Islamic holy texts, etc. – *Pari* steers clear of commonplace Islamophobia; that the threat belongs to a particular religious formation is presented, but not especially underlined in any way. And, while intensely local in significant ways, *Pari* simultaneously draws from a plethora of western horror texts, including *Rosemary's Baby* (Polanski, 1968), *Saw* (Wan, 2004) and torture porn more generally, *The Exorcist* (Friedkin, 1973), and *Let the Right One In* (Alfredson, 2008), to name a few. The citations are brief, but deftly woven into the narrative and instantly recognizable to attentive viewers of horror films, a fact that may ensure the film an audience outside India.

This essay suggests that *Pari* departs radically from what Bollywood has historically and conventionally produced in the horror genre, especially in its

---

12   Casey Ryan Kelly writes of *It Follows* (Mitchell, 2014), 'the film constructs a monster that embodies the characteristics of precarity in postindustrial age: a slow yet ceaseless force that delivers to its victim not only inevitable mortality but consciousness of their ever-present vulnerability. Ambient horror – where the source of dread is atmospheric and structural – shifts the audience's focal point from specific monsters to one that can be neither eradicated nor domesticated, and, thus, to structural forces of fear and violence that have no easy solution.' While markedly different in content, tone, and texture, *Pari* similarly evokes a pervasive evil that goes beyond the murderous lust of the *ifrit*; in a sense, the horror of Rabia and Ruksana's existence is conditioned by their relationship to a malevolent nation-state, and not simply the supernatural.

treatment of space, gender/sexuality, and religion. Although the film grounds itself in spaces and folklore that remain robustly South Asian, it eschews the typical excesses associated with the popular form, relying instead on ambience, atmospherics, and unusual narrative/ideological contortions. Whether the film signals an overhauling of the genre – or remains an isolated experiment – remains to be seen.

Dana Och

Jalmari Helander's *Rare Exports* (2003–2010)

While the transnational circulation of films has long been a part of any consideration of film history – and indeed was de rigueur prior to the coming of sound – the distribution circuit often still excluded the products of smaller nations. The coming of sound in conjunction with a rise in nationalism resulted, from the end of the Second World War, in various language policies internationally, whereby nations would try to protect their own industries through quota systems. Currently, the domination of the world market by a few mega-industries results in many small national industries struggling for transnational visibility and viability. Transnational success in these cases often ends up taking the form of an 'art cinema' mode of narrative and image-making that is popularly considered 'high' culture and beyond commercial concerns. Alternately, genre filmmaking can export well to a transnational audience especially when dealing with core generic elements but exoticized with a defamiliarized approach to some element of cinematic construction (e.g. colour, shift from three-act structure, or music). Genre cinema circulating as art cinema due to its foreign origin is not unusual and can be seen not only with examples such as Mexican cinema in the 1960s but also with Italian horror in 1980s or, more recently, South Korean horror.

The three versions of the Finnish Santa horror story – the two web-distributed shorts, *Rare Exports Inc* (Helander, 2003) and *Rare Exports: The Official Safety Instructions 2005* (Helander, 2005) and one full-length fiction film *Rare Exports: A Christmas Tale* (Helander, 2010) – under discussion in this chapter highlight techniques of transferring meaning in a transnational context for a small national industry that is not particularly visible in terms of its films in general or its horror output in particular. While Finnish cinema is more than just the social-realist art cinema for which it is most readily identified, *Rare Exports* still stands as one of its only popular film successes in terms of domestic and foreign box office totals. The film's reception is marked by a sense of the 'exotic' by its various audiences, in that its American reception focused on exoticism and cultural specificity while the Finnish audiences regard its Hollywoodization as exotic (Kääpä 2012: 10–11). These shifted modes of reception reflect the complexity of transnational circulation and attest to the ways that hybridized genres deliberately address diversified audiences.

Given the invisibility of Finland's industry on the international market, also evident here is how transmedia distribution of short films online prior to the festival circuit can work as a form of publicity and reputation building. The double-pronged approach allowed the feature film to circulate simultaneously as a popular genre film and a foreign art film with its combination of horror, ecological, fairy-tale, anthropological, and youth film elements. This simultaneous appeal to multiple audiences is further evident with how the mode of cinematic address shifts from the English voiceover comedic short films (distributed on Vimeo) to the full-length Finnish-language film in theatrical distribution. Notably, though, the opening credits for the full-length film are in English with the interesting caveat that a drawn symbol of Santa is used instead of the words 'Rare Exports'. Thus, *Rare Exports*, generically and linguistically, taps into multiple categories simultaneously to hail various audiences with shifted reading modes. While hybrid genres are not unique to transnational films, this approach to filmmaking can be understood as a deliberate technique by small national industries and minority cinemas to make money, to ensure distribution, to diversify audiences, and to become viable on the world stage.

In terms of its most visible transnational reading modes, *Rare Exports* taps into an existing horror cycle with Santa horror, while simultaneously invoking the fairy-tale horror cycle and nodding to art cinema in its critique of cultural imperialism. Released just prior to the reinvigorated mainstream interest in Krampus as a fairy-tale/folk-tale figure that emerged fully into the mainstream around 2013 after smaller spikes in interest starting around 2006 and which resulted in the release of *Krampus* (Dougherty, 2015) among other playful and serious horror films, these three versions of *Rare Exports* mark a significant shift in the treatment of Santa Claus in mainstream culture. These films experiment not only with genre but also directly reintegrate pagan/folklore roots of Santa (or Stallo) mythology. Santa/Father Christmas is reclaimed as an essentially animal/human hybrid god/fairy-tale figure who eats children. By setting it in Lapland, where the Stallo figure has consistently been regarded as a monstrous threat well into the twentieth century,[1] the films rethink transnational commerce, tradition, and patriarchal authority in different ways across the texts while rewarding completionist viewers because each film stars the same three men and the child featured in the second short stars in the full-length film.

Essential to establishing this series of recognizable reading modes is the inclusion of larger recognized motifs; here, the invocation and intertwining of horror and fairy tales make the film legible, yet still exotic. In this case, holiday horror emerges as the primary genre given its history of the monstrous Santa cycle of horror that had its main genre cycle in the 1970s and 1980s with films such as *Silent Night, Deadly Night* (Sellier Jr, 1984), *Black Christmas* (Clark, 1974), and *Christmas Evil* [You Better Watch Out] (Jackson, 1980). Even though *Silent Night, Deadly Night* was not the first film in the genre cycle, upon its release in 1984, parent protests and letter writing campaigns resulted in theatres in New York, New Jersey, and Wisconsin pulling the film, as the violent reimagining of the mythological figure was condemned for sullying the Christmas tradition. The generic shift offered in the *Rare Exports* films brings together Santa horror and fairy-tale horror by claiming that the sanitizing of Santa into a 'Coca-Cola Santa' that erases his monstrous threat is itself sullying the Christmas tradition. The accusation extends to a larger implication of American cultural contamination through commodification.

While a large number of the recently reimagined fairy tales focus on female characters – and gesture, supposedly, to a reclaiming of feminist potential[2] – these Santa Claus retellings allow for a shift in the fairy-tale and horror film tropes by depicting males centring the deconstruction and/or recuperation of patriarchal authority that is brought into focus not only by the notable absence of women in the diegesis but also through invoking the Santa figure and his modern paternalist persona in capitalism. In the feature-length film, the child Peitari's knowledge and bravery are eventually recognized and embraced by

---

1   See Siefker 1997: 161.
2   See Bacchilega (2013) for a discussion of the 'faux feminism' of many of the recent fairy-tale adaptations in popular culture.

his community as he enters into adult masculinity and successfully reforms patriarchy from within, renewing it for a new era and a new world.[3] The web distributed short films that preceded the full-length film are much more overt in how they link genre shifts to the destabilizing of patriarchy, nation, and transnational capitol; web media's greater freedom in terms of direct political content can be accounted for by the differing pressures of marketing and audience cultivation between web-based and theatrical distribution.[4] The first six-minute short, *Rare Exports, Inc*, takes the form of a nature documentary, though one that adopts an elevated and epic tone that is in awe of the three traditional Lapp trackers who pursue the most elusive of prey. The suspense builds for two of the five minutes before the prey is revealed. Father Christmas, naked and completely animal in appearance, is eventually captured, but not before the English-speaking narrator (Jonathan Hutchings, who also plays the main American contractor who unearths the evil mega Santa Claus in the full-length film) establishes him as both vicious but also the 'most precious of the free-roaming wild beasts of the whole of the wilderness'. Once the trackers, whose dialogue is never translated, capture the Father Christmas, a montage highlights how they train and then eventually ship him out to Tanzania (see Figure 45).

Rare Exports, Inc, in this version is the transnational company that, since 1793, hires Lapps to capture and domesticate hundreds of Stallos to export to 150 countries around the world. Of particular note here is the use of language in the film: the titles and the voiceover are in English, but the dialogue of the trackers is not translated. This indicates an embrace of the exoticized treatment of the local traditions, indicating that the short film's primary audience is imagined as English-speaking, a suspicion confirmed by the faux-documentary training video style of the short which balances between a joke about corporate training videos, transnational corporations with offshore companies and labour forces, and faux documentary sitcom style humour.

---

3 Kääpä points out that the domestic audience would also recognize how the film invokes Finnish *junti* films, which are comedies about the adventures of immature men (Kääpä 2012: 10).

4 See Chapter 3 in Bacchilega (2013) for a larger discussion of this issue.

Jalmari Helander's *Rare Exports* (2003–2010)   195

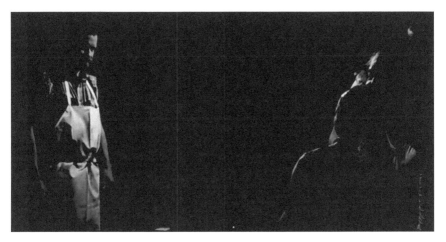

Figure 45. A Father Christmas can't control his urge to eat children during the training montage. *Rare Exports Inc,* dir. Jalmari Helander (Woodpecker Film, 2003).

Rare Exports: The Official Safety Instructions 2005 elaborates that the Father Christmases are never truly domesticated, which becomes clear through a series of events where the distributors and delivery people break the rules and cause the Father Christmases to punish (murder) them. This ten-minute short – a training video for employees of businesses involved in the transnational exchange of culture as goods – features the same three Lapp experts being called in to deal with Father Christmases. However, this time a small child is also brought along, as the Lapp patriarchal tradition is being taught. The video marked 'for distributors and importers only', runs through the list of rules (for example, 'Make No Loud Noises', 'Always Behave') by having the Lapps break every one of the rules and then highlighting the dangerous reactions of Father Christmases in training (see Figure 46).

The narrator shows little pity for anyone who breaks the rules, calling out the audience of distributors and importers as 'irresponsible fools' who invoke such rage in this 'beast with no concept of mercy': 'his eyes blinded by rage, it will not be able to tell who's naughty or nice'. While the short film ends on a high note (the child lures Father Christmas close with a gingerbread cookie and then the men shoot out his knees, lasso him, and shoot him in the head) marking the child's entry into adult masculinity, the narrator chides

Figure 46. Lapp trackers deal with rampaging Father Christmas while the narrator observes that by breaking the rules 'these irresponsible fools got what they deserved'. *Rare Exports: The Official Safety Instructions 2005*, dir. Jalmari Helander (Woodpecker Film, 2005).

the distributors and importers for bringing the Santas closer to extinction. A great irony is visible throughout the two short films in that the Western corporation profits greatly by the exporting of Santas across the globe, but their lack of understanding of history and the danger represented by Stallo (not to mention their inability to deal with his anger like the Lapps can) results in mayhem spreading around the world.

When these short films were adapted into the full-length film in 2010, the element of the 'long tradition' of the Lapps exporting Santas was eliminated, replaced instead with the claim that the Western world's sanitized Santa is a scam. The true Santa Claus, buried in ice by Lapps hundreds of years previously, has actually been forgotten by the townspeople, a narrative decision which posits a similar ignorance between audiences regardless of the country of origin (see Figure 47).

Only when a transnational corporation drilling on Russian territory, though completely staffed by Americans, is hired to explore and excavate an unknown 'product' from the mountain does the trouble begin. The child Pietari (Onni Tommila), researching fairy-tale books, is the only one who realizes the true nature of the evil Santa being released and tries to alert the adults about what the corporation is unleashing, but his warnings are ignored. Echoing the short films, the workers are told to follow the Safety Instructions, but they

Jalmari Helander's *Rare Exports* (2003–2010)

Figure 47. As Pietari learns about Santa's vicious history, so does the film's transnational audiences. *Rare Exports: A Christmas Tale*, dir. Jalmari Helander (Cinet et al., 2010).

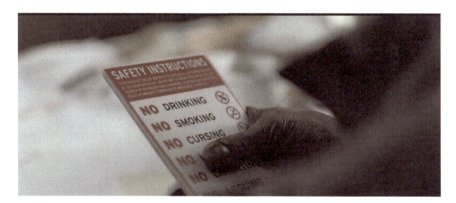

Figure 48. A reference to the second film (re-)establishes the rules that the American workers will ignore. *Rare Exports: A Christmas Tale*, dir. Jalmari Helander (Cinet et al., 2010).

ignore them (see Figure 48). The horned, mega Santa (he is more than 100 feet tall and encased in ice) begins to exert his mind control.

He turns all of the American workers, as well as numerous other men, into his 'elves': each looks like Santa Claus but runs around barefoot and naked, kidnapping all the children from the town to feed to the real Santa Claus once they thaw him out. Catching one elf accidentally (he falls into the wolf pit), the Lapp men decide to ransom 'Santa' off for $85,000 to the transnational corporation, looking to recoup their lost revenue from the reindeer massacre performed by what they mistakenly had assumed were Russian wolves. The situation culminates in Pietari realizing that he must lure the zombie-like hoard of mentally controlled zombie elves away from Santa so that the three Lapp men can blow him up ('Ever wonder how Santa can be in a zillion places at once?'), thus releasing the elves from his mind control and allowing the Lapps to dominate the market by training the elf beasts for export into the international market.

Rare Exports in its three forms work to reclaim the pagan and fairy-tale roots of the Santa Claus figure in combination with Santa horror. In the process, the films put a new inflection (or reclaim an old one) on an internationally known figure to localize while remaining legible. Through genre hybridization and 'creolization' (Bacchilega 2013: 131), these films balance competing demands and needs of its domestic and global audiences. In an allegorical reading invited by the story's commentary on transnational commerce and cultural imperialism, Pietari's orchestrated killing of Santa Claus allows him to not only serve as the saviour of all the children in town, but to reconstitute Lapland's economic future while still being able to cynically reflect on transnational capitalism. To be sure, Santa may sometimes become a bit psychotic, but the Finnish choice to play along is a deliberate and savvy intervention that allows them to claim ownership of the Santa figure in both his psychotic and benign formulations.

Part V

Horror Authors and their Contemporary Afterlives

Dara Downey

Laeta Kalogridis' *Altered Carbon* (2018–present)

In Season 1 of the cyberpunk series *Altered Carbon* (2018–present), the protagonist, Takeshi Kovacs (Joel Kinneman), checks himself into what is known in the show as an 'A.I. hotel'. After over 200 years in prison, Kovacs' consciousness has recently been released into a borrowed body, by a billionaire who hires him to solve a murder. The hotel that Kovacs chooses is called 'The Raven', a gothic fantasy stuffed with gloomy carvings and vaulted ceilings, run by an artificial-intelligence projection who calls himself Edgar A. Poe (Chris Conner; see Figure 49). Dressed in the formal dark suits and stiff collars of

Figure 49. The Raven Hotel. *Altered Carbon*, created Laeta Kalogridis (Virago Productions, 2018–present).

Figure 50. Poe as a poker-playing AI. *Altered Carbon*, created by Laeta Kalogridis (Virago Productions, 2018-present).

nineteenth-century America and marked by the dark moustache and soulful eyes familiar from photographs of the writer Edgar Allan Poe, the writer's namesake is perfectly in keeping with his surroundings.

In the second episode ('Fallen Angel'), we see the hotel proprietor join other A.I.s at a poker game, where his fellow projections mock him for what they see as his unhealthy and dated fascination with all things human (see Figure 50). The exchange takes on a darker tone as we come to understand that A.I.s were originally little more than servants, designed to serve unquestioningly the needs of the 'living'. Poe is, they feel, stuck in the past, having not had a guest at his hotel for nearly fifty years, while the other A.I.s have turned to exploiting the exploiters, peddling virtual sex to their corporeal masters. Poe, then, is a double anachronism – dressed in the garb of an earlier age and outmoded in his fascination with humans. This Poe simulacrum clings morbidly to a power dynamic that the rest of his kind have reversed; one of the AIs boasts gloatingly of using 'live' humans in recordings of high-tech, evidently violent 'sexperiences'. Yet, it is Poe who is criticized by the group for allowing a recent bloody shoot-out to take place in the lobby of The Raven; they taunt him by asking if the corpses were devoured by rats. While the other A.I.s are depicted as dangerously amoral, it is, consequently, Poe, having chosen a form of historical drag, aping humanity in the process, who is associated with abjection, the macabre, and messy, painful, spectacular death. In other words, the historical Poe's own reputation overwrites what is actually happening in this scene – very dark deeds are hinted at, but it is the urbane, waistcoat-clad hotel proprietor who is accused of subjecting the dead to repulsive indignities.

Altered Carbon therefore functions as a generic hybrid (see Leeder 2018: 98–106), punctuating its science-fictional/noir *mise-en-scène* with elements of horror (gore, sexualized violence, and extended scenes of torture), and of the gothic iconography associated with Edgar Allan Poe. In doing so, the show raises a number of issues central to contemporary popular-culture depictions of Poe and his work. In particular, the scene discussed above mobilizes ideas relating to definitions of humanity, the autonomy of the conscious subject, and the representation of Poe himself in popular culture, motifs identifiable in a number of other recent texts in which he features. A full exploration of the films, television programmes, graphic novels, music videos, and other media products that evoke Poe, his writings and legacy (see Peeples 2004, and Perry and Sederholm 2012) is far beyond the scope of this article. However, examining a small selection of such texts – specifically *The Raven* (2012), *Twixt* (2011), and *Altered Carbon* – helps elucidate some of the ways in which Poe's image and the popular understanding of his writings continue to be employed into the twenty-first century, within and beyond the horror genre proper.

These three texts exploit, respectively, the association of Poe with murder, mayhem, torture, and the burial alive of beautiful young women; the critical tendency to reduce secondary characters and even locations in Poe's work to functions or projections of the central male character's troubled psyche; and the ways in which these motifs and critical strategies can be employed to trouble definitions of humanity, selfhood, and autonomy. Arguably, though, what is demonstrated most clearly by *Altered Carbon* is the sheer recognizability of the historical figure of Poe as what Scott Peeples calls a 'cultural signifier' (Peeples 2004: 126–53), and his usefulness as a means of inserting horror tropes into non-horror texts. For example, the ghost of Poe appears in a 2013 episode of *South Park* ('Goth Kids 3: Dawn of the Posers'), where he is described as 'the creator of all that is dark, the godfather of death and despair' (see Crosby 2014: 513). His name and image have become cultural shorthand for dark tales about obsession, alcoholism, murder, incest, dead women and live burial, excessive mourning, unsolved crimes and inexplicable events, uncanny animals, dream states and skewed mental perceptions (Peeples 2004: 142–3, Perry and Sederholm 2012: 1, and Stashower 2006: 323–38). Scott Peeples argues that this has largely been the result of popular film adaptations of Poe's work in the first half of the twenty-first century; from the mid-nineteenth century to the early decades of the twentieth, he asserts, depictions of Poe 'shifted decisively from the tortured romantic poet to the godfather of the macabre' (Peeples 2004: 134). In the process, however, film adaptations and fictionalizations of his life often both misconstrue the plots and concerns of Poe's stories, and portray the man himself as 'the Marquis de Sade', revelling in the horrors he conjures up in his fiction, 'making "Poe" signify torture, murder, insanity, and perversity' (Peeples 2004: 135–6). 'Poe' therefore serves as a means of gesturing outward towards an overdetermined but vaguely evoked vision of 'horror', which, in *Altered Carbon*, is metonymized by a set of spectacular but outmoded visual motifs that have, like the A.I. himself, been superseded by the new horrors of a violent future.

Peeples focuses primarily on the 1963 Roger Corman film *The Raven*, in which a serial killer uses the writings of Poe as (very loose) inspiration. *The Raven*, from 2012, goes one step further, pitting the murderous fan (who re-stages 'The Murders in the Rue Morgue' (1841) and 'The Pit and the Pendulum' (1845)) against the writer himself (John Cusack). The more recent film re-imagines the final, largely undocumented days of Poe's life, figuring him as plagued by writer's block, alcoholism, debt, and grief; we are told that that 'every woman he's ever loved has died in his arms'. The film seeks to give Poe one more shot at true love in the form of the entirely fictional Emily Hamilton (Alice Eve), and at redemption, by saving her from the copycat killer. Emily is attracted to Poe because she finds his focus on death and decay 'romantic'. When her father's yearly masked ball (during which Poe plans to propose to her publicly) is threatened by the murderer, she refuses to let him postpone the proposal, as she thinks it 'thrilling' that Poe should 'commit himself to eternal love ... under threat of death'. Even his love interest, then, is caught up in the image of what 'Poe' signifies.

Her romanticizing of Poe's own romanticizing of death is rocked, however, when the killer uses the ball to kidnap her and bury her alive, giving the

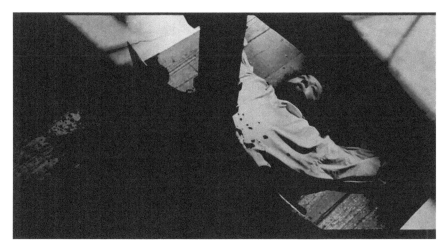

Figure 51. Rufus Griswold's murder. *The Raven*, dir. James McTeigue (Relativity Media, 2012).

poet the opportunity to play the hero by offering his own life for hers. Indeed, rescuing 'Poe' as cultural signifier from adverse associations seems to be a major project of the film as a whole. A fictionalized Rufus Griswold, often accused of misrepresenting Poe and of negatively influencing later accounts (see <https://www.eapoe.org/geninfo/poegrisw.htm>), is brutally murdered by a giant pendulum in a sort of fictional retribution before the fact (see Figure 51).

From here, the plot as a whole strives to renovate Poe's reputation, even while exploiting the images of grisly death and depravity that his name conjures up. Although the opening scenes appear to establish Poe himself as a suspect, the other characters seem to forget this, and quickly accept him as a credible authority on the murders. At the same time, however, we are not allowed to forget that this is all merely a reconstruction of a past that never 'really' existed. *The Raven* opens with Poe expiring on a park bench, having taken a fatal dose of poison from the killer, and we return to this scene in the closing moments; the film therefore situates Poe as always already dead and irrevocably in the past, even as the majority of the film plays out as 'real' and in 'the present'. Despite *The Raven*'s insistence on his innocence in the murders, then, one possible reading is that, like Ambrose Bierce's 'An Occurrence at Owl Creek Bridge' (1890), the entire plot has been a sort of pre-death hallucination.

Figure 52. Poe's death as framing image. *The Raven*, dir. James McTeigue (Relativity Media, 2012).

Had McTeigue's production rendered this interpretation more explicitly, it would not have been an unprecedented move, considering how many literary critics have insisted that secondary characters and even locations in many of Poe's best-known tales are nothing more than projections or subcategories of the male protagonists' troubled psyche. Perry and Sederholm, for example, assert that Poe 'would take a tale with classic gothic elements and trim its rambling plot, hackneyed ghosts, and out-of-place humor, turning it into a brooding, surreal, minimalist gothic nightmare that focuses with laser sharpness on the inexplicabilities of psychological aberration' (Perry and Sederholm 2012: 2; see Figure 52).

Analogous assessments abound among critical responses to Poe's works. To cite but one example, Benjamin F. Fisher, writing about 'The Fall of the House of Usher' (1839), also dismisses the 'outward Gothic trappings [which] lie at the surface' of what is, for him, a psychological tale plain and simple (Fisher 2002: 84). He goes on to claim that '[t]he Usher twins represent the states of the narrator's own emotional-physical constitution. That they are ill indicates that all is not well with the visitor's soul' (Fisher 2002: 90; see also Griffith 1987, 128–9). Working from similar assumptions, numerous critics read Roderick Usher in particular as nothing more than the embodiment of a hidden part of the narrator's mind, his sister Madeline as the repressed part of Roderick's consciousness, and the house itself as the manifestation either of Roderick's or the narrator's psyche (see Thompson 1987: 151, and Lloyd-Smith 1989: 36).

Coppola's *Twixt* might follow *The Raven* in situating a struggling, alcoholic writer of gothic tales as the heroic saviour of young women who have been buried alive, but it does so entirely through the lens of such interpretive strategies. The film packs in suspected vampirism, threatening goth teenagers, a sensationalized mass murder, a fanatical, child-abusing clergyman, a vertiginous clock-tower, a waifish female ghost, live burial, a creepy hotel, suspicious, semi-comic law-enforcement agents, and the ghost of Poe himself, who appears in stylized, black-and-white dream sequences. The protagonist, Hall Baltimore (Val Kilmer), is a writer of increasingly unsuccessful thrillers about witch hunters. During a book-signing tour, he stumbles across a sleepy Southern town with an abandoned hotel where Poe once allegedly stayed. Learning that the town harbours some nasty secrets, Baltimore begins to realize that his attempts to drag these horrors into the light might provide a convenient premise for his next, long-overdue novel.

It is only as he begins to encounter the ghost of Poe, in a series of dream-hallucinations, that Baltimore comes to understand that he harbours his own dark secrets, and that unearthing them is the key to overcoming his writer's block (see Figure 53). Consequently, in attempting to connect a body in the

Figure 53. Hall Baltimore meets the ghost of Poe. *Twixt*, dir. Francis Ford Coppola (American Zoetrope, 2011).

morgue (with a stake through its heart) to the ghost of Virginia (Elle Fanning) – a young girl who he also meets in his dreams – Baltimore ultimately forges a figurative association between these dead girls and his own daughter, killed in a tragic boating accident while he was sleeping off a hangover. The boundaries between various characters begin to break down further, as it emerges that Virginia was walled up alive by a zealous local pastor, who also murdered several orphans in the belief that he was saving them from vampirism. Sequences in which Baltimore talks to Poe cut away to reveal him talking to himself, and, in a climactic scene, Hall (while dreaming) scribbles frantically in his notebook about his sins, while a tortured Pastor Allan Floyd (Anthony Fusco) confesses to child abuse and murder. The camera cuts between the two men, and occasionally to Virginia in a bloody white dress, striking the air angrily, actions which seem to hurt both Baltimore and the pastor. Finally, just before we see Baltimore waking up, he and Poe are shown sitting above a river, onto which is projected images both of Virginia and of Baltimore's daughter in her final dying moments (see Figure 54).

Here then, multiple characters gradually merge into one another – Baltimore is both Floyd and Poe, and Virginia is both Baltimore's daughter and

Figure 54. Baltimore's projection of his dead daughter. *Twixt*, dir. Francis Ford Coppola (American Zoetrope, 2011).

an avatar of Virginia Clemm, Poe's wife, as well as, arguably, a personification of the American South (see Anderson, Hagood, and Turner 2015, and Street and Crow 2016) and of Baltimore's guilt. As in the scholarly responses to Poe's work quoted above, then, the film refuses to grant autonomy to individual characters, reducing them instead to projections of a single male psyche. Clark Griffith takes this critical manoeuvre to its logical end point, asserting that, unless the central, organizing imagination is working upon them, the fictional objects and characters in Poe's stories essentially cease to exist, becoming inert, lifeless, and meaningless (Griffith 1987: 128).

And it is here that we return to *Altered Carbon*, which can be read as a critique of such assessments, depicting as it does a post-human world (Graham 2002) in which computer programs have life, and where the human consciousness can be downloaded into the body of another living host. A full exploration of the relationship between the Poe A.I. and the post-human is beyond the scope of this article. However, as one of the least violent, most sympathetic characters in the show, he does prompt viewers to question the ethics of employing the name and face of a once-living human being to signal all the darkness of the human soul, or to function as a mere signifier of old-fashioned horror. Edgar Allan Poe was, after all, once human too.

Carl H. Sederholm

Crafteon's *Cosmic Reawakening* (2017)

Throughout Crafteon's debut album *Cosmic Reawakening*, there is a persistent sense that something is terribly wrong. Initially, that feeling comes from the band's bass-heavy approach to black metal, a technique that gives even more weight to the music's already heavy use of guitars, fast tempos and rasped or shrieked vocals. As listeners approach the album with even more attention to its lyrics and themes, they quickly discover that its nagging sense of wrongness deepens. This is because the album is an example of the weird, a type of expression concerned with challenging human perception in ways that render everything strange or unsettled. Cosmic in scope, the weird examines things in light of the tension between what can be known and what can be represented. Mark Fisher describes the weird as a 'particular kind of perturbation' because of the ways it makes common-sense notions of life hard to sustain (Fisher 2016: 15). Like corrosive worry, the weird invades one's thoughts and feelings with hints of grim possibilities. Crafteon captures this broad sense of the weird not only by adapting multiple stories by H. P. Lovecraft but also by preserving as much of his language and his mood as possible (see Figure 55). Throughout its run time, *Cosmic Reawakening* questions the reality of what human beings see, hear and experience in ways that suggest there is something more to the world and the cosmos than merely human interests.

The album opens with 'The Outsider', a song that adapts Lovecraft's 1921 tale about an unnamed individual who lives apart from society and decides to seek greater knowledge about himself and others. As the character journeys upward (he does not know that he lives underground), he finds himself in an old castle, only to encounter a creature he partly describes as 'a compound of all that is unclean, uncanny, unwelcome, abnormal, and detestable' (Lovecraft 1999: 48). Reaching out to this awful creature, the character discovers that he

Figure 55. Band members from left to right: Rhagorthua, Lord Mordi, Ithaqua, Fthaggua. Image reproduced with permission of Crafteon and Boutte Photography and Design.

is not touching a living body at all. Instead, he is touching his reflection in a mirror. The song's final verse captures the climactic moment this way: 'With arms outstretched / To a carrion thing before me / Unnameable creature / My touch collides with polished glass' (Crafteon 2017). After a short musical interlude, the band's vocalist growls the words 'It's me' in a way that suggests the character's simultaneous confusion and acceptance that he is a monster, not a man. This moment illustrates a general tendency within weird texts to equate knowledge with the shattering of assumptions as they pertain to the self, other and cosmos.

In the weird, knowledge is devastating. The best place to start thinking about this problem comes from Lovecraft's introductory paragraph to 'The Call of Cthulhu' where he suggests:

> The most merciful thing in the world, I think, is the inability of the human mind to correlate all its contents. We live on a placid island of ignorance in the midst of black seas of

infinity, and it was not meant that we should voyage far. The sciences, each straining in its own direction, have hitherto harmed us little; but some day the piecing together of dissociated knowledge will open up such terrifying vistas of reality, and of our frightful position therein, that we shall either go mad from the revelation or flee from the deadly light into the peace and safety of a new dark age. (Lovecraft 1999: 139)

Lovecraft's point is that reality cannot be experienced without losing one's mind completely. Even the slightest glimpse into alternative realities drives his characters insane, leaving them alone, anxious and despairing.

It should seem obvious by now that Lovecraft – and those, like Crafteon, who adapt his work into other media – was not dealing with everyday setbacks or unfortunate circumstances. Instead, the weird creates an atmosphere that encourages audiences to worry about what would happen if they encountered conditions or entities that are impossible to process, describe or understand. In a classic definition of the weird tale, Lovecraft explains that it cannot be bound by convention because it always requires 'something more', something built on an atmosphere leading to 'a malign and particular suspension or defeat of those fixed laws of Nature which are our only safeguard against the assaults of chaos and the daemons of unplumbed space' (Lovecraft 1945: 15).

Given these broad ambitions, weird tales are sometimes described in philosophical terms. For example, S. T. Joshi suggests, 'the weird tale is an inherently philosophical mode in that it frequently compels us to address directly such fundamental issues as the nature of the universe and our place in it' (Joshi 2003: 11). Joshi is right to underscore these aspects of the weird tale, but his definition falls short by framing it in human terms. The weird obviously poses fundamental human questions, but it also grapples with ideas outside of the human, including wondering whether or not human beings matter in the first place. Michael Saler captures this point best when he writes that, in Lovecraft, 'knowledge shatters anthropocentrism' (Saler 2012: 133). Similarly, Graham Harman argues that the weird undermines human primacy by emphasizing just how unknowable everything is. As he puts it, 'reality itself is weird because reality itself is incommensurable with any attempt to represent or measure it' (Harman 2012: 51). Weird tales are thus doubly unsettling; not only do they frighten audiences with strange and twisted narratives, but they also provoke fears that nothing is as it seems. In that light, anyone, or anything, could be the monster in the mirror.

In the decades since Lovecraft produced his major tales, interest in his work – and in the larger subset posthumously known as the 'Cthulhu Mythos' – has grown so much that there have been hundreds of adaptations, appropriations, and echoes of his work across media. Michel Houellebecq memorably describes Lovecraft as a *'generator of dreams,'* someone whose artistic vision 'is not limited to literature alone' but ranges far and wide (Houellebecq 2005: 51). One aspect of this growing interest in Lovecraft stems from a wish to stay connected to his mood, atmosphere, settings and monsters. Saler captures the sheer range of this interest when he explains that, over the last several decades, 'The Mythos continued to acquire a mythic reality of its own. New fiction, films, role-playing games, computer games, comic books, and other forms of mass culture have extended Lovecraft's Secondary World, amplifying it while usually remaining true to the rational and secular parameters he established' (Saler 2012: 147).

Unfortunately, Saler does not mention that one of the most common connections between Lovecraft and other media is in heavy metal music, especially in extreme forms such as death metal and black metal. Interest in Lovecraft within heavy metal dates to at least the 1980s with tracks like Metallica's 'The Call of Ktulu' from *Ride the Lightning* (1984) or 'The Thing That Should Not Be' from *Master of Puppets* (1985). Special mention should also be made of the cover art to Iron Maiden's *Life After Death* (1985), which included a passage from Lovecraft.[1] Within the scholarly literature, Jeffrey Weinstock and Carl Sederholm (2016) comment on multiple points of intersection between Lovecraft and heavy metal to establish some of the reasons behind his renewed popularity. They also discuss important ties between Michael Whelan's iconic covers for the Del Rey paperback editions of Lovecraft's tales and the cover art of popular albums by influential bands Obituary and Demolition Hammer. Sederholm (2016) also addresses connections between Lovecraftian cosmicism and extreme metal in his discussion of music by the Swedish band Head of the Demon. Similarly, Joseph Norman (2013) surveys and evaluated multiple significant points of connection between Lovecraft's Cthulhu Mythos and extreme metal. Norman has subsequently developed a blog dedicated to evaluating performances and recordings that fall within what he calls 'weird metal' (2018).

1 See also Gary Hill 2006.

Establishing all these connections between Lovecraft and heavy metal is important, but we should add to them a better understanding of what makes those connections significant. To do that, we must remember that the weird evokes feelings of unease that lead to serious doubts about the nature of the world and the universe. Like free-floating anxiety, the weird plays on insecurities and doubts but twists them toward higher, even more frightening, concerns. A black metal album like Crafteon's *Cosmic Reawakening*, I am arguing, not only connects to Lovecraft, but also joins him by searching even more deeply into the weird itself.

Norman helps establish the weird qualities of black metal in by contrasting them against Timo Airaksinen's broadly anthropocentric reading of 'The Music of Erich Zahn'. Whereas Airaksinen suggests Zahn compulsively plays his viol 'to fill the void with music ... to distinguish himself from the nothingness', Norman argues that black metal 'seeks to fill the music *with the void*, allowing its listeners themselves to be absorbed into the nothingness' (Norman 2013: 198). Black metal makes no effort to ward off the dark or to preserve any sense of human significance. It is weird in that it provokes readers into thinking that everything is subject to destruction.

No musical style should have that kind of power, but that is precisely the point. It explores the void so that others have no need of doing so. As a form of weird expression, black metal reaches beyond the borders of human understanding, including staring into that awful void. As Eugene Thacker argues, black metal should be understood as a significant instance of what he calls 'Cosmic Pessimism' which he defines as 'the difficult thought of the world as absolutely unhuman, and indifferent to the hopes, desires, and struggles of human individuals and groups' (Thacker 2011: 17). Although Thacker never draws an explicit connection to Lovecraft in his discussion, his discussion echoes Lovecraft's own dark cosmicism.

Of all the Lovecraft-inspired black metal bands, Crafteon stands out because of their explicit interest in preserving the strangeness of Lovecraft's language while also retaining a strong commitment to his tales (see Figure 56). In the liner notes to the album *Cosmic Reawakening*, Crafteon explains, 'Lyrics are an attempt to remain as true as possible to the original text of each H. P. Lovecraft short story (via excerpts from the Public Domain) and where such attempts prove difficult, Lord Mordi [Lord Mordiggian, the band's lyricist] has supplied lyrical contributions and revisions while striving to at least mirror

Figure 56. Members of Crafteon in performance. Image reproduced with permission of Crafteon and Boutte Photography and Design.

Lovecraft's style and diction'. This statement could be read simply as a means to recognize Lovecraft's work (and an attempt to avoid copyright problems), but the effort at capturing 'or at least mirror[ing] Lovecraft's style and diction' suggests that the band understands the significant connection between Lovecraft's style and the weird (Crafteon 2017).

When I asked Lord Mordiggian to comment on his approach to writing lyrics, he explained that he originally hoped to write his own Lovecraft-inspired words but quickly determined that he wanted to capture Lovecraft's style as much as his substance. He thus began to imitate the way Lovecraft expressed himself even though he was forced to adapt things, so they would fit within the general parameters of writing song lyrics. His aim was to adapt the stories in such a way that listeners would not readily notice 'where Lovecraft ends, and I begin, or vice-versa' (Sederholm 2018).[2] Evidence of Lord Mordiggian's

---

2   See 'Journey into Lovecraft-ian Worlds', <https://www.seaoftranquility.org/article.php?sid=3764>.

imitations appears in several ways, including his use of archaic adjectives (e.g. using 'caliginous' in 'The Outsider' even though it does not appear in the original story), his emphasis on mood and atmosphere, and his frequent suggestion that things are not as they seem.

This emphasis on Lovecraft's prose reflects Lovecraft's own interest in how language conveys the weird. As Roger Luckhurst explains, Lovecraft's prose style is much more deliberate than people realize: 'the power of the weird crawls out of these sentences *because* of the awkward style. These repetitions build an incantatory rhythm, tying baroque literary form to philosophical content' (Luckhurst 2013: xx). Graham Harman also characterizes Lovecraft's prose as demonstrating a philosophical 'gap' between the world and any human attempt to represent it (Harman 2012: 3). According to Harman, 'no other writer is so perplexed by the gap between objects and the power of language to describe them, or between objects and the qualities they possess' (3).

Because the lyrics on *Cosmic Reawakening* adapt and imitate Lovecraft's language, they may also be understood as creating a similar suspicion about the nature of language itself. For example, on the album's closing track 'The Whisperer in the Darkness', the lyrics point directly to problems with representation by referring to a series of 'indescribable' events and how they connect with 'old rustic superstitions' and 'whispered legends' concerning strange creatures and what they signify (Crafteon 2017). As things build toward the chorus, the lyrics turn away from making sense of things to a series of boldly shouted Lovecraftian incantations. Specifically, in the moments when Lord Mordiggian shouts 'Ia! Shub-Niggurath!' and 'Ia! Yuggoth!' the words may be read as signs that human understanding has broken down and some new order of understanding is taking over. As the song concludes with the words, 'This can't be real …', they suggest that a nagging sense of doubt associated with the weird has done its work. In the weird, whether expressed in short fiction or in song lyrics, nothing is ever as it seems.

Cosmic Awakening evokes cosmic dread through its effective blend of Lovecraftian language and its bleak and pessimistic approach to black metal. Like Eugene Thacker, Lord Mordiggian believes that black metal inherently conveys a dark and cosmic perspective, one that invites audiences to meditate on the possibility of nothingness. As Lord Mordiggian puts it, 'Black metal soundscapes tend to bathe listeners in a wide, ambient void of cold space that is daunting and isolating, which I believe aligns with the sense of cosmic dread prevalent in Cthulhu Mythos stories and in other weird fiction' (Sederholm 2018). By combining such awful soundscapes with an explicit attention to Lovecraftian language and style, Crafteon's music will influence bands that also want to draw on the weird in order to understand how unstable things are. In that light, albums like *Cosmic Reawakening* demonstrate that Lovecraft's influence on metal is far deeper than any single fleeting allusion or passing reference might suggest. As I have been suggesting, his influence lies at the heart of an ongoing human attempt to understand an unstable world and an indifferent cosmos.

Todd S. Garth

Damián Szifron's *Relatos salvajes* (2014)

Four severely disabled boys, neglected by their middle-class parents, behead their little sister to delight in her blood. A self-effacing bride is gradually and mysteriously drained of life by a bloodsucking creature hidden in her bedding. An impoverished, unprepossessing jeweller endures the hysterics of his venal wife until he can stand it no longer and plunges a diamond stickpin into her heart. A boy ignorant of nature's dangers gorges on a cache of wild honey that turns out to be poisonous, paralysing him while a horde of ants devours him live. These are four of the more memorable stories in *Cuentos de amor, de locura y de muerte* [Tales of Love, Madness and Death] (1917), by Latin America's master of the gothic and the grotesque, Horacio Quiroga (Uruguay 1878-Argentina 1936).

Guillermo del Toro, Latin America's current master of horror film, acknowledges the importance of Quiroga to his work and to the horror genre, pointing specifically to the first two stories above, 'La gallina degollada' [The Decapitated Chicken] and 'El almohadón de plumas' [The Feather Pillow] (@RealGDT). Gabriel Eljaiek-Rodríguez expands on this reference, noting the variation on vampirism in 'El almohadón de plumas' (Eljaiek-Rodríguez 2015: 147–8) and pointing out that Quiroga's interest in vampirism was directly linked to his obsession with silent film. The blurring of the frontier between life and death, the role of the vampire in violating that frontier, and force of erotic passion compelling those crossings repeatedly figure in Quiroga's vampire stories and in his reviews of Hollywood movies, published between 1913 and 1928 (Garth 2016: 77–96).

Yet despite evidence that during this period conventional horror movies were widely viewed and publicized in Buenos Aires, Quiroga apparently ignored them (Garth 2016: 89–90).[1] This neglect reflects Quiroga's particular take on horror: a focus less on the graphic carnal terrors resulting from repression, perversion or thwarting of human and natural forces and more on the revenge wrought by those forces. Revenge, as the centrepiece of much horror fiction in Argentina, follows a line from Quiroga to the present through Jorge Luis Borges (despite Borges's disdain for Quiroga, see Lafforgue 1996: xxxvii), Roberto Arlt, Silvina Ocampo, and Luisa Valenzuela, to name a few. *Relatos selvajes* [*Wild Tales*], the 2014 film by director Damián Szifron, is the cinematic epitome of this tradition.[2]

Relatos selvajes comprises six vignettes relating to a central conceit: 'getting back' – at individuals, at one's own misfortune, at the system, but most of all at those who wield power. Each vignette contains a terrifying moment of violent, often bloody, revenge. Each such moment is the culmination of abuses – in a single encounter, during a protracted period, or over a lifetime – that push one person over the edge.

While Szifron never mentions Horacio Quiroga's influence, numerous threads – thematic, descriptive, and philosophical – connect Argentina's master of the gothic short story with this contemporary filmmaker. Most salient is the trope of the pariah wreaking revenge, simultaneously heroic and abject, on a repressively conformist society; an ordinary citizen made outcast suddenly transformed by rage, indignation, or bravery into a perverse, destructive monster. A notable exception in *Relatos salvajes* is the vignette titled 'La propuesta' [The Proposition], in which an enraged, indigent public takes harrowing revenge on a humble conforming individual.

But where Quiroga was consistent in revealing the pariah inherent in the traditional heroic individual, Szifron begins his anthology with the reverse: the tragic potential inherent in the societal shaping of a pariah. In 'Pasternak', which unfolds before the beginning credits, it emerges, to growing horror, that an airline bursar with a troubled past has arranged to trap everyone who has ever wronged him on a doomed charter flight. This initial episode ends in a

---

1 See Finkielman 2004: 172–4, on the first sound version of *Drácula* shown in Argentina, in 1930.
2 See also Risner's, three studies of Argentine horror films (2012a and 2012b) and Heller-Nicholas's summary of rape-revenge films in Argentina (2012: 104–7).

Figure 57. Érica Rivas as Romina, in vignette six, 'Hasta que la muerte nos separe' [Till Death Do Us Part]. *Relatos salvajes* [*Wild Tales*] dir. Damián Szifron (Sony Pictures Classics, 2014).

blood chilling twist, setting the pattern for each of the tales that follows. The method is not new, nor does it originate with Quiroga, but it was Quiroga who enshrined it in Spanish American fiction, explicitly appropriating it from Edgar Allan Poe.[3] In contrast to Poe, however, Quiroga's twists are often a direct result of the pariah's unexpected – and, to onlookers, inexplicable – transformation into a raging avenger.

Relatos salvajes's last vignette, 'Hasta que la muerte nos separe' [Till Death Do Us Part] is most provocative in this regard, partly because the avenger is a young woman, and partly because the setting, a posh Jewish wedding, as well as the crime – the bride suddenly realizes that her groom has not been completely faithful – are comparatively benign. The enraged bride, Romina, reveals just what monstrosities she is capable of in two awful moments (see Figure 57). The first is on the rooftop of a Buenos Aires hotel, as she declares

3   Quiroga, "Decálogo del perfecto cuentista' [Decalogue of the Perfect Storyteller], *Todos los cuentos* (1996: 1194).

to the stunned groom that she intends to make his life a living hell, spending his last penny, screwing every man who looks at her, and exploiting the legal system to insure he cannot divorce her. Ariel, the husband, reacts by vomiting directly into the camera. In the second such moment, Romina grabs the offending other woman, who has had the audacity to attend the wedding and, forcing her into a two-woman spin to klezmer music, releases her hurling into a plate-glass window then walks unconcernedly away.

Quiroga's women, while not so violent, are capable of equal cruelty, particularly in marriage. Indeed, their capacity for cruelty is directly proportionate to their identification with bourgeois values, values that Quiroga regularly impales. A central conflict in Quiroga's fiction is between the domestic idyll a woman desires – afforded by wealth and encouraged by her family, particularly her mother – and the unpretentious aims of an unattached hardworking male. It usually results in one of two outcomes: the possession of the bride by the groom in an access of sexual awakening or the destruction of both by the groom's inevitable despair, incomprehension or outrage, as with the jeweller, referenced above, in the story 'El solitario' [The Solitaire]. Szifron favours the more peaceable first option of romantic and erotic reconciliation, but not before making it clear that in modern times a woman's capacity for physical and psychological terror is real and omnipresent.

Szifron is also in sympathy with Quiroga, and with his legacy of resentment against bourgeois values, in his treatment of racial prejudice, though his technique has more in common with cinematic precedent. 'El más fuerte' [The Fittest], the most violent of the film's episodes, features close-ups of two men fighting hand-to-hand to the death in a closed car. The shaky, hand-held-like footage, the eerie music, the tight visuals of an aggressor's soot-smeared enraged face, set against the backdrop of a transcendentally majestic landscape, all make use of the filmic vocabulary of horror.[4] But it is in almost glossed-over details that the social and philosophical weight of this tragedy lies. The car is a brand-new BMW; its driver a wealthy urbanite who, speeding along the highway, is cut off by a local hick driving a jalopy. The annoyed yuppie yells an insult at the implacable yokel, '¿sabés que sos un negro resentido? ¡forro!'

4   Thanks to my students in FS202 (Intermediate Spanish II) at the US Naval Academy for pointing out these conventions.

This insult has generated much internet commentary, in which Argentines confirm that it is a highly offensive slur with a primarily classist, and secondarily racist and homophobic, message. One viable, though not entirely satisfactory, translation is 'You know you're an uppity mongrel? Cocksucker!'[5] The critical analysis that links these prejudices in Argentine cultural discourse, particularly in their guise as the 'civilization versus barbarism' tradition, is too lengthy and rich to summarize here (see Lusnich 2005: 12). This is a tradition that Quiroga firmly rejected, and his portrayals of violent revenge against bourgeois abuse and prejudice can be seen as a direct precedent to Szifron's. One of the most chilling is the story 'Las fieras cómplices' [Beasts in Collusion], in which the honest Italian overseer of a logging camp and the indigenous labourer most loyal to him are left maimed and disfigured in a brutal punishment by the Brazilian owner of the camp. With the help of a tamed lioness, they carry out a merciless and bloody revenge, described in hair-raising detail.

One of only two Argentine full-length movies based directly on Quiroga's fiction is *Prisioneros de la tierra* [Prisoners of the Land]. The movie is an amalgam of stories detailing the brutal abuse of rural labourers in the subtropical Argentine back country at the hands of interests represented by white, urban professionals, bearers of the *civilización y barbarie* mentality that Quiroga relentlessly assailed – an assault that Szifrón continues. Szifrón even echoes Quiroga's insistence on questioning the boundaries between the human and the animal – on blurring the definition of 'beasts' in tales of European man, indigenous man and wild animal colluding to exact cruel revenge. The opening credits of *Relatos salvajes* are shown against images of wild animals, each presumably reflecting personal characteristics of the people credited. (Szifron's name accompanies the close-up of a fox.)

In Argentina today, Quiroga is best known for his children's stories, which, while arguably gentler than his gothic fiction, are also replete with violence and revenge. One of Quiroga's most striking revenge stories is 'Juan Darién', evidently aimed at young adults, which combines numerous ingredients of today's horror genre. These include the trope of a savage creature as an apparent human's true, hidden identity. Instead of a vampire or werewolf

---

5 '*Forro*,' literally slang for 'condom', is often used to impugn masculinity.

masquerading as a noble man, however, Quiroga gives us a tiger disguised as a kind, honest and diffident orphan boy. For Juan's antagonist, instead of a doctor, scientist or detective – the symbol of rational science against human depravity and animality – we have the consummate bureaucrat, a government school inspector. And the mob 'justice' unleashed on Juan, in lieu of villagers or bystanders who have a legitimate fear of incomprehensible monstrosity, we have the entire population of a backcountry town hounding a small boy until he literally shows his stripes, reverting to a tiger, so that they can 'legitimately' torture and crucify him, then blast him with fireworks. Juan's revenge, following a Christ-like return to life as a full-fledged beast, cannily inflicts the same method of torture in his retribution on the school's inspector.[6]

Examined alongside 'Juan Darién', *Relatos salvajes* reveals ways in which horror conventions, while applied to the challenging of classism and racism, also concomitantly resonate with certain contemporary theories on the limits of the human and the bearing those limits have on class and race prejudice. In addition to the recalibration of the relationship between the human and the nonhuman demanded by cultural ecocriticism (Heffes 2014: 15), and the questioning of human moral codes against the animality of mass human violence (Gunnells 2006: 350–4), the horror in both works raises the question of how the hallmarks of civilization – the evidence of a sacred moral exceptionalism pertaining to humans – occupy the same space as the hallmarks of savagery. Quiroga, by revealing the essentially savage inherent in the ostensibly civilized, sheds light on how the conventions of civilization effectively perpetuate the brutalizing of subjects made subaltern by the conventions of race and class.

This fusing of civilization and barbarism, characteristic of contemporary Argentine challenges to their cultural tradition, is analogous to the process Giorgio Agamben elaborates in his theory of 'bare life': individuals who are simultaneously inside and outside the human community, simultaneously profane and sacred and thus subjects for sacrifice – morally prescribed homicide (Agamben 1998: 102–3). Just as werewolves and vampires, when dispensed with, confirm the moral exceptionalism of humans, Juan Darién and a sacrificial

---

6   On the relationship between vampires in Argentine literature and film and the dynamics of mob justice and bureaucratic abuse ('the administrative grotesque'), see Braham 2015: 129–40.

groundskeeper in *Relatos salvajes*'s fourth vignette, 'La propuesta', reveal the speciousness of this form of justice. An important aspect of Agamben's approach to this phenomenon is that *homo sacer*, the object of sacrifice, is forbidden a voice to articulate their own 'sacred' value – it is conferred upon them by 'civilized' language. Quiroga and Szifron both suggest that the animality in humans obscured by social conventions is the same force needed to save humans from class, race and economic exploitation. In other words, their savages talk back.

Juan Darién's actions are particularly provocative because the narrator makes it clear that Juan is morally pure; indeed, the story implies that moral purity is only attainable *outside* of human experience. Such is not entirely the case with the humble gardener subjected to mob justice in *Relatos salvajes*. In 'La propuesta', the victim of the crowd demanding retribution is a *willing* scapegoat, the loyal groundskeeper of a wealthy entrepreneur whose young son has committed hit-and-run manslaughter. Naïve about the risks involved, the groundskeeper agrees to take the boy's rap in exchange for payment; his demand of a beach apartment in addition to the agreed-upon half million dollars attests to the fact that although the pawn of a social and economic system rigged against him, he is not free of human greed. In both 'La propuesta' and 'Juan Darién', the bourgeois values of wealthy urbanites shape the crimes of the masses against the scapegoat – crimes of shocking violence against individuals whose lives are *de facto* disposable.

The voice of the pariah circumscribed by the dynamics of horror in these stories emerges especially loudly in 'Bombita', the fifth episode of *Relatos salvajes*. In a realistic, though heightened, tale of frustration and rage against a corrupt, abusive bureaucracy, Szifron gives us Simón Fischer, an explosives engineer who, having received one too many bogus parking fines, simply cannot take it anymore. Unable to make his voice heard, he sacrifices everything – career, family, reputation – in a spectacular detonation of noise, light and heat, shattering glass and twisting metal. This is a heroic response to dehumanization that could be straight out of Quiroga, except that in Quiroga animals are also capable of pyrotechnics, and human revenge is more likely to resemble the blood-soaked outcome of 'Las ratas' [Mice], *Relatos salvajes*'s second episode, or the gasp-inducing finale of 'La propuesta'.

A film dealing so directly with the economic, social and cultural problems of its Argentine context is not going to fit neatly into the horror genre; the occasional Argentine films that correspond more obviously to the genre take their cues more directly from Hollywood and popular horror conventions.[7] But many aspects of this film most in sympathy with the genre reveal the extent to which Horacio Quiroga's home-grown gothic and naturalist fiction informs Latin American horror. The indelible images of pain, aggression, rage, fear and disgust that make Quiroga's stories so compelling today continue to be an important source of vocabulary – visual, linguistic and thematic – for horror in the Southern Cone.

---

7   One example is *Plaga zombie* series (Zombie Plague: 1997–2018) a series of ultra-low-budget comic horror films by Pable Parés, Berta Muñiz and Hernán Saenz.

Kristopher Woofter

Caitlín R. Kiernan's *The Drowning Girl* (2012)

A critically acclaimed, bestselling writer in her time, Shirley Jackson produced a body of work that is of immense importance to the American Gothic and horror traditions, and to American literature more generally. Her 1948 short story 'The Lottery' is still one of the most anthologized stories in American literature – and in many ways the Rosetta Stone for scholars seeking the 'essence' of Jackson's philosophy and aesthetic. Yet, the bulk of Jackson's work has remained largely under-appreciated, perhaps due to its stunning originality and hybridity. Consequently, Jackson sits only at the margins of the American literary canon. As Alexis Shotwell White (2013) has noted, it is a common lament that Jackson's work remains so under-studied (cited in Anderson and Kröger, 2016: 14); and her influence on twentieth- and twenty-first-century popular culture is equally understated, even muted.[1] Scholars seeking ways into Jackson's work have taken pains, in their tracing of ostensible 'Jacksonian' themes, to avoid reducing the author or her work to something *essential*. Darryl Hattenhauer sees in Jackson's oeuvre a 'proto-postmodern' aesthetics of ambiguity, particularly evinced by the author's intertextual nods to 'nonrealist modes', as well as by her unreliable narrators and her creation of 'disunified' and 'entropic' characters in an 'undecidable world' (2003: 2, 5, 3, 4). More recently, S. T. Joshi finds in Jackson a satirical, misanthropic apocalypticism echoing the work of Ambrose Bierce (2016: 37). And Eric Savoy traces a 'poetics of dark

---

1   In Autumn 2018, Netflix released a critically lauded ten-episode series, *The Haunting of Hill House* (Mike Flanagan), which takes its title, character names, and ostensibly its inspiration from Jackson's novel (though little of its tone, subtlety, and intelligence). And a recent adaptation of *We Have Always Lived in the Castle* (Stacie Passon) had its premiere at the LA Film Festival in September of 2018 but has not yet found distribution.

potentiality' in Jackson's work – an inarticulable, disturbing *something* which lies 'between the ordinary day and the "thing" that can blow that day apart' (2017: 837). Michael T. Wilson, writing in 2015 on Jackson's *The Haunting of Hill House* (1959), also has noted this sense of the 'ineffable' and the pleasurable *frisson* affected when characters confront things uncategorizable and unrepresentable. This essay, too, claws towards a sense of something integral to Jackson's work, here via the concept of writing-as-haunting, and the construction of self-as-ghost. Characters in Jackson's work often turn away from reality to fantasy in a triumphant annihilation of self. This thematic strain of writing oneself into another (or 'othered') existence is rooted in proto-feminist works such as Charlotte Perkins-Gilman's 'The Yellow Wall Paper' (1892), and is apparent in the titling of the most recent posthumous collection of Jackson's work, *Let Me Tell You* (2015). It also resonates with one of the twenty-first-century's greatest conjurers of darker realities, Caitlín R. Kiernan – particularly her 2012 novel, *The Drowning Girl*.

In *The Drowning Girl*, Kiernan offers both a compelling act of writing oneself into existence and a sustained investigation of the memoir as a literary form. To reconcile with a traumatic past and a present diagnosis of paranoid schizophrenia, Kiernan's protagonist India Morgan Phelps (Imp) writes a ghost story, where the ghost is less an unbidden manifestation of the return of the repressed than a *conjuring* by the protagonist. Imp bases this ghostly creation on Eva Canning, a real woman whom she helped to commit suicide, before reconstructing Eva in her memoir as both a folkloric wolf and a mythical mermaid-siren – two potentially monstrous forms in that they may or may not exist simultaneously, and that they may or may not be versions of Imp herself. Thus, Imp collapses into multiple, fantastical bodies and perspectives. In Kiernan's rendering, the beckoning details of the past lead not to Imp's eventual annihilation, as the siren metaphor would suggest, but instead to an acceptance of the multiplicities and slippages of the fractured self. For, as Imp writes, 'There's always a siren, singing you to a shipwreck' (Kiernan, 2012: 277). Imp's conjuring of the ghost is less as a supernatural force than a kind of weirding or queering of reality, resisting both supernatural and cruder psychoanalytical readings. Hauntings here are things 'unfinished' (Kiernan, 2012: 29), the memories, thoughts, and experiences from which we try to wrest meaningful narratives. 'Dead people and dead thoughts and supposedly dead moments are never, ever truly dead', writes Imp, 'and they shape every moment of our lives. We discount them, and that makes them mighty' (Kiernan, 2012: 110). The idea of memory as a haunting or possession is built directly into Kiernan's theory of the memoir itself as a narrative form, voiced through the sustained mirroring of self-consciousness and formal reflexivity that characterizes Imp's storytelling: 'One does not find closure, resolution', Imp writes, 'One is never unhaunted, no matter how much self-help happy-talk purveyors of pop psychology and motivational speaking ladle on' (2012: 278). Kiernan's narrative goals mirror Imp's fully embodied outlook on reality, where the irrational, dreamlike, and gut-churningly emotional are valued as much as the so-called mental clarity gained by contemplative, objectively distanced back-looking. Accordingly, Kiernan frames her novel as a highly self-aware attempt by a 'haunted' woman to construct a meaningful, truthful account of her struggle through often blatantly non-factual strands. As Imp puts it, 'The story's not factual, but it's true' (Kiernan, 2012: 126). Imp's is a narrative where ghosts, sirens, fairy-tale allusions, paintings, dreams, hallucinations, multiple selves, and multiple fictional narratives all cohere into a semblance of the self-as-haunted. It is in Kiernan's complex reworking of the spectral self that *The Drowning Girl* most recalls the work of Shirley Jackson. For both authors, a state of haunted-ness captures experience in a way that is more 'true' than 'factual', where the ghost is less a mediating presence between the living and the dead or the past and present, but between *possible realities*.

Jackson announces this liminal space of possibility in the famous opening paragraph of her 1959 novel *The Haunting of Hill House*: 'No live organism can continue for long to exist sanely under conditions of absolute reality' (1984: 3). The line is something of a summation of the author's aesthetic stance in all her fiction to this point, and a pronouncement of further exploration in this vein. In 'absolute reality', the stark truth of existence stares the subject in the face – though, in Jackson's work, it most often comes to the characters in glimpses and shades that cause nausea, paranoia and anxiety. The line recalls Emily Dickinson's invocation to 'tell all the Truth but tell it slant –', or else 'every man be blind' ([1868] 1960: 506–7). As in Dickinson, 'absolute reality' is bald, mind-scrambling Truth – variously imminent and immanent, and yet resistant to the subject's clutching for meaning. Hints of such a truth appear across Jackson's collection *The Lottery and Other Stories* (1948), for example, as a vague eschatological sense of decay and degeneration in stories like 'Pillar of Salt', 'The Renegade', and 'The Daemon Lover'. Here, protagonists find themselves trapped in a reality of near-fantastical repetitions of collective violence, and of not-so-subtle taunting, and sinister collusion in their families and communities – all factors that leave them paralysed, stranded on the edge of awareness. In *Hill House*, against a reality that will not have her (at least in part because it cannot contain her), Eleanor Vance will literally become a ghost, melding with the fantasy construct that is the only place (reality, world) she could ever really call home: Hill House. Possibly tragically, possibly heroically, and possibly both, Eleanor's eventual suicide offers her the materialization of that fantastic 'magic oleander square' (Jackson, 1984: 19) she imagines will contain both her lost, vaunted hopes for love and belonging, and her simultaneous vehement desire to be cordoned off from society, alone, 'protected poisonously from the eyes of people passing' (Jackson, 1984: 20). In her follow-up novel, *We Have Always Lived in the Castle* (1962), Jackson would carry the active conjuring of a wholesale fantasy even further, showing it to be the construct of not only the ghostly surviving members of the Blackwood family, but also the town that holds them at abject distance – a necessary mythical monster to their wretched normalcy. In Merricat Blackwood, Jackson extends the irrationality of Eleanor Vance to monstrous, murderous proportions that are not necessarily unpleasant to behold. Merricat's totalizing destruction of the old world where she and her sister Constance were the pariahs of the community, also orchestrates an all-consuming, oddly appealing fantasy, where the sisters live like enigmatic ghosts, a necessary foil to the town's impoverished 'absolute reality'. *We Have Always Lived in the Castle* takes the folkloric ritual beliefs of the community in 'The Lottery' to their (ironically) logical conclusion, with Merricat and Constance becoming an essential myth, living like ghosts in the burned-out shell of the Blackwood estate – on 'the Moon', as Merricat dubs it – the townspeople bringing them daily meals to sustain an illusion to which they, also, desperately need to cling.

In these, Jackson's two most masterful works, there is a progression: from a kind of triumphant annihilation in Eleanor's final semi-conscious act of driving her car into a tree to avoid being ejected from Hill House's 'poisonous protection', to a kind of immortality in the similarly triumphant, quasi-posthumous existence of the Blackwood sisters – a wholesale erasure from 'absolute reality' to transcend into the powerful realm of story. If these works read tragically (Hattenhauer, 2003: 6), it is arguably less due to the protagonists' active turn towards fantasy as a form of insanity (or death), and more due to the hostile reality that cannot integrate them. In a letter to her editor for *Hill House*, Jackson takes up the notion of the ghost as less the mark of tragic trauma and failure than as a form of self-fulfilling reconciliation or reconstitution: 'The ghost promotes a consummation deeply desired by the percipient. ... [The] ghost is a *statement* and a *resolution* of a problem that cannot be faced or solved *realistically*' (quoted in Franklin, 2016: 173, emphases mine). It is this 'deeply desired' aspect of ghostliness as a 'statement' and a 'resolution' that Kiernan picks up in *The Drowning Girl*. Yet, where Kiernan's echoing of Jackson *most* resonates is less in these works of dead and living ghostly 'consummations', than in the promise of the novel Jackson left unfinished after her untimely death: *Come Along with Me*, published posthumously in 1965, along with a selection of stories, by her widower, Stanley Edgar Hyman.

'No story has a beginning', writes Kiernan's Imp. 'All beginnings are arbitrary' (2012: 6). Yet Imp rather decidedly begins with a convention: 'I'm going to write a ghost story now' (2012: 1). In darkly comical fashion, *Come Along with Me* embraces this arbitrariness of beginnings – of names and locations and new starts – with its initial tracing the steps of a middle-aged woman who is more than happy to have buried her husband, dispensed with her home and most of its contents, and moved to an unnamed city to start a new life with a new name that she chooses at random. The first six chapters of *Come Along with Me* are all that we have, and in them, there is already the suggestion of another shift in Jackson's work. As if to take its cue from the two masterworks preceding it, the novel *begins* with an act of self-annihilation that reads like a reinvention or resurrection: 'I erased my old name and took my initials off everything, and I got on the train and left', she says. 'I can't say I actually chose the city I was going to; it was actually and truly the only one available at the moment; I hadn't ever been there and it seemed a good size and I had enough in my pocket to pay the fare' (1995: 5). Essentially an act of self-annihilation reminiscent of Eleanor's melding with Hill House, or Constance and Merricat Blackwood's transcendence into myth, the journey of this woman, who will eventually dub herself Mrs Angela Motorman, is already an act of both resistance to the rational and a retreat into a totalizing fantasy where reality serves as raw material out of which to fashion a new self. Mrs Motorman tells us that she is 'starved for strangers' and thus heads to a 'proper little city, correct and complete, set up exactly for my private use, fitted out with quite the right people, waiting for me to come. I slid around on the streetcar seat and thought that they had done it all very well' (1995: 8). Shades of the megalomaniacal Merricat Blackwood appear in Mrs Motorman's vision of a reality fashioned for her 'private use', but the moment feels like an awakening.

As a clairvoyant, Mrs Motorman lives in a present full of possible ghosts – a conceit that might have formed this novel's version of the sinister Crowd – yet she welcomes the opportunity for reality-testing, remembering a time prior to marriage when she 'never really knew [...] whether what I was doing was real or not' (1995: 18). How Jackson might have followed through on this vision of a woman at play in the space between fantasy and 'absolute reality' is uncertain; what is clear is that the *breakdown* of any distinction between the two is necessary for the character to exist – 'sanely', or otherwise. Both Mrs Motorman and Kiernan's Imp construct a series of readings and renderings of reality that suit their story, that suit their identity. 'It isn't what we see', writes Imp. 'It's what we are left to envision' (2012: 168). The active courting of fantasy in these works reveals characters – and authors – bringing the force of their will to bear upon 'absolute reality' in the form of adventurous storytelling. In this sense, both authors are self-conscious fantasists, encouraging an investigation of the spaces between realities – the ones where we *really* exist. In interviews, Kiernan identifies more as a fabulist than a horror writer, even to the point of having remarked upon her 'loathing for the label "horror"', arguing that 'horror' is one of a range of emotions evoked by fiction that typically falls under the name, which she sees as 'an – increasingly unsuccessful – marketing category' (quoted in VanderMeer, 2012: n.p.) more than a coherent genre. The idea is not to position herself against a 'crude' genre, but to acknowledge a range of emotions characterized in her fiction that rests uncomfortably within categorical definitions of genre – definitions that also make it difficult to 'label' the work of authors like Jackson. As is the case with so much of Jackson's work, Kiernan's masterful novel deserves major scholarly attention as an investigation into the concept of repression, as a work resistant to vulgar renditions of psychoanalysis, and as an artistic negotiation of the self against the epistemology of the horror tale. *The Drowning Girl* is no mere echo of Jackson's concerns, but insofar as it does echo Jackson's preoccupation with summoning the self into existence out of the strands of fantasy, it is essential to understanding Jackson's own narrative experiments in conjuring ghosts. Imp reconciles with a past haunted by 'madwomen' through an act of conjuring a fragmented female ghost of her own. And *Come Along with Me* suggests Jackson moving into a future dictated by a powerfully reconstitutive female voice, one surrounded by other voices, but negotiating them in a realm all her own.

Simon Brown

Stephen King's *Full Dark No Stars* (2010)

As the title implies, Stephen King's novella collection *Full Dark No Stars* is an uncharacteristically bleak work from a writer who, as described by Deborah Notkin, usually presents 'people doing the right thing' and whose 'primary theme is one of hope and survival' (1990: 132, 142). In contrast the four tales in this volume offer a pessimistic depiction of humanity as self-serving, morally ambiguous and murderous. '1922' is set in Nebraska where farmer Wilfred James narrates how he co-opted his son, Henry, into murdering his wife, Arlette, and dropping her body down a well. The event traumatizes Henry, who becomes an outlaw and robs a series of banks until he and his young sweetheart are killed. Eight years later, after telling his story, Wilfred commits suicide. In 'Big Driver', Tess, a writer of mystery novels, takes a short cut home after a public appearance and is raped by a truck driver and left for dead by the roadside. She recovers and seeks revenge on the man who attacked her. 'Fair Extension', involves a dying man named Streeter, who stops at a roadside stand with a sign that reads 'Fair Extension, Fair Price'. Behind the stand is George Elvid, who offers Streeter a fifteen-year reprieve from his cancer. The price is 15 per cent of his income over the same period, plus someone else has to take the weight of Streeter's misfortune. He nominates his friend, Tom Goodhugh, and the rest of the story chronicles Streeter's rising fortunes alongside the catalogue of disasters that befall Goodhugh. In the final tale, 'A Good Marriage', happily married Darcy Anderson is shocked to discover that her husband of twenty-five years is a notorious serial killer known as Beadie.

What makes *Full Dark* an important King book is that in contrast to King's reputation as a writer of supernatural horror stories, these four tales have only the merest whiff of the paranormal about them. Wilfred in '1922' is beset by rats that are scratching their way through the walls of the hotel room in which he writes his confession. The rats are presented in his first-person narration as a supernatural manifestation of his guilt, although in reality they do not exist. In 'A Good Marriage' Darcy believes she sees in the mirror a darker version of herself in a parallel world, which is presented literally as if there really is a world beyond the mirror, but which is also a metaphor for the darkness in all of us. While George Elvid is obviously the devil, his deal with Streeter is largely a mundane business transaction stripped of its supernatural overtones (Elvid says to Streeter, 'I wouldn't...know a soul if it bit me on the buttocks' King 2010: 235), while in 'Big Driver' Tess' revenge is both actually and metaphorically guided by her GPS system, which offers her advice on where to go but also what to do. These are typical King traits. A deal with the devil as a financial matter also appears in *Needful Things* (1991), while the rendering of everyday objects into talismans with mythic properties appear throughout his work, for example Eddie Kaspbrak's asthma inhaler, which he uses to help to defeat the monster in *IT* (1986).

King states in the afterward of *Full Dark* that fiction is 'one of the vital ways in which we try to make sense of our lives, and the often terrible world we see around us,' (King 2010: 337) and while his reputation as a horror writer has led to the perception that it is through supernatural monsters that he represents a 'terrible world', in fact their impact is most often felt through the deeds of the men (and occasionally women) who are in their thrall. This is for instance the basis of *Needful Things*, in which the devil in the form of Leland Gaunt opens a curio shop where the citizens of Castle Rock can find what they believe their heart desires, the price for which is to turn on their neighbours. While the greed of the people brings about the ruin of the town, it is the entity Gaunt who is the real antagonist. In *Full Dark* the situation is reversed, and the supernatural remains subtext while human evil drives the stories. *Full Dark* is emphatic evidence that Stephen King is as much a chronicler of the human condition as the supernatural world, and while Notkin argues that 'the overwhelming impression to be gained from reading King's books is that the kinks and the sadists are the exception, not the rule' (Notkin 1990: 132), *Full Dark No Stars* turns this on its head, presenting four portraits of a humankind that has lost its humanity.

'1922' is narrated by Wilfred, and so King thrusts the reader into the mind of a man who slits his wife's throat because she wants to sell off some of the farmland,

and also because simply 'I had come to hate her, you see. I had come to wish her dead' (King 2010: 4). Claiming that 'there is inside every man, a stranger, a Conniving Man' who takes control of his actions (4), Wilfred's narrates his deeds in a matter of fact manner, his interior monologue concentrating upon the details of what happened, rather than the moral implications of his actions. Only the mysterious rats betray his tortured soul. The law never catches him, but the rats do, and ultimately he dies believing he is being eaten by them, when in fact he is biting his own flesh. The story ends with a newspaper report about the discovery of his body. Without next of kin, he is to be buried in public ground, his wife unavenged. An anonymous end to a terrible crime.

'A Good Marriage' similarly concludes on an unresolved note. Darcy discovers her husband has been a serial killer for two decades and kills him by pushing him down the stairs and making it look like an accident. His death is not investigated, but weeks later a retired detective visits her, and she admits to him who her husband was. He decides that making it public wouldn't bring back the dead, so to protect Darcy he goes on his way. The victims again are robbed of justice, while the reader, who has experienced the events through Darcy's innocent perspective, is left to question the ethics of this resolution. 'Big Driver' sees Tess take a gun and shoot both her rapist, his brother and his mother (who was responsible for telling her about the short cut that seals her fate). It ends with Tess telling the whole story to another woman, Betsy, a bartender who she meets after she was raped. They too agree to say nothing, Betsy supporting Tess because 'my gran loves your books and would be very disappointed if you went to jail for a triple murder' (226).' Fair Extension' concludes with Streeter and his wife discussing their good fortune while his wife also comments on Goodhugh's disastrous luck. 'Some people get a run of sevens, some people … get snake eyes' says Streeter. His wife tells him she has everything she wants in the world. 'Me too' says Streeter, and then looking up at the stars, he wishes for more (258). In the world of these stories the authorities are powerless, and good people like Tess and Darcy are driven to murder. While they, like many of King's protagonists, are fighting the forces of evil, the difference here is that those forces are human rather than monster, turning Tess and Darcy into vigilantes and muddying the moral waters. Wilfred's guilt finally catches up with him, but Streeter remains unrepentant, despite the misfortune of his friend. This is a book about the evil that men do.

With its ambiguous endings and emphasis on human evil rather than the supernatural, *Full Dark* seems on the surface to be uncharacteristic of King's work. Yet this is not the case, for what the virtual absence of supernatural elements achieves is to highlight that his reputation has eclipsed the fact that King's primary focus, and his strength as a writer, lies not in his marshalling of the monstrous, but rather in his depiction of the everyday. Many King scholars including Jonathan P. Davis (1994), Douglas Winter (1989) and Michael Collings (2006), have argued that his phenomenal appeal stems from his ability to create a recognizable and accessible world of Americana, rather than from the paranormal creatures that have come to define him. King's work is rooted in the ordinary and the familiar, his stories littered with common brand names, from Coke to Pabst, from Mr Coffee machines to La-Z-Boy armchairs. As Tony Magistrale points out, this draws the readers into the story, because if they can 'be convinced that King's characters are actually functioning in our world, that they ingest the same foods, drive upon the same interstate highways ... then the horror they experience becomes ours' (Magistrale 1988: 54).

This process of identification is augmented by King's characters. His (mostly male) heroes are straightforward blue-collar folk who go to work and watch the ball-game, right up until they are confronted by the paranormal. In *The Dead Zone* (1979) John Smith is a high school teacher suddenly imbued with precognitive powers after a car accident. In *11.22.63* (2011) Jake Epping is another high school teacher, who finds himself charged with using a portal to travel back in time and prevent the assassination of John F. Kennedy. In *Dreamcatcher* (2001) the main protagonists, Beaver, Pete, Henry and Jonesy, are just four friends hanging out in a cabin in the woods when the Earth is invaded by aliens. Sometimes, like the foursome in *Dreamcatcher* or the adult members of The Losers Club in *IT*, they share a past supernatural event. In others, King's principal characters are figures of authority (for instance Sherriff Pangbon in *Needful Things* or Detective Bill Hodges in the *Mr Mercedes* trilogy, 2014–16) or people who have achieved notable success (such as writer Thad Beaumont in *The Dark Half*, 1989). Overwhelmingly however King's protagonists are ordinary people, working normal jobs on regular salaries, whose main weapon in the fight against evil is decency and integrity. This makes them relatable, which forms an essential ingredient to King's appeal. As Randall D. Larson points out 'By spending a little more time with his characters we get to know more about them and, consequently, care more for them. As a result the horrors they face become more real' (Larson 1985: 103–4). Mark Jancovich states, one of the main ways that King builds character identification is to give the reader access to their thoughts. His stories are 'highly personal and interior novels in which we watch his characters' thought processes. The drama of the novels takes place as much within these thought processes as within the moments of action and violence (Jancovich 1992: 99). In *Full Dark* the stripping away of the supernatural allows for the strengths of King's world building and characterization to stand out, especially through the internal narration of Tess, Darcy and Wilfred. Furthermore, while Tess and Darcy are confronted by evil, the fact that '1922' is told from the perspective of Wilfred's warped psyche concentrates the readers' attention on how the narratives are driven by the actions of very human monsters. Relatable characters and human-driven stories have always been part of his writing, but these are often overwhelmed by the uncanny elements, not just in the stories themselves but also in critical discussions of them, making *Full Dark* a significant text that highlights these essential, but often overlooked, aspects of King's work.

The fact that King writes about people as well as the supernatural is particularly noticeable in the film and TV adaptations, where the most acclaimed texts not only focus on people rather than monsters, but also are often not horror at all. *The Shawshank Redemption* (1994) and *The Green Mile* (1999) are both magic realist tales set in a harsh and unforgiving prison world into which is injected an element of hope in the form of a mysterious, serene force for good, the preternaturally patient Andy Dufresne in *Shawshank* and the healer John Coffey in *The Green Mile*. Rob Reiner's *Stand by Me* (1986) tells a nostalgic tale of four boys on the cusp of adolescence who go on a journey to find the body of a boy who has been hit by a train. Although death waits for them in the form of the body, the film celebrates life through the interactions of these four characters, each of whom are damaged when the journey begins, but are healed during their odyssey. In all three films, and the stories from which they were adapted, the main characters face a human enemy in the form of corrupt Warden Norton (*Shawshank*), bully Ace Merrill (*Stand by Me*) and brutal and stupid prison guard Percy (*The Green Mile*). As in *Full Dark* the supernatural is downplayed, although in contrast these three tales offer a message of hope rather than ambiguous despair. *Stand by Me*, *Shawshank* and

The Green Mile all avoided association with King's name on their release to distance themselves from his reputation as a writer of horror, and thus allowed audiences to discover King's skilful characterizations without the horror label, which is applied to King and King adaptations whether they warrant it or not.

Released in 2017 *IT* is the most successful King film to date, and it offers a blending of the nostalgic, human centred coming of age story from *Stand by Me* and the supernatural horrors for which King is so famous, in the form of the iconic Pennywise the Dancing Clown. Although it was sold as a horror film by an ad campaign teasing the appearance of Pennywise, the pleasure for the majority of *IT*'s running time stems from the interaction of the seven members of The Losers Club. In addition, while the Losers' primary antagonist is supernatural, the film is full of examples of human evil, most notably the abuse suffered by Beverly and Henry at the hands of their fathers. *IT* is able to balance these elements because the message that King is more than the writer of supernatural horrors that he has been branded to be is beginning to be heard. *Full Dark No Stars*, along with other recent books like *Mr Mercedes*, *Under the Dome* (2009) and *11.22.63* sees King exploring the horrors that humans do without the help of monsters, rendering as text the subtext that underlies all his work. He has not abandoned the supernatural, as his recent sequel to his 1977 novel *The Shining*, *Doctor Sleep* (2013) attests, but what *Full Dark No Stars*, with its dark characters and grim pessimism clearly indicates is that King should not be seen solely as a writer of supernatural horror, for that is something he has never been.

Bibliography

10 Cloverfield Lane, dir. Dan Trachtenberg (Paramount Pictures, 2016).
À l'intérieur [Inside], dir. Alexandre Bustillo and Julien Maury (BR Films and La Fabrique de Films, 2007).
Abbott, Stacey, *Undead Apocalypse: Vampires and Zombies in the Twenty-first Century* (Edinburgh: Edinburgh University Press, 2016).
Abbott, Stacey, Darren Elliott-Smith, Rebecca Janicker and Lorna Jowett, 'A new golden age of TV horror: a round table discussion'. Panel Presentation presented to: *Cine-Excess X: Cult Genres, Traditions and Bodies: A Decade of Excess*, Birmingham, UK, 10–12 November 2016 (Unpublished).
Abbott, Stacey, and Lorna Jowett, *TV Horror: Investigating the Dark Side of the Small Screen* (London: I. B. Tauris, 2012).
Abraham, Nicolas, and Maria Torok, *The Wolf-Man's Magic Word: A Cryptonomy*, trans. Nicholas Rand (Minneapolis: University of Minnesota Press, 1994).
Adlakha, Siddhant, 'Jigsaw Review: A Muddled, Pointless Game of "Who Cares?"' in *Birth. Movies. Death*, 30 October 2017 <http://birthmoviesdeath.com/2017/10/30/jigsaw-review-a-muddled-pointless-game-of-who-cares> accessed 30 October 2017.
Agamben, Giorgio, *Homo Sacer: Sovereign Power and Bare Life*, trans. Daniel Heller Roazan (Stanford, CA: Stanford University Press, 1998).
Alaimo, Stacy, *Bodily Natures: Science, Environment, and the Material Self* (Bloomington: Indiana University Press, 2010).
Alberta Filmmakers Podcast, 'Cowboy Smithx and Noirfoot Narrative Labs.' <https://abfilmcast.ca/season-2/s02e32-cowboy-smithx-and-noirfoot-narrative-labs/> accessed 12 July 2018.
Aldana Reyes, Xavier, *Horror Film and Affect: Towards a Corporeal Model of Viewership* (Abingdon and New York: Routledge, 2016).
——, 'The [*REC*] Films: Affective Possibilities and Stylistic Limitations of Found Footage Horror,' in Linnie Blake and Xavier Aldana Reyes, eds, *Digital Horror: Haunted Technologies, Network Panic and the Found Footage Phenomenon* (London and New York: I. B. Tauris, 2015a), 149–60.
——, 'Reel Evil: A Critical Reassessment of Found Footage Horror,' in *Gothic Studies*, 17/2 (2015b), 122–36.
Altered Carbon, created by Nick Hurran (Netflix 2018).
Altman, Rick, *Film/Genre* (London: BFI, 1999).

Amanti d'oltretomba [Nightmare Castle], dir. Mario Caiano (Cinematografica Emmeci, 1965).

American Horror Story, created by Ryan Murphy and Brad Falchuk (FX, 2011–present).

Amnesia: The Dark Descent, dir. Thomas Grip (Frictional Games, 2010).

Amnesty International, 'No More Stolen Sisters: The Need for a Comprehensive Response to Discrimination and Violence Against Indigenous Women in Canada,' 30 September 2009 <https://www.amnesty.ca/news/no-more-stolen-sisters-need-comprehensive-response-discrimination-and-violence-against> accessed 25 November 2018.

——, 'Violence Against Indigenous Women and Girls in Canada: A Summary of Amnesty International's Concerns and Call to Action,' February 2014 <https://www.amnesty.ca/sites/amnesty/files/iwfa_submission_amnesty_international_february_2014_-_final.pdf> accessed 1 July 2018.

Ancuta, Katarzyna, 'Kaosu Means Chaos: the Japanese Sense of Fear and its Consequences for Contemporary Horror Cinema,' in Malgorzata Nitka and Piotr Dziedzic, eds, *Fire and Ice: The Dialectics of Chaos and Order* (Katowice: Silesia University Press, 2008), 90–106.

Anderson, Eric Gary, Taylor Hagood and Daniel Cross Turner (eds), *Undead Souths: The Gothic and Beyond in Southern Literature and Culture* (Baton Rouge: Louisiana State University Press, 2015).

Anderson, Jason, 'Saw VI, a Cut Above its Predecessors,' in *The Toronto Star* (25 October 2009).

Andersen, Kara, and Karra Shimabukuro, 'European Horror Games: Little Red Riding Hood's Zombie BBQ and the European Game Industry,' in Dana Och and Kirsten Strayer, eds, *Transnational Horror Across Visual Media: Fragmented Bodies* (London, Routledge, 2013), 96–116.

Anderson, Kim, Maria Campbell and Christie Belcourt, *Keetsahnak: Our Missing and Murdered Indigenous Sisters* (Edmonton: AB, University of Alberta Press, 2018).

Anderson, Melanie R., and Lisa Kröger, 'Introduction' in Melanie R. Anderson and Lisa Kröger eds, *Shirley Jackson: Influences and Confluences* (London and New York: Routledge, 2016), 12–17.

Andrew, Paul, '8th Fire Dispatch: Sacred Heart Residential School – Part 1,' *CBC*, 5 January 2012 <http://www.cbc.ca/player/play/2183547330> accessed 11 July 2018.

Angulo, Ana Gabriela, and Sandra Pamela Stemberger, 'La ciudad monstruo(sa) en cuentos de Mariana Enríquez,' in *Jornaler@s: Revista científica de estudios literarios y lingüísticos* 3.3 (2017), 309–18.

Anon., *#StrangerThursdays*, <https://twitter.com/hashtag/strangerthursdaysvertical=default&src=hash&lang=en> accessed 27 April 2018.

Anon., 'Box Office History for Saw Movies,' in *The Numbers*, 3 February 2018 <http://www.the-numbers.com/movies/franchise/Saw#tab=summary> accessed 3 February 2018.

Bibliography

Anon., 'Edgar Allan Poe and Rufus Wilmot Griswold', *Edgar Allan Poe Society of Baltimore*, 22 January 2009 <https://www.eapoe.org/geninfo/poegrisw.htm> accessed 9 May 2018.

Anon., 'Food Dye and Snags Do Not a Movie Make,' in *Canberra Times* (25 October 2008).

Anon., 'Franchise Looks a Bit Rusty; Saw V,' in *Daily Record* (24 October 2008).

Anon., 'Healing the Legacy of the Residential Schools,' in *Where are the Children*, <http://wherearethechildren.ca/en/> accessed 11 July 2018.

Anon., 'Homepage,' *Truth and Reconciliation Commission of Canada*, <http://www.trc.ca/websites/trcinstitution/index.php?p=4> accessed 11 July 2018.

Anon., 'Indigenous filmmaking set to rise in Canada in 2018 and beyond,' *CBC*, 28 December 2017. <https://www.cbc.ca/news/indigenous/indigenous-filmmakers-canada-funding-1.4466278> accessed 11 July 2018.

Anon., 'It Follows', *IMDBPro.com*, 2018 <https://pro.imdb.com/title/tt3235888/?ref_=instant_tt_1&q=it%20follows> accessed 10 December 2018.

Anon., 'Movie Review: Jigsaw,' in *The New Zealand Herald* (2 November 2017).

Anon., 'The Purge: Anarchy', *IMDBPro.com*, 2018 <https://pro.imdb.com/title/tt2975578/?ref_=instant_tt_1&q=purge%20an> accessed 10 December 2018.

Anon., 'Saw Far it's so Gruesome – For Fans Only, in *Daily Record* (23 October 2009).

Anon., 'Señalizan como Sitio de la Memoria a Comisaría de San Blas de los Sauces,' in *El independiente: Un pueblo hecho noticia*, 24 March 2017 <http://www.elindependiente.com.ar/pagina.phpid=134350> accessed 14 March 2018.

Anon., 'SMART HORROR: THE EVOLUTION OF THE GENRE' in *Morbidly-Beautiful*, 16 June 2018 <http://morbidlybeautiful.com/smart-horror/> accessed 12 December 2018.

Anon., 'Suicide Squad', *IMDBPro.com*, 2018 <https://pro.imdb.com/title/tt1386697/?ref_=instant_tt_1&q=suicide%20squ> accessed 10 December 2018.

Anon., 'Transformers: Age of Extinction', *IMDBPro.com*, 2018 <https://pro.imdb.com/title/tt2109248/?ref_=instant_tt_1&q=transformers%20ag> accessed 10 December 2018.

Anon., 'The women missing from the silver screen and the technology used to find them,' *Google*, 2017 <https://www.google.com/about/main/gender-equality-films/> accessed 14 July 2017.

Aquilina, Tyler, 'Why horror is having its moment', *The Hollywood Reporter*, 28 August 2018 <https://www.hollywoodreporter.com/heat-vision/suspiria-why-horror-is-thriving-once-more-1137706> accessed 28 November 2018.

Arcade, dir. Albert Pyun (Full Moon Entertainment, 1993).

Bacchilega, Cristina, *Fairy Tales Transformed?: Twenty-First-Century Adaptations and the Politics of Wonder* (Detroit, MI: Wayne State University Press, 2013).

Baise-moi, dir. Virginie Despentes and Coralie Trinh Thi (Pan-Européenne, 2000).

Baker, David, 'Seduced and Abandoned: Lesbian Vampires on Screen, 1968–74,' in *Continuum* 26/4 (2012), 553–63.

Balmain, Colette, *Introduction to Japanese Horror Film* (Edinburgh: Edinburgh University Press, 2008).
Barber, Nicholas, 'Is horror the most disrespected genre?', *BBC.com*, 14 June 2018 <http://www.bbc.com/culture/story/20180614-is-horror-the-most-disrespected-genre> accessed 6 December 2018.
Barham, Jeremy, 'Incorporating Monsters: Music as Context, Character and Construction in Kubrick's *The Shining*,' in Philip Hayward, ed., *Terror Tracks: Music, Sound and Horror Cinema* (Sheffield: Equinox, 2009), 137–70.
Barnes, Brooks, 'Audiences Laughed to Forget Troubles,' in *The New York Times* (30 December 2009).
Bates Motel, created by Carlton Cuse, Kerry Ehrenreich and Anthony Cipriano (A&E 2013–17).
Beal, Timothy K., *Religion and its Monsters* (New York: Routledge, 2002).
Beem, Katherine, and Andy Paciorek, *Folk Horror Revival Field Studies* (Durham: Wyrd Harvest Press, 2015).
Benshoff, Harry M., 'Horror Before "The Horror Film,"' in Harry M. Benshoff, ed., *A Companion to the Horror Film* (Malden, MA: Wiley-Blackwell, 2014), 207–24.
Bett, Alan, 'Mariana Enriquez: Black Magical Realism,' in *The Skinny: Independent Cultural Journalism*, 5 April 2017 <http://www.theskinny.co.uk/books/features/mariana-enriquez> accessed 25 March 2018.
Bierce, Ambrose, 'An Occurrence at Owl Creek Bridge,' in E. F. Bleiler, ed., *Ghost and Horror Stories of Ambrose Bierce* (New York: Dover, 1964), 50–8.
Billson, Anne, 'Crash and Squirm,' *The Guardian* (31 October 2008).
Black Christmas, dir. Bob Clark (Film Funding Ltd of Canada et al., 1974).
Blade 2, dir. Guillermo del Toro (New Line Cinema, 2002).
Blake, Linnie, and Xavier Aldana Reyes, eds, *Digital Horror: Haunted Technologies, Network Panic and the Found Footage Phenomenon* (London and New York: I. B. Tauris, 2015).
The Blair Witch Project, dir. Daniel Myrick and Eduardo Sánchez (Haxan Films, 1999).
Blowup, dir. Michelangelo Antonioni (Metro-Goldwyn-Mayer and Bridge Films, 1966).
Booth, Paul, '*Saw* Fandom and the Transgression of Fan Excess,' in David J. Gunkel and Ted Gournelos, eds, *Transgression 2.0: Media, Culture and the Politics of a Digital Age* (London and New York: Continuum, 2011), 69–83.
Bordwell, David, and Noël Carroll, *Post-Theory: Reconstructing Film Studies* (Madison: University of Wisconsin Press, 2016).
Botting, Fred, *Gothic* (London: Routledge, 1996).
Braham, Persephone, *From Amazons to Zombies: Monsters in Latin America* (Lewisburg, PA: Bucknell University Press, 2015).
Brainscan, dir. John Flynn (Admire Productions Ltd/Coral Productions, 1994).
Bram Stoker's Dracula, dir. Francis Ford Coppola (American Zoetrope, 1993).

Brereton, Pat, *Smart Cinema, DVD Add-Ons, and New Audience Pleasures* (London: Palgrave Macmillan, 2012).
Briger, Sam, 'Stranger Things 2: Creators Wanted a Sequel that Topped the Original,' *National Public Radio*. 4 November 2017 <https://www.npr.org/2017/11/14/564049997/stranger-things-2-creators-wanted-to-scale-up-for-the-show-s-return> accessed 25 May 2018.
The Brood, dir. David Cronenberg (Canadian Film Development Corporation, 1979).
Brottman, Mikita, *Offensive Films: Toward an Anthropology of Cinéma Vomitif* (Westport, CT: Greenwood Press, 1997).
Brown, Marshall, *The Gothic Text* (Stanford, CA: Stanford University, 2005).
Buckley, Chloé Germaine, *Twenty-First-Century Children's Gothic* (Edinburgh: Edinburgh University Press, 2018).
Burke, Edmund, *A Philosophical Enquiry Into the Origin of Our Ideas of the Sublime and Beautiful* [1757] (Oxford: Oxford University Press, 2015).
Butler, Judith, *Gender Trouble: Feminism and the Subversion of Identity* (New York: Routledge, 1990).
Byron, Glennis, 'Slasher Movies,' in William Hughes, David Punter and Andrew Smith, eds, *The Encyclopaedia of the Gothic* (Oxford: Wiley Blackwell, 2016), 627–9.
Campbell, James, 'Cosmic Indifferentism in the Fiction of H. P. Lovecraft,' in *American Supernatural Fiction: From Edith Wharton to the Weird Tales Writers* (New York: Garland Publishing, 1996), 167–228.
Candy Meister, dir. Cowboy Smithx (Noirfoot Narrative Labs, 2014) <https: youtu.beUPzVPDgWZkw> accessed 1 July 2018.
Candyman, dir. Bernard Rose (Polygram, 1992).
Cannibal Holocaust, dir, Ruggero Deodato (F. D. Cinematografica, 1980).
Carreño, Paulina, 'Recuperación de centros clandestinos: un debate todavía pendiente,' *Data Rioja*, year 11, edition #542 <http://www.datarioja.com/index.phpmodulo=notas&accion=ver&id=521> accessed 14 March 2018.
Carrie, dir. Brian De Palma (Red Bank Films, 1976).
Carroll, Noel, *The Philosophy of Horror, or Paradoxes of the Heart* (London: Routledge, 1990).
Cavarero, Adriana, *Horrorism: Naming Contemporary Violence* (New York: Columbia University Press, 2011).
Cell, dir. Tod Williams (Benaroya Pictures, 2016).
Chatroom, dir. Hideo Nakata (Ruby Films, 2010).
Cherry, Brigid, *Horror* (London: Routledge, 2009).
——, *The Female Horror Film Audience: Viewing Pleasures and Fan Practices* (PhD thesis, University of Stirling, 1999).
Christmas Evil, dir. Lewis Jackson (Edward R Pressman Film, 1980).

Church, David, 'The Return of the Return of the Repressed: Notes on the American Horror Film 1991–2006', *Offscreen* 10: 10 (October 2006) <http://offscreen.com/view/return_of_the_repressed> accessed 20 February 2018.

Clark, Timothy, *The Cambridge Introduction to Literature and the Environment* (Cambridge: Cambridge University Press, 2011).

Clarke, Cath, 'Jigsaw Review – No Shock, No Horror in Tame Torture-Porn Reboot', in *The Guardian* (27 October 2017).

Clasen, Mathias, *Why Horror Seduces* (Oxford: Oxford University Press, 2017).

——, 'The Horror! The Horror!,' in *The Evolutionary Review* (2010), 112–19.

Clover, Carol J., *Men, Women and Chain Saws: Gender in the Modern Horror Film* (Princeton, NJ: Princeton University Press, 1992).

Clute, John, *A Darkening Garden: A Short Lexicon of Horror* (Cauheegan, WI: Payseur & Schmidt, 2006).

Code, David J., 'Rehearing *The Shining*: Musical Undercurrents in the Overlook Hotel,' in Neil Lerner, ed., *Music in the Horror Film: Listening to Fear* (London: Routledge, 2010), 133–51.

Collings, Michael, *The Films of Stephen King* (Rockville: Wildside Press, 2006).

The Collingswood Story, dir. Michael Costanza (Beverly Burton/Calum Waddell, 2002).

CONADEP, *Nunca Más*, 'Informe de la Comisión Nacional Sobre la Desaparición de Personas' (Buenos Aires: Eudeba, 1984).

Conrich, Ian, 'Puzzles, Contraptions and the Highly Elaborate Moment: The Inevitability of Death in the Grand Slasher Narratives of the Final Destination and Saw Series of Films,' in Wickham Clayton, ed., *Style and Form in the Hollywood Slasher Film* (Basingstoke and New York: Palgrave Macmillan, 2015), 106–17.

——, *Horror Zone: The Cultural Experience of Contemporary Horror Film* (New York: I. B. Tauris & Co. Ltd, 2010).

Costorphine, Kevin, 'Introduction,' in Kevin Costorphine and Laura R. Kremmel, eds, *The Palgrave Handbook to Horror Literature* (Cham: Palgrave Macmillan, 2018), 1–18.

Crafteon, 'The Outsider,' in Cosmic Reawakening (CD Baby, 2017).

——, 'The Whisperer in the Darkness,' Cosmic Reawakening (CD Baby, 2017).

Creed, Barbara, *The Monstrous-Feminine: Film, Feminism, Psychoanalysis* (London: Routledge, 1993).

Croot, James, 'Saw-did Horror: How to Ruin a Great Movie's Legacy,' in *The Dominion Post* (30 October 2017).

Crosby, Sarah J., 'Beyond Ecophilia: Edgar Allan Poe and the American Tradition of Ecohorror,' in *Interdisciplinary Studies in Literature and Environment* 21/3 (Summer 2014), 513–25.

Cumming, Ed, 'The Week's Best Films,' in *The Daily Telegraph* (19 June 2010).

Das Cabinet des Dr Caligari [The Cabinet of Dr Caligari], dir. Robert Wiene (Decla-Bioscop AG, 1920).
Davis, Jonathan, *Stephen King's America* (Bowling Green: Bowling Green State University Press, 1994).
de Vos, Gail, *What happens next?: Contemporary Urban Legends and Popular Culture* (Santa Barbara: Libraries Unlimited, 2012).
——, *Tales, Rumors, and Gossip: Exploring Contemporary Folk Literature in Grades 7–12* (Englewood, CO: Libraries Unlimited, 1996).
Death Tube: Broadcast Murder Show, dir. Yôhei Fukuda (2010).
Death Tube 2: Broadcast Murder Show, dir. Yôhei Fukuda (2010).
The Den, dir. Zachary Donohue (Cliffbrook Films/Onset Films, 2013).
Der Student von Prag [The Student of Prague], dir. Stellan Rye (Deutsche Bioscop GmbH, 1913).
Detroit, dir. Kathryn Bigelow (Annapurna Pictures, 2017).
Di Fonzo, Carla, 'Gross Cinema: Waiting for the Gore Fad To Pass,' in *Intelligencer Journal* (26 October 2007).
The Diary of the Dead, dir. George A. Romero (Artfire Films/Romero-Grunwald Productions, 2007).
Dickinson, Emily, 'Tell all the Truth but tell it slant –', in Thomas H. Johnson, ed., *The Complete Poems of Emily Dickinson* (Boston, MA and Toronto: Little, Brown and Company, 1960), 506–7.
Die Marquise von Sade, dir. Jesús Franco (Elite Film, 1976).
Doane, Mary Ann, *The Desire to Desire* (Bloomington and Indianapolis: Indiana University Press, 1987).
Dobbs, Sarah, 'Get Out,' in *SFX* 286 (June 2017), 96.
Donnelly, Kevin, *The Spectre of Sound: Music in Film and Television* (Basingstoke: BFI Publishing, 2005).
Due, Tananarive, *Ghost Summer: Stories* (Gathersburg, MD: Prime Books, 2015).
——, *My Soul to Take* (New York: Washington Square Press, 2011).
——, *Blood Colony* (New York: Atria Books, 2008).
——, *Joplin's Ghost* (New York: Washington Square Press, 2006).
——, *The Living Blood* (New York: Washington Square Press, 2001).
——, *My Soul to Keep* (New York: Harper Collins, 1997).
Edelstein, David, 'Now Playing at Your Local Multiplex: Torture Porn,' in *New York* (28 January 2006).
Edwards, Justin D., 'The Abyss,' in William Hughes, David Punter and Andrew Smith, eds, *The Encyclopaedia of the Gothic* (Oxford: Wiley Blackwell, 2016), 4–6.
Egan, Kate, *Trash or Treasure? Censorship and the Changing Meaning of the Video Nasties* (Manchester: Manchester University Press, 2007).

Eljaiek-Rodríguez, Gabriel, 'Bloodsucking Bugs: Horacio Quiroga and the Latin American Transformation of Vampires', in John W. Morehead, ed., *The Supernatural Cinema of Guillermo del Toro: Critical Essays* (Jefferson, NC: McFarland, 2015), 146–62.

Elliott-Smith, Darren, *Queer Horror Film and Television: Sexuality and Masculinity at the Margins* (New York and London: I. B. Tauris & Co. Ltd, 2016).

Enríquez, Mariana, 'Terror de Mariana Enríquez', in *La Clé des Langues* [en ligne] June 2017 <http://cle.ens-lyon.fr/espagnol/litterature/entretiens-et-textes-inedits/textes-inedits/terror-de-mariana-enriquez> accessed 25 March 2018.

———, *The Things We Lost in the Fire: Stories*, trans. Megan McDowell (New York: Hogarth, 2017).

The Entity, dir. Sidney J. Furie (American Cinema Productions, 1982).

Eraserhead, dir. David Lynch (American Film Institute, 1977).

Estok, Simon C., 'Theorising in a Space of Ambivalent Openness: Ecocriticism and Ecophobia', in *International Studies in Literature and the Environment* (ISLE), Vol. 16, Issue 4 (Spring 2009) 203–25.

The Exorcist, dir. William Friedkin (Warner Bros, 1972).

Eyes of My Mother, dir. Nicolas Pesce (Tandem Pictures, 2016).

Fern, Ong Sor, 'Not at All Fun and Games', in *The Straits Times* (16 April 2008).

Finkielman, Jorge, *The Film Industry in Argentina: An Illustrated Cultural History* (Jefferson, NC: McFarland, 2004).

Fisher, Benjamin Franklin, 'Poe in the Gothic Tradition', in Kevin J. Hayes, ed., *The Cambridge Companion to Edgar Allan Poe* (Cambridge: Cambridge University Press, 2002), 72–91.

Fisher, Lucy, 'Birth Traumas: Parturition and Horror in "Rosemary's Baby"', *Cinema Journal*, Vol. 31, No. 3 (Spring, 1992), 3–18.

Fisher, Mark, *The Weird and the Eerie* (London: Repeater, 2016).

Five Nights At Freddy's, created by Scott Cawthorn (2014).

Floyd, Nigel, 'Close Up – Could Critics of "Torture Porn" at Least Watch the Movies?' in *Time Out* (20 June 2007).

Follows, Stephen, *The Horror Report* (London: The Film Data Fund, 2017).

The Forbidden Files, dir. Jean-Teddy Filippe (MBA Films, 1989).

Foy, Joseph J., 'It Came from Planet Earth: Eco-Horror and the Politics of Postenvironmentalism in *The Happening*', in Timothy M. Dale and Joseph J. Foy, eds, *Homer Simpson Marches on Washington: Dissent Through American Popular Culture* (Lexington: The University Press of Kentucky, 2010).

Franklin, Ruth, *Shirley Jackson: A Rather Haunted Life* (2016).

Freaks, dir. Tod Browning (Metro-Goldwyn-Mayer, 1931).

Freeland, Cynthia, *The Naked and the Undead: Evil and the Appeal of Horror* (Oxford and Boulder, CO: Westview Press, 2002).

Freeman, Elizabeth, *Time Binds: Queer Temporalities, Queer Histories* (Durham, NC and London: Duke University Press, 2010).
Freud, Sigmund, 'The Uncanny,' in *The Uncanny* [1919] (London/New York: Penguin, 2003), 121–62.
Friend Request, dir. Simon Verhoeven (Wiedemann & Berg Film, 2016).
Garforth, Lisa, 'Green Utopias: Beyond Apocalypse, Progress and Pastoral', *Utopian Studies*, Vol. 16, No. 3 (Winter 2005), 393–427.
Garth, Todd S., *Pariah in the Desert: The Heroic and the Monstrous in Horacio Quiroga* (Lewisburg, PA: Bucknell University Press, 2016).
Gaynor, Stella, '"We Want to Out HBO, HBO" said Reed Hastings, Netflix CEO: Micro-genres, Money Shots and Murder in Netflix's Hemlock Grove,' in unpublished conference paper, *Fear 2000* (6–7 April 2017).
Gelder, Ken, *The Horror Reader* (London: Routledge, 2000).
Geller, Theresa L., and Anna Marie Banker, '"That Magic Box Lies": Queer Theory, Seriality, and American Horror Story' in *The Velvet Light Trap*, Number 79 (Spring 2017), 36–49.
Gent, James. 'Robin Hardy, The Wicker Man and Folk Horror,' in *We Are Cult*, 1 July 2017 <http://wearecult.rocks/robin-hardy-the-wicker-man-and-folk-horror> accessed 29 June 2018.
Gerow, Aaron, 'The Empty Return: Circularity and Repetition in Recent Japanese Horror Films,' in *Minikomi* 64/2 (2002), 19–24.
Get Out, dir. Jordan Peele (Blumhouse, 2017).
Ghosh, Bishnupriya, 'The Security Aesthetic in Bollywood's High-Rise Horror,' in *Representations*, Vol. 126, No. 1 (Spring 2014), 58–84.
Ghostwatch, dir. Lesley Manning (BBC, 1992).
Glee, created by Ryan Murphy, Brad Falchuk and Ian Brennan (FOX; 2009–15).
Gleiberman, Owen, 'Film Review: Jigsaw,' in *Variety*, 26 October 2017 <http://variety.com/2017/film/reviews/jigsaw-review-tobin-bell-1202600173/> accessed 26 October 2017.
Gopal, Sangita, 'Fearful Habitations: Upward Mobility and the Horror Genre,' in *Conjugations: Marriage and Form in New Bollywood Cinema* (Chicago: University of Chicago Press, 2011), 91–123.
'Goth Kids 3: Dawn of the Posers,' *South Park*, dir. Trey Parker (South Park Studios 2013).
Graham, Elaine L., *Representations of the Post/human: Monsters, Aliens, and Others in Popular Culture* (Manchester: Manchester University Press, 2002).
Grave [Raw], dir. Julia Ducournau (Petit Film, 2016).
Griffith, Clark, 'Poe and the Gothic', in Eric W. Carlson, ed., *Critical Essays on Edgar Allan Poe* (Boston, MA: G. K. Hall, 1987), 127–32.

Gunnels, Bridget, 'Blurring Boundaries Between Animal and Human: Animalhuman Rights in 'Juan Darien' by Horacio Quiroga,' in *Romance Notes* 45.3 (Spring 2006), 349–58.

Hall, Stuart, *Modernity and Its Future* (Cambridge: Polity Press, 1992).

Han, Angie, 'George A. Romero explains why he won't do The Walking Dead,' in slashfilm. com, 14 November 2013 <http://www.slashfilm.com/george-a-romero-explains-why-he-wont-do-the-walking-dead/> accessed 20 April 2018.

Hanich, Julian, *The Audience Effect: On the Collective Cinema Experience* (Edinburgh: Edinburgh University Press, 2018).

——, *Cinematic Emotion in Horror Films and Thrillers: The Aesthetic Paradox of Pleasurable Fear* (Abingdon and New York: Routledge, 2010).

Hantke, Steffen, 'Introduction: They Don't Make 'Em Like They Used To: On the Rhetoric of Crisis and the Current State of American Horror Cinema,' in Steffan Hantke, ed., *American Horror Film: The Genre at the Turn of the Millennium* (Jackson: University of Mississippi Press, 2010), vii-xxxii.

——, 'Monstrosity without a Body: Representational Strategies in the Popular Serial Killer Film,' in *PostScript: Essays in Film and the Humanities* 22.2 (Winter/Spring 2003), 34–55.

Hare, Breeanna, 'The Most Disturbing Movie Ever Made?' *CNN*, 11 May 2010 <http://edition.cnn.com/2010/SHOWBIZ/Movies/05/10/centipede.torture.movie/index.html> accessed 26 November 2017.

Hargreaves, Allison, *Violence against Indigenous Women: Literature, Activism, Resistance* (Waterloo, ON: Wilfrid Laurier University Press. 2017).

Harman, Graham, *Weird Realism: Lovecraft and Philosophy* (Washington, DC: Zero Books, 2011).

Hattenhauer, Darryl, *Shirley Jackson's American Gothic* (Albany: SUNY Press, 2003).

Haunting of Hill House, dir. Mike Flanagan (Netflix, 2018).

Haute tension [High Tension], dir. Alexandre Aja (Alexandre Films and EuropaCorp, 2003).

Hawkins, Joan, *Cutting Edge: Art-Horror and the Horrific Avant-garde* (Minneapolis: University of Minnesota Press, 2000).

Heffes, Gisela, 'Introducción: Para una crítica latinoamericana: entre la postulación de un ecocentrismo crítico y la crítica de un antropocentrismo hegemónico,' in *Revista de Crítica Literaria Latinoamericana* 40.79 (Spring 2014), 11–34.

Hellboy, dir. Guillermo del Toro (Columbia Pictures, 2004).

Heller-Nicholas, Alexandra, *Found Footage Horror: Fear and the Appearance of Reality* (Jefferson, NC: McFarland & Co., Inc., 2015).

——, *Rape-Revenge Films: A Critical Study* (Jefferson, NC: McFarland, 2011).

Heumann, Joseph K., and Robin L. Murray, *Monstrous Nature: Environment and Horror on the Big Screen* (Lincoln: University of Nebraska Press, 2016).

Hill, Claire, 'Welcome to the Meat Factory,' in *The Western Mail* (22 June 2007).
Hill, Gary, *The Strange Sound of Cthulhu: Music Inspired by the Writings of H. P. Lovecraft* (N.p.: lulu.com., 2006).
Hill, Joe, and Gabriel Rodriguez, *Locke and Key: Heaven and Earth* (New York: IDW, 2017).
——, *Locke and Key: Alpha & Omeg*, Volume 6 (New York: IDW, 2014).
——, *Locke and Key: Keys to the Kingdom*, Volume 4 (New York: IDW, 2013).
——, *Locke and Key: Crown of Shadows*, Volume 3 (New York: IDW, 2013).
——, *Locke and Key: Clockworks*, Volume 5 (New York: IDW, 2012).
——, *Locke and Key: Head Games*, Volume 2 (New York: IDW, 2011).
——, *Locke and Key: Welcome to Lovecraft*, Volume 1 (New York: IDW, 2011).
Hills, Matt, 'Horror Reception/Audiences', in Harry M. Benshoff, ed., *A Companion to the Horror Film* (Oxford and Malden, MA: Wiley Blackwell, 2014), 90–108.
——, *The Pleasures of Horror* (London and New York: Continuum, 2005).
Holland-Toll, Linda, *As American as Mom, Baseball and Apple Pie: Constructing Community in Contemporary American Horror Fiction* (Bowling Green, OH: Bowling Green State University Popular Press, 2001).
Hopkinson, Nalo, and Uppinder Mehan, 'Introduction', in *So Long Been Dreaming: Postcolonial Science Fiction & Fantasy* (Vancouver: Arsenal Pulp Press, 2004).
Horeck, Tanya, and Tina Kendall, eds, *The New Extremism in Cinema: From France to Europe* (Edinburgh: Edinburgh University Press, 2011).
#Horror, dir. Tara Subkoff (Lowland Pictures/AST Studios, 2015).
Houellebecq, Michel, *H. P. Lovecraft: Against the World, Against Life*, trans. Dorna Khazeni (San Francisco, CA: Believer/McSweeny's, 2005).
Hounds of Love, dir. Ben young (Factor 30 Films, 2016).
House on Haunted Hill, dir. William Castle (William Castle Productions, 1959).
How to Make a Monster, dir. George Huang (Creature Features Productions, 2001).
Hu, Jane, 'Can Horror Movies Be Prestigious?', *The Ringer*, 15 June 2018 <https://www.theringer.com/movies/2018/6/15/17467020/hereditary-elevated-horror-get-out-a-quiet-place-the-witch> accessed 12 December 2018.
Hudson, Dale, *Vampires, Race, and Transnational Hollywood* (Edinburgh: Edinburgh University Press, 2017).
Humphries, Reynold, *The American Horror Film: An Introduction* (Edinburgh: Edinburgh University Press, 2002).
The Hunger, dir. Tony Scott (Metro-Goldwyn-Mayer, 1983).
Hunt, Leon, *Cult British TV Comedy: From Reeves and Mortimer to Psychoville* (Oxford: Oxford University Press, 2013).
——, *The League of Gentlemen* (London: BFI TV Classics, 2008).
Hutchings, Peter. *The Horror Film* (Harlow: Pearson Educational, 2004).

Jackson, Gita, 'What We Loved About Annihilation, an Ecological Horror Story', *Kotaku*, 28 February 2018 <https://kotaku.com/what-we-loved-about-annihilation-an-ecological-horror1823404894> accessed 12 March 2018.
Jackson, Michael, 'Thriller' (video), dir. John Landis (Epic Records, 1983).
——, 'Thriller' (song), in *Thriller* (Epic Records, 1982).
Jackson, Shirley, *Let Me Tell You* (New York: Random House, 2015).
——, *Come Along with Me* (New York: Penguin, 1995).
——, *The Haunting of Hill House* (New York: Penguin, 1984).
——, *We Have Always Lived in the Castle* (New York: Penguin, 1984).
——, *The Lottery and Other Stories* (New York: Farrar, Straus and Giroux, 1982).
Jacobs, Tom, 'How Humans Evolved to Love Horror Movies', *Pacific Standard*, 11 January 2019 <https://psmag.com/education/why-we-flocked-to-bird-box> accessed 13 January 2019.
Jameson, Fredric, 'Metacommentary', in *PMLA* 86.1 (January 1971), 9–18.
Jancovich, Mark, *Horror* (London: B. T. Batsford, 1992).
Janicker, Rebecca, ed., *Reading American Horror Story: Essays on the Television Franchise* (Jefferson, NC: McFarland, 2017).
Jaworowski, Ken, 'Killing Ground', in *The New York Times* (21 July 2017).
Jenks, Carol, 'The Other Face of Death: Barbara Steele and La maschera del demonio', in Richard Dyer and Ginette Vincendeau, eds, *Popular European Cinema* (London and New York: Routledge, 1992), 149–62.
Jigsaw, dir. Michael Spierig and Peter Spierig (Twisted Pictures, 2017).
Johnson, Kevin, 'Dissecting Torture', in *St Louis Post-Dispatch* (26 October 2007).
Johnston, Trevor, 'Film of the Week: Get Out, a surreal satire of racial tension', in *Sight and Sound*, 17 March 2017 <http://www.bfi.org.uk/news-opinion/sight-sound-magazine/reviews-recommendations/get-out-jordan-peele-surreal-satire-racial-tension> accessed 20 April 2018.
Jones, Darryl, *Sleeping with the Lights On: The Unsettling Story of Horror* (Oxford: Oxford University Press, 2018).
Jones, Steve, *Torture Porn: Popular Horror After Saw* (London: Palgrave-Macmillan: 2013).
——, '"Time is wasting": Con/sequence and S/pace in the Saw Series', in *Journal of Horror Studies* ½ (2010), 225–39.
Joshi, S. T., 'A Failed Experiment: Family and Humanity in *The Sundial*', Melanie R. Anderson and Lisa Kröger, eds, *Shirley Jackson: Influences and Confluences* (London and New York: Routledge, 2016), 36–45.
——, *The Weird Tale* (Austin: University of Texas Press, 1990).
Jowett, Lorna, 'Whedon, Feminism, and the Possibility of Feminist Horror on Television', in Kristopher Woofter and Lorna Jowett, eds, *Joss Whedon vs. The Horror Tradition: The Production of Genre in Buffy and Beyond* (London and New York: I. B. Tauris, 2018).

Jowett, Lorna, and Stacey Abbott, *TV Horror: Investigating the Dark Side of the Small Screen* (London and New York: I. B. Tauris, 2013).

Kääpä, Pietari, 'Film of the Year: Rare Exports,' in Pietari Kääpä, ed., *Directory of World Cinema: Finland* (Bristol: Intellect, 2012), 9–11.

Kelly, Casey Ryan, '*It Follows*: Precarity, Thanatopolitics, and the Ambient Horror Film,' in *Critical Studies in Media Communication*, Volume 34, no. 3 (2017), 234–49.

Kermode, Mark, 'It review – enthusiastic, cine-literate retelling of Stephen King's horror novel,' in *The Guardian*, 10 September 2017 <https://www.theguardian.com/film/2017/sep/10/it-review-enthusiastic-cine-literate-stephen-king-adaptation> accessed 20 April 2018.

Kiernan, Caitlín R., *The Drowning Girl* (New York: ROC Books, 2012).

Killing Ground, dir. Damien Power (Hypergiant Films, 2017).

King, Stephen, *End of Watch* (London: Hodder and Stoughton, 2016).

——, *Finders Keepers* (London: Hodder and Stoughton, 2015).

——, *Mr Mercedes* (London: Hodder and Stoughton, 2014).

——, *Doctor Sleep* (London: Hodder and Stoughton, 2013).

——, *11.22.63* (London: Hodder and Stoughton, 2011).

——, *Full Dark No Stars* (London: Hodder and Stoughton, 2010).

——, *Under the Dome* (London: Hodder and Stoughton, 2009).

——, *Dreamcatcher* (London: Hodder and Stoughton, 2001).

——, *Needful Things* (London: Hodder and Stoughton, 1991).

——, *The Dark Half* (London: Hodder and Stoughton, 1989).

——, *IT* (London: Hodder and Stoughton, 1986).

——, *Danse Macabre* (London: Future, 1982).

——, *The Dead Zone* (New York. The Viking Press, 1979).

——, *The Shining* (London: New English Library, 1977).

Kingston, Anne, 'Ever Hear the One about the Chick Who Got Raped?' in *Maclean's* (9 July 2007).

Kirkland, Ewan, 'Storytelling in Survival Horror Videogames', in Bernard Perron, ed., *Horror Video Games: Essays on the Fusion of Fear and Play* (Jefferson, NC: McFarland, 2009), 62–78.

Klein, Amanda Ann, *American Film Cycles: Reframing Genres, Screening Social Problems, and Defining Subcultures* (Austin: University of Texas Press, 2011).

Krampus, dir. Michael Dougherty (Universal Pictures, 2015).

Kristeva, Julia, *Strangers to Ourselves* (New York: Columbia University Press, 1988).

——, *The Powers of Horror: An Essay on Abjection*, trans. Leon Roudiez (New York: Columbia University Press, 1982).

Krzywinska, Tanya, 'Hands-on Horror,' in Harmony Wu, ed., *Axes to Grind: Re-Imagining the Horrific in Visual Media and Culture*, Special Issue of *Spectator*, 22:2 (Fall 2002) 12–23.

La frusta e il corpo [The Whip and the Body], dir. Mario Bava (Vox Film, 1963).
La maschera del demonio [Black Sunday], dir. Mario Bava (Galatea Film and Jolly Film, 1960).
La morte vivante [The Living Dead Girl], dir. Jean Rollin (Films A.B.C., 1982).
La novia ensangrentada [The Blood Spattered Bride], dir. Vicente Aranda (Morgana Films, 1972).
La piel que habito [The Skin I Live In], dir. Pedro Almodóvar (FilmNation Entertainment, 2011).
Lacey, Liam, 'There's a Reason for All This Torture Porn: It Makes Money,' *The Globe and Mail* (30 October 2009).
Lafforgue, Jorge, 'Actualidad de Quiroga', in Napoleón Bacciono Ponce de León and Jorge Lafforgue, eds, *Todos los cuentos*, by Horacio Quiroga (Madrid: ALLCA XX, 1996), xxxv–xlvi.
Larson, Randall, 'Cycle of the Werewolf and the Moral Tradition of Horror', in Darrell Schweitzer, ed., *Discovering Stephen King* (Mercer Island: Starmont House, 1985), 102–8.
The Lawnmower Man, dir. Brett Leonard (Allied Vision, 1992).
Lazic, Elena, 'Jigsaw', in *Little White Lies*, 28 October 2017 <http://lwlies.com/reviews/jigsaw/> accessed 28 October 2017.
LeBar, Rachel, 'Universal releases details on "American Horror Story" maze at Halloween Horror Nights 27', *The Gist*, 29 March 2017 <https://www.orlandoweekly.com/Blogs/archives/2017/03/29/universal-releases-details-on-american-horror-story-maze-at-halloween-horror-nights-27> accessed 1 May 2018.
Lee, Benjamin, 'Saw Too Much: Why the Horror Genre Doesn't Need a Torture Porn Comeback,' in *The Guardian* (24 October 2017).
Leeder, Murray, *Horror Film: A Critical Introduction* (New York and London: Bloomsbury, 2018).
Les lèvres rouges [Daughters of Darkness], dir. Harry Kümel (Showking Films, 1971).
Les yeux sans visage [Eyes without a Face], dir. Georges Franju (Champs-Élysées Productions and Lux Film, 1960).
Lidz, Franz, 'Limbs Pile Up, and Money, Too,' in *The New York Times* (25 October 2009).
Lloyd-Smith, Allan Gardner, *Uncanny American Fiction: Medusa's Face* (Basingstoke and London: Macmillan, 1989).
Lodhi, Adnan, 'Anushka Sharma's Pari Banned in Pakistan,'in *The Express Tribune*, 2 March 2018 <https://tribune.com.pk/story/1648860/4-anushka-sharmas-pari-banned-pakistan/> accessed 4 June 2018.
Lorde, Audre, *Black Women Writers at Work*, ed. Claudia Tate (New York: Continuum, 1983), 100–16.
Los otros [The Others], dir. Alejandro Amenábar (Cruise/Wagner Productions, 2001).

Love at First Bite, dir, Stan Dragoti (American International Pictures, 1979).
Lovecraft, H. P., 'The Call of Cthulhu,' in *H. P. Lovecraft: The Complete Fiction* (New York: Barnes & Noble, 2008a), 355–79.
——, 'The Unnamable,' in *H. P. Lovecraft: The Complete Fiction* (New York: Barnes & Noble, 2008b), 256–61.
——, 'The Call of Cthulhu,' in S. T. Joshi, ed., *The Call of Cthulhu and Other Weird Tales* (New York: Penguin, 1999a), 139–69.
——, 'The Outsider,' in S. T. Joshi, ed., *The Call of Cthulhu and Other Weird Tales* (New York: Penguin, 1999b), 43–9.
——, *Supernatural Horror in Literature* (New York: Ben Abramson, 1945).
Lowenstein, Adam, *Shocking Representations: Historical Trauma, National Cinema, and the Modern Horror Film* (New York: Columbia University Press, 2005).
Luckhurst, Roger, 'Introduction,' in Roger Luckhurst, ed., *H. P. Lovecraft: The Classic Horror Stories* (Oxford: Oxford University Press, 2013), vii–xxviii.
Lui, John, 'Reviews: Jigsaw Does Not Offer New Scares,' in *The Straits Times* (1 November 2017).
Lusnich, Laura, 'Introduction', in Laura Lusnich, ed., *Civilización y barbarie en el cine argentino y latinoamericano* (Buenos Aires: Biblios, 2005), 16–38.
McCall, Sophie, Deanna Reder, David Gaertner, and Gabrielle L'Hirondelle Hill, eds, *Read. Listen. Tell: Indigenous Stories from Turtle Island* (Waterloo: Wilfrid Laurier University Press, 2017).
McCartney, Jenny, 'The Films Get Sicker – So Does Society,' in *The Sunday Telegraph* (22 April 2017).
Mcfarlane, Robert, 'The eeriness of the English countryside', *The Guardian*, 10 April 2015 <https://www.theguardian.com/books/2015/apr/10/eeriness-english-countryside-robert-macfarlane> accessed 12 December 2018.
McRoy, Jay, 'Spectral Remainders and Transcultural Hauntings: (Re)iterations of the Onryō in Japanese Horror Cinema', in Murray Leeder, ed., *Cinematic Ghosts: Haunting and Spectrality from Silent Cinema to the Digital Era* (London: Bloomsbury, 2015), 199–217.
Magistrale, Tony, *Landscape of Fear: Stephen King's American Gothic* (Bowling Green, OH: Bowling Green State University Press, 1988).
Marble Hornets, created by Joseph DeLage and Troy Wagner, YouTube Channel, 2009–14 <https://www.youtube.com/user/MarbleHornets> accessed 30 January 2018.
Martyrs, dir. Pascal Laugier (Eskwad, 2008).
Maseda, Mood R., 'Silence and Ghostly Words: Female Trauma in Isabel Coixet's *The Secret life of Words*,' in *Studies In European Cinema*, 11, 1 (2014), 48–63.
Mathijs, Ernest, and Xavier Mendik, eds, *Alternative Europe: Eurotrash and Exploitation Cinema since 1945* (London and New York: Wallflower, 2004).

Matthew Hall, *Plants as Persons: A Philosophical Botany* (New York: SUNY Press, 2011).

Medak-Saltzman, D, 'Coming to You from the Indigenous Future: Native Women, Speculative Film Shorts, and the Art of the Possible', *Studies In American Indian Literatures: The Journal Of The Association For The Study Of American Indian Literatures*, 2017, 29, 1, pp. 139–71, MLA International Bibliography, EBSCOhost, viewed 11 July 2018.

Mee, Laura, *Reanimated: The Contemporary American Horror Remake* (Edinburgh: Edinburgh University Press, forthcoming 2019).

Megan is Missing, dir. Michael Goi (Trio Pictures, 2011).

Metal Gear Solid 5, created by Hideo Kojima (Konami, 2014–15).

Metallica, 'The Thing That Should Not Be,' in *Master of Puppets* (Elektra Records, 1985).

——, 'The Call of Ktulu,' in *Ride the Lightning* (Megaforce Records, 1984).

Mitchell, Wendy. 'What's driving the new wave of indigenous filmmaking?', *ScreenDaily*, 29 March 2018. <https://www.screendaily.com/features/whats-driving-the-new-wave-of-indigenous-filmmaking/5127820.article> accessed 11 July 2018.

Miyamoto, Ken, 'How to Sell Your TV Series the Stranger Things Way,' *Huffington Post*, 3 November 2017 <https://www.huffingtonpost.com/entry/how-to-sell-your-tv-series-the-stranger-things-way_us_59fcb17ae4b05e3e1f0a00d1> accessed 25 May 2018.

Monahan, Mark, 'Why I Love Gore-Free Scary Movies,' in *The Daily Telegraph* (29 October 2010).

Morrison, Toni. *Beloved* (New York: Alfred A. Knopf, 1987).

Mother!, dir. Darren Aronofsky (Protozoa Pictures, 2017).

Mubarki, Meraj Ahmed, *Filming Horror: Hindi Cinema, Ghosts and Ideologies* (New Delhi: SAGE Publications, 2016).

Muir, Kate, 'It's LA, Jim, but Not as We Know It,' in *The Times* (11 June 2010).

Mumford, Gwilym, 'Get Political and Have Great Scares,' in *The Guardian* (6 May 2017).

Mundell, Ian, 'Euros Face H'wood Onslaught,' in *Daily Variety* (16 June 2008).

Myers, Ben, 'Folk horror, a history: from the Wicker Man to the League of Gentlemen.' In *New Statesman*, 26 July 2017 <https://www.newstatesman.com/culture/books/2017/07/folk-horror-history-wicker-man-league-gentlemen> accessed 12 December 2018.

Nashawaty, Chris, 'Jennifer Lawrence Gets Put Through the Torture-Porn Wringer in mother!' in *Entertainment Weekly*, 8 September 2017 <http://ew.com/movies/2017/09/08/jennifer-lawrence-mother-review/> accessed 8 September 2017.

National Inquiry into Missing and Murdered Indigenous Women, 'Executive Summary from the intern report: Our Women and Girls are Sacred,' May 2018 <http://www.mmiwg-ffada.ca/wp-content/uploads/2018/05/MMIWG-Executive-Summary-ENG.pdf> accessed 25 November 2018.

Nekromantik, dir. Jörg Buttgereit (Manfred Jelinski, 1987).

Nelson, Rob, 'Saw 3D,' in *Daily Variety* (1 November 2010).
Newton, Michael, 'Cults, human sacrifice and pagan sex: how folk horror is flowering again in Brexit Britain', in *The Guardian*, 30 April 2017 <https://www.theguardian.com/film/2017/apr/30/folk-horror-cults-sacrifice-pagan-sex-kill-list> 12 December 2018.
Niemeyer, Katharina, ed., *Media and Nostalgia: Yearning for the Past, Present and Future* (London: Palgrave Macmillan, 2014).
Nip/Tuck, created by Ryan Murphy (FX; 2003–10).
Norman, Joseph, '"Sounds Which Filled Me with an Indefinable Dread": The Cthulhu Mythopoeia of H. P. Lovecraft and "Extreme" Metal,' in David Simmons, ed., *New Critical Essays on H. P. Lovecraft* (New York: Palgrave Macmillan, 2013), 193–208.
Nosferatu, dir. F. W. Murnau (Prana-Film GmbH, 1922).
Nosferatu the Vampyre, dir. Werner Herzog (20th Century Fox, 1979).
Notkin, Deborah, 'Stephen King: Horror and Humanity for our Time', in Tim Underwood and Chuck Miller, eds, *Fear Itself: The Horror Fiction of Stephen King (1976–82)* (London: Pan, 1990), 131–44.
Och, Dana, and Kirsten Strayer, *Transnational Horror Across Visual Media: Fragmented Bodies* (London: Routledge, 2014).
Olney, Ian, *Euro Horror: Classic European Horror Cinema in Contemporary American Culture* (Bloomington: Indiana University Press, 2013).
One Flew Over the Cuckoo's Nest, dir. Milos Forman (Fantasy Films, 1975).
One Missed Call, dir. Takashi Miike (Kadokawa-Daiei Eiga, 2004).
Orange, Michelle, 'Taking Back the Knife: Girls Gone Gory,' *The New York Times* (6 September 2009).
Ordona, Michael, 'Saw Has Seen Better Days', in *Los Angeles Times* (30 October 2010).
Orosz, Demian, 'Cuentos de terror de Mariana Enríquez,' in *La voz*, 3 December 2009, n.p. <http://vos.lavoz.com.ar/content/cuentos-de-terror-de-mariana-enriquez-0> accessed 23 February 2018.
O'Sullivan, Charlotte, 'Also Showing,' in *The Evening Standard* (29 September 2017).
Otto, Rudolph, *The Idea of the Holy: An Inquiry into the Non-Rational Factor in the Idea of the Divine and Its Relation to the Rational* [1917], trans. John W. Harvey (Oxford: Oxford University Press, 1980).
P.T., dir. Hideo Kojima & Guillermo Del Toro (Konami, 2014).
Paranormal Activity, dir. Oren Peli (Blumhouse Productions, 2007).
Pastor, Heraldo Alfredo, 'Diana Beláustegui: El género del terror en Santiago del Estero,' in *Revista Cifra 7* (2012), 65–74.
Peeples, Scott, *The Afterlife of Edgar Allan Poe* (New York: Camden House, 2004).
Perez, Gilberto, *The Material Ghost: Films and Their Medium* (Baltimore, MD: Johns Hopkins University Press, 2000).

Perkins, Claire, *American Smart Cinema* (Edinburgh: Edinburgh University Press, 2012).
Perkins-Gilman, Charlotte, 'The Yellow Wall Paper', in Peter Straub, ed., *American Fantastic Tales: Terror and the Uncanny from Poe to the Pulps* (New York: Library of America, 2009), 131–47.
Perry, Dennis R., and Carl H. Sederholm (eds), *Adapting Poe: Re-Imaginings in Popular Culture* (New York: Palgrave, 2012).
Personal Shopper, dir. Oliver Assayas (CG Cinéma, 2016).
Phillips, Kendall R., *Projected Fears: Horror Films and American Culture* (Westport, CT: Praeger, 2005).
Phone, dir. Ahn Byeong-ki (Toilet Pictures, 2002).
Pinedo, Isabel C., 'Torture Porn: 21st Century Horror', in Harry M. Benshoff ed., *A Companion to the Horror Film* (Malden, MA: Wiley Blackwell, 2017), 345–61.
——, 'Recreational Terror: Postmodern Elements of the Contemporary Horror Film,' in *Journal of Film and Video*, 48.1–2 (1996), 17–31.
Plantinga, Carl, *Moving Viewers: American Film and the Spectator's Experience* (London, Berkeley and Los Angeles: University of California Press, 2009).
Poe, Edgar Allan, 'The Pit and the Pendulum,' in *Broadway Journal* 1/20 (17 May 1845), 3–7.
——, 'The Murders in the Rue Morgue,' in *Graham's Magazine* 18/4 (April 1842), 166–79.
——, 'The Fall of the House of Usher,' in *Burton's Gentleman's Magazine* 5/3 (September 1839), 145–52.
Poltergeist, dir. Tobe Hooper (Metro-Goldwyn-Mayer, 1982).
Potton, Ed, 'The Eyes of My Mother,' in *The Times* (24 March 2017a).
——, 'Film Review: Jigsaw,' in *The Times* (27 October 2017b).
Powell, Anna, *Deleuze and Horror Film* (Edinburgh: Edinburgh University Press, 2005).
Preacher, created by Sam Catlin, Seth Rogan and Evan Goldberg (AMC 2016–present).
Prince, Stephen, *A New Pot of Gold: Hollywood Under the Electronic Rainbow, 1980–1989* (New York: Scribner's, 2000).
Profondo rosso [Deep Red], dir. Dario Argento (Rizzoli Film and Seda Spettacoli, 1975).
Psycho, dir. Alfred Hitchcock (Shamley Productions, 1960).
Puig, Claudia, 'Last House is condemnable; No Curb Appeal in Uber-Violent Film,' in *USA Today* (13 March 2009).
Pulse, dir. Jim Sonzero (Distant Horizon, 2006).
Quinn, Karl, 'Cutting Through the Gloom; Slasher Flicks Don't Have to Be All Dark and Depressing,' in *The Age* (3 November 2017).
Quiroga, Horacio, *Todos los cuentos*, eds Napoleón Baccio Ponce de León and Jorge Lafforgue (Madrid: ALLCA XX, 1996).
——, *The Decapitated Chicken and Other Stories*, trans. Margaret Sayers Peden (Austin: University of Texas Press, 1976).

Radcliffe, Ann, 'On the Supernatural in Poetry,' in *New Monthly Magazine*, Volume 16, no. 1 (1826), 145–52.
Rapold, Nicolas, 'Interview with Julia Ducournau,' in *Film Comment* 53/2 (2017), 45–6.
Rare Exports: A Christmas Tale, dir. Jalmari Helander (Cinet, 2010).
Rare Exports: The Official Safety Instructions 2005, dir. Jalmari Helander (Woodpecker Film, 2005) <https://vimeo.com/16878867> accessed 1 June 2018.
Rare Exports Inc., dir. Jalmari Helander (Woodpecker Film, 2003) <https://vimeo.com/16878465> accessed 1 June 2018.*Rasen* [Spiral], dir. Jôji Iida (Basara Pictures, 1998).
Ratter, dir. Branden Kramer (Start Motion Pictures, 2015).
The Raven, dir. James McTeigue (FilmNation Entertainment, 2012).
The Raven, dir. Roger Corman (Alta Vista, 1963).
@RealGDT, 'Recomiendo enormemente a Horacio Quiroga. Pueden empezar con LA GALLINA DEGOLLADA y EL ALMOHADON DE PLUMAS. Genial. Ciudadseva.com/textos/cuentos...' Twitter, 25 September 2015, 8:15 am, <https://twitter.com/realgdt/status/647791571719426049>.
[REC], dir. Jaume Balagueró and Paco Plaza (Filmax International/Castelao Productions, 2007).*Rear Window*, dir. Alfred Hitchcock (Paramount, 1954).
Reinstein, Mara, 'Drew Barrymore and Timothy Olyphant Preview "Santa Clarita Diet" Season 2: "The Stakes Are Crazy,"' in *Variety*, 16 March 2018 <http://variety.com/2018/tv/news/santa-clarita-diet-drew-barrymore-timothy-olyphant-season-2-interview-1202704553/> accessed 27 April 2018.
Relatos salvajes, dir. Damián Szifron (Warner Sogefilms, 2014).
Resident Evil, dir. Shinji Mikami (Capcom, 1996).
Ring (Ringu), dir. Hideo Nakata (Toho, 1998).
Ring 0: Birthday (Ringu 0: Bâsudei), dir. Norio Tsuruta (Toho, 2000).
Ring 2 (Ringu 2), dir, Hideo Nakata (Toho, 1999).
The Ring Virus, dir. Dong-bin Kim (South Korea: AFDF, 1999).
Risner, Jonathan, 'Is it There? Specters of the Dirty War in Contemporary Argentine Horror Cinema,' in Daniela Gruber and Ursula Prutsch, eds, *Filme in Argentien/Argentine Cinema* (Berlin: LIT Verlang, 2012a), 93–104.
——, 'Killers on the Pampa: Gender, Cinematic Landscapes, and the Transnational Slasher in Adrián García Bogiano's *Habitaciones para turistas* (2004) and *36 Pasos* (2006),' in *Hispanet* 4 (2012b).
——, 'This City is Killing Me: The Circulation of Argentine Horror Cinema and Buenos Aires in Pablo Parés and Daniel de la Vega's *Jenniver's Shadow* (2004) and De la Vega's *Death Knows Your Name* (2007),' in *Studies in Hispanic Cinema* 7.1 (2011), 23–34.
Robben, Antonius C. G. M., *Political Violence and Trauma in Argentina* (Philadelphia: University of Pennsylvania Press, 2007).

Robey, Tim, 'It's Not Scary – Just Revolting,' in *The Daily Telegraph* (27 June 2007).
Rosemary's Baby, Roman Polanski (William Castle Productions, 1968).
Rust, Stephen A., and Carter Soles, 'Ecohorror Special Cluster: "Living in Fear, Living in Dread, Pretty Soon We'll all be Dead,"' in *ISLE*, Vol. 21.3 (2013), 509–12.
Ryan, Michael, and Douglas Kellner, *Camera Politica: The Politics and Ideology of Contemporary Hollywood Film* (Bloomington: Indiana University Press, 1988).
Rymer, James Malcolm, *Varney the Vampire* [1845–7] (Mineola, Dover Publishing, 2015).
Sadako 2 3D, dir. Tsutomu Hanabusa (Japan: Kadokawa Pictures, 2013).
Sadako 3D, dir. Tsutomu Hanabusa (Japan: Kadokawa Pictures, 2012).
Sadako vs. Kayako, dir. Kôji Shiraishi (Kadokawa, 2016).
Safire, William, 'As Gorno Ankles, Zitcoms Roll Out,' in *The New York Times* (11 November 2007).
Saler, Michael, *As If: Modern Enchantment and the Literary Prehistory of Virtual Reality* (Oxford: Oxford University Press, 2012).
Sandel, Michael J., *Democracy's Discontent: America in Search of a Public Philosophy* (Cambridge, MA: Harvard University Press, 1996).
Savoy, Eric, 'Between As If and Is: On Shirley Jackson', in *Women's Studies* 46, no. 8 (2017), 827–44.
Saw III, dir. Darren Lynn Bousman (Twisted Pictures, 2006).
Saw IV, dir. Darren Lynn Bousman (Twisted Pictures, 2007).
Saw V, dir. David Hackl (Twisted Pictures, 2008).
Saw VI, dir. Kevin Greutert (Twisted Pictures, 2009).
Saw, dir. James Wan (Twisted Pictures, 2004).
Scheck, Frank, 'Jigsaw: Film Review', in *Hollywood Reporter*, 26 October 2017.<http://www.hollywoodreporter.com/review/jigsaw-1052289> accessed 26 October 2017.
Schneider, Steven Jay (ed.), *Horror Film and Psychoanalysis: Freud's Worst Nightmare* (Cambridge: Cambridge University Press, 2004).
——, 'Introduction: Psychoanalysis in/and/of the Horror Film,' in Steven Jay Schneider, ed., *Horror Film and Psychoanalysis; Freud's Worst Nightmare* (Cambridge: Cambridge University Press, 2001), 1–16.
Sconce, Jeffrey, 'Irony, nihilism, and the new American "smart" film', *Screen*, 43.4 (2002), 349–69.
Scovell, Adam, *Folk Horror: Hours Dreadful and Things Strange* (New York: Columbia University Press, 2017).
——, *Haunted Media: Electronic Presence from Telegraphy to Television* (Durham, NC: Duke University Press, 2000).
Se7en, dir. David Fincher (New Line Cinema, 1996).
Sederholm, Carl H., 'H. P. Lovecraft, Heavy Metal, and Cosmicism,' in *Rock Music Studies* 3.3 (2015). 266–80.

Sederholm, Carl H., and Jeffrey Andrew Weinstock, 'Introduction: Lovecraft Rising,' in Carl H. Sederholm and Jeffrey Andrew Weinstock, eds, *The Age of Lovecraft* (Minneapolis: University of Minnesota Press, 2016), 1–42.
Sélavy, Virginie, 'Fresh Meat,' in *Sight & Sound* 27/5 (2017), 52–3.
Semley, John, 'The Bigelow Dilemma,' in *The Globe and Mail* (4 August 2017).
Sen, Meheli, *Haunting Bollywood: Gender, Genre, and the Supernatural in Hindi Commercial Cinema* (Austin: University of Texas Press, 2017).
Sevenich, Robert, '"Come Out, Come Out, Wherever You Are": Queering American Horror Story', in *Gender Forum*, Special issue, Issue 54 (2015), 35–51.
Sexton, Jamie, 'U.S. "indie-horror": Critical reception, genre construction, and suspect hybridity', *Cinema Journal*, 51.2 (2002), 67–86.
Shaviro, Steven, *The Cinematic Body* (London and Minneapolis: University of Minnesota Press, 1993).
The Shining, dir. Stanley Kubrick (Warner Bros., 1980).
Shoen, Sarah, 'Santa Clarita Diet Is About More Than a Flesh-Eating Realtor, Says Drew Barrymore,' in *Vanity Fair*, 20 March 2018 <https://www.vanityfair.com/hollywood/2018/03/drew-barrymore-santa-clarita-diet-interview-92nd-street-y> accessed 27 April 2018.
Short, Sue, *Misfit Sisters: Screen Horror as Female Rites of Passage* (Basingstoke and New York: Palgrave Macmillan, 2006).
Siefker, Phyllis, *Santa Claus, Last of the Wild Men: The Origins and Evolution of Saint Nicholas, Spanning 50,000 Years* (Jefferson, NC: McFarland and Co., 1997).
Silent Hill, dir. Keiichiro Toyama (Konami, 1999).
Silent Hill 4: The Room, dir. Suguru Murakoshi (Konami, 2004).
Silent Night, Deadly Night, dir. Charles E Sellier Jr (Tri Star Pictures and Slayride, 1984).
Slotek, Jim, 'Welcome Back, Sam!' in *The Toronto Sun* (29 May 2009).
Smiley, dir. Michael J. Gallagher (Level 10 Films, 2012).
Smith, Anna, 'Horrorwood!' in *The Guardian* (14 September 2017).
Smith, Ariel, 'This Essay Was Not Built On an Ancient Indian Burial Ground: Horror Aesthetics within Indigenous Cinema as Pushback Against Colonial Violence,' in *Off Screen*, Vol. 18, issue 8, August 2014 <https://offscreen.com/view/horror-indigenous-cinema> accessed 25 November 2018.
Smithx, Cowboy, *Napi and the Prettiest Girl in the Village*. <http://www.angelfire.com/theforce/eccentric/prettiestgirl.> accessed 11 July 2018.
Smuts, Aaron, 'Cognitive and Philosophical Approaches to Horror,' in Harry M. Benshoff ed., *A Companion to the Horror Film* (Chichester: Wiley Blackwell, 2017), 3–20.
Sobchack, Vivian, *Carnal Thoughts: Embodiment and Moving Image Culture* (Berkeley: University of California Press, 2004).

Soles, Carter, 'Sympathy for the Devil: The Cannibalistic Hillbilly in 1970s Rural Slasher Films,' in Stephen Rust, Salma Monani, and Sean Cubitt, eds, *Ecocinema: Theory and Practice* (New York: Routledge, 2012), 233–50.
Sontag, Susan, 'The Imagination of Disaster,' in *Commentary 40* (October 1965), 42–8.
Stashower, Daniel, *The Beautiful Cigar Girl: Mary Rogers, Edgar Allan Poe, and the Invention of Murder* (New York: Berkeley Books, 2006).
Stay Alive, dir. William Brent Bell (Hollywood Pictures, 2006).
Stratton, David, 'Well-Crafted Torture Tale,' in *The Australian* (3 June 2017).
Street, Susan Castillo, and Charles L. Crow (eds), *The Palgrave Handbook of the Southern Gothic* (London: Palgrave, 2016).
Suspiria, dir. Dario Argento (Seda Spettacoli, 1977).
Suzuki, Koji, *S*, trans. Greg Gencorello (New York: Vertical, 2017).
——, *Birthday*, trans. Glynne Walley (New York: Vertical, 2007).
——, *Loop*, trans. Glynne Walley (New York: Vertical, 2006).
——, *Spiral*, trans. Glynne Walley (London: Harper, 2005).
——, *Ring*, trans. Robert B. Rohmer and Glynne Walley (New York: Vertical, 2004).
Sweet Home, dir. Tokuro Fujiwara (Capcom, 1989).
Tallerico, Brian, 'The 12 Most Terrifying TV Episodes to Watch This Halloween,' *Vulture*, 18 October 2017 <http://www.vulture.com/2017/10/scariest-tv-episodes-to-watch-on-halloween.html> accessed 25 April 2018.
Tateishi, Ramie, 'The Japanese horror film series: Ring and Eko Eko Azarak,' in Steven Jay Schneider, ed., *Fear without Frontiers* (Godalming: FAB Press, 2003), 295–304.
Telegraph Reporters, 'Stranger Things credits designer explains the new logo, and the ones that were rejected,' in *The Telegraph*, 26 October 2017 <http://www.telegraph.co.uk/on-demand/0/stranger-things-credits-designer-explains-new-logo-ones-rejected/> accessed 27 April 2018.
Thacker, Eugene, *In the Dust of This Planet: Horror of Philosophy Vol. 1* (Winchester: Zero Books, 2011).
Thompson, G. R., 'Explained Gothic ["The Fall of the House of Usher"]' in Eric W. Carlson, ed., *Critical Essays on Edgar Allen Poe* (Boston, MA: G. K. Hall, 1987), 142–52.
Tidwell, Christy, 'Ecohorror', in Rosi Braidotti and Maria Hlavajova, eds, *Posthuman Glossary* (London: Bloomsbury Academic, 2018).
Timerman, Jacobo, *Prisoner Without a Name, Cell Without a Number*, trans. Toby Talbot (Madison: University of Wisconsin Press, 2002).
Tohill, Cathal, and Pete Tombs, *Immoral Tales: European Sex and Horror Movies, 1956–84* (New York: St Martin's Griffin, 1995).
Tookey, Chris, 'Viggo's Mobster Delivers on His Promise,' in *Daily Mail* (26 October 2007).
Trouble Every Day, dir. Claire Denis (Arte France Cinéma, 2001).

Tudor, Andrew, *Monsters and Mad Scientists: A Cultural History of the Horror Movie* (Oxford: Basil Blackwell, 1989).
Twin Peaks, dir. David Lynch (Propaganda Films, 1990–91).
Twisted Nerve, dir. Roy Boulting (Charter Film Productions, 1968).
Twixt, dir. Francis Ford Coppola (American Zoetrope, 2011).
Tybjerg, Casper, 'Shadow-Souls and Strange Adventures: Horror and the Supernatural in European Silent Film,' in Stephen Prince, ed., *The Horror Film* (New Brunswick, NJ: Rutgers University Press, 2004), 15–39.
Unfriended, dir. Lee Gabriadze (Bazelevs Company/Blumhouse Productions, 2014).
VanderMeer, Jeff, 'Interview: Caitlín R. Kiernan on Weird Fiction', in *Weird Fiction Review*. Last modified 12 March 2012 <http://weirdfictionreview.com/2012/03/interview-caitlin-r-kiernan-on-weird-fiction/> accessed 10 December 2018.
Vertigo, dir. Alfred Hitchcock (Alfred J. Hitchcock Productions, 1958).
The Video Dead, dir. Robert Scott (Highlight Productions, 1987).
Videodrome, dir. David Cronenberg (Canadian Film Development Corporation, 1983).
Virtue, Graeme, 'Why smart horror is putting the fear into sequel-addicted Hollywood,' in *The Guardian*, 12 April 2018 <https://www.theguardian.com/film/2018/apr/12/horror-quiet-place-get-out-hollywood> accessed 27 April 2018.
Vlog, dir. Joshua Butler (Twisted Pictures/Iceblink Films, 2008).
Walker, Johnny, *Contemporary British Horror Cinema: Industry, Genre and Society* (Edinburgh: Edinburgh University Press, 2018).
The Walking Dead, created by Frank Darabont (AMC, 2010–present).
Wallace, David, 'Mariana Enríquez on the Fascination of Ghost Stories,' in *The New Yorker*, 12 December 2016 <https://www.newyorker.com/books/page-turner/this-week-in-fiction-mariana-on-the-fascination-of-ghost-stories> accessed 23 February 2018.
Waller, Gregory A., *The Living and the Undead* (Chicago: University of Illinois Press, 1986).
We Have Always Lived in the Castle, dir. Stacie Passon (Further Film, 2018).
Weaver, James B., and Ron Tamborini (eds), *Horror Films: Current Research on Audience Preferences and Reactions* (Mahwah, NJ: Lawrence Erlbaum Associates, 1996).
West, Alexandra, *Films of the New French Extremity* (Jefferson, NC: McFarland, 2016).
Whannell, Leigh, 'Writer's Commentary,' in *Saw III: Director's Cut* DVD (Lionsgate 2008).
Wheatley, Helen, *Gothic Television* (Manchester, Manchester University Press, 2006).
White, James, 'IT: Big shoes to fill,' in *SFX* 291 (October 2017), 98–9.
Willis, Andrew, 'From the Margins to the Mainstream: Trends in Recent Spanish Horror Cinema,' in Antonio Lázaro Reboll and Andrew Willis, eds, *Spanish Popular Cinema* (Manchester: Manchester University Press, 2004), 237–49.
Wilson, Michael T. '"Absolute Reality" and the Role of the Ineffable in Shirley Jackson's *The Haunting of Hill House*', in *The Journal of Popular Culture* 48, no. 1 (2015), 114–23.

Wilson, Staci Layne, 'Jigsaw (2017),' in *Dread Central*, 26 October 2017 <http://www.dreadcentral.com/reviews/257810/jigsaw-2017/> accessed 27 October 2017.

Winter, Douglas, *The Art of Darkness: The Life and Fiction of the Master of the Macabre, Stephen King* (London: New English Library, 1989).

Wisker, Gina, *Horror Fiction: An Introduction* (London: Continuum, 2005).

Wolfe, April, 'With "A Quiet Place" and "Get Out", horror film is having a mainstream moment. Will that alienate fans?', *The Washington Post*, 13 April 2018 <https://wapo.st/2qtIl7b?tid=ss_tw&utm_term=.9adcbc562aa5> accessed 30 November 2018.

Wolfreys, Julian, 'Spectrality,' in William Hughes, David Punter and Andrew Smith, eds, *The Encyclopaedia of the Gothic* (Oxford: Wiley Blackwell, 2016), 638–44.

——, *Victorian Hauntings: Spectrality, Gothic, the Uncanny and Literature* (Basingstoke: Palgrave Macmillan, 2001).

Wood, Robin, *Hollywood from Vietnam to Reagan ... and Beyond* (New York: Columbia University Press, 2003).

Yoshida, Emily, 'Jigsaw Is a Gruesome, Facile Reboot of a Gruesome, Facile Franchise,' in *Vulture*, 27 October 2017 <http://www.vulture.com/2017/10/jigsaw-review.html> accessed 27 October 2017.

The X-Files, created by Chris Carter (Fox 1993–present).

Zinoman, Jason, *Shock Value: How a Few Eccentric Outsiders Gave Us Nightmares, Conquered Hollywood, and Invented Modern Horror* (New York: Penguin, 2012).

Zone of the Enders, dir. Hideo Kojima (Konami, 2001).

Notes on Contributors

STACEY ABBOTT is Reader in Film and Television Studies at the University of Roehampton. She is the author of *Celluloid Vampires* (2007), *Angel* (2009), *Undead Apocalypse: Vampires and Zombies in the 21st Century* (2016), and co-author, with Lorna Jowett, of *TV Horror: Investigating the Dark Side of the Small Screen* (2013). She has written extensively on horror film and TV, including recent articles on *Hannibal* and *The Purge* franchise. She is currently writing the BFI Film Classic on *Near Dark*.

XAVIER ALDANA REYES is Senior Lecturer in English Literature and Film at Manchester Metropolitan University and a founder member of the Manchester Centre for Gothic Studies. He specializes in Gothic and horror film and fiction. He is the author of *Spanish Gothic* (2017), *Horror Film and Affect* (2016) and *Body Gothic* (2014) and the editor of *Horror: A Literary History* (2016).

KATARZYNA ANCUTA is a lecturer at Chulalongkorn University in Thailand. Her research interests oscillate around the interdisciplinary contexts of contemporary Gothic/Horror, currently with a strong Asian focus. Her recent publications include contributions to *Neoliberal Gothic* (2017), *Ghost Movies in Southeast Asia and Beyond* (2016), *The Routledge Handbook to the Ghost Story* (2017), *B-Movie Gothic* (2018), and a co-edited collection, *Thai Cinema: The Complete Guide* (2018).

SIMON BACON has co-edited books on various subjects including *Undead Memory: Vampires and Human Memory in Popular Culture* (2014), *Little Horrors: Interdisciplinary Perspectives on Anomalous Children and the Construction of Monstrosity* (2016), *Growing Up with Vampires: Essays on the Undead in Children's Media* (2018), and *The Gothic: A Reader* (2018). He has published two monographs, *Becoming Vampire: Difference and the Vampire in Popular Culture* (2016), and *Dracula as Absolute Other: The Troubling and Distracting Specter of Stoker's Vampire on Screen* (2019), and is currently working on his third, *Eco-Vampires: The Vampire as Environmentalist and Undead Eco-activist*."

SIMON BROWN is Associate Professor of Film and Television at Kingston University. He is the author of *Screening Stephen King: Adaptation and the Horror Genre in Film and Television* (Austin: University of Texas Press) and *Creepshow* (Devil's Advocates Series, Leighton Buzzard: Auteur Press, 2019).

GERRY CANAVAN is Associate Professor of Twentieth- and Twenty-first-century Literature in the Department of English at Marquette University. He is the co-editor, with Kim Stanley Robinson, of *Green Planets: Ecology and Science Fiction* (2014) and, with Eric Carl Link, of *The Cambridge Companion to American Science Fiction* (2015). His first monograph is *Octavia E. Butler* (University of Illinois Press, 2016).

GAIL DE VOS specializes in telling contemporary legends to young adults. She teaches online courses on Storytelling, Comic Books and Graphic Novels in school and public libraries, Canadian Children's Literature for the School of Library and Information Studies (University of Alberta), where she is an adjunct professor, and Canadian Indigenous Literature for the Aboriginal Teacher Education Program. She is the author of nine award-winning books about storytelling and contemporary folklore in popular culture.

DARA DOWNEY is Visiting Lecturer in the School of English, Trinity College Dublin, and on the Trinity Access Programme. She is the author of *American Women's Ghost Stories in the Gilded Age* (Palgrave, 2014), co-editor of *Landscapes of Liminality: Between Space and Place* (Rowman and Littlefield, 2016), and editor of *The Irish Journal of Gothic and Horror Studies*. She is currently researching servants and slaves in American gothic.

DARREN ELLIOTT-SMITH is Senior Lecturer in Film and Gender at the University of Stirling and is the author of *Queer Horror Film and TV: Masculinity and Sexuality at the Margins* (I. B. Tauris 2016). His research and publications centre on the study of gender, sexuality and identity in the horror genre and extend to cult film/TV, experimental film, psychoanalysis and cinema, and screen curation and genre programming. His forthcoming collection entitled *New Queer Horror Film and TV* is co-edited with Dr John Edgar Browning and will be published by University of Wales Press.

TRACY FAHEY is Head of Department in Fine Art and Head of the Centre of Postgraduate Studies at the Limerick School of Art and Design, LIT. Her research into Gothic and the visual arts has been published in edited collections. Her short fiction has appeared in fifteen Irish, UK and US anthologies. Her first collection, *The Unheimlich Manoeuvre* (2016), was nominated for a British Fantasy Award in 2017.

THOMAS FAHY is Professor of English at Long Island University, Post, and has published sixteen books, including *Dining with Madmen: Fat, Food, and the Environment in 1980s Horror*, *The Writing Dead: Talking Terror with TV's Top Horror Writers*, *The Philosophy of Horror*, *Understanding Truman Capote*, and the young adult horror novels *Sleepless* and *The Unspoken*. He is also a classical pianist and lives in Brooklyn with his family.

TODD S. GARTH is the author of two books and multiple articles on early and mid-twentieth-century Latin American fiction, including the work of Argentine authors Roberto Arlt, Jorge Luis Borges, Macedonio Fernández, Horacio Quiroga and Alfonsina Storni and on Brazilian writer Machado de Assis. He is a professor at the US Naval Academy, teaching Spanish, Portuguese and Latin American Studies, also serving as Associate Chair of the Languages and Cultures Department.

STEPHANIE A. GRAVES is a film and television scholar whose research interests include horror, the grotesque, and the southern gothic, particularly when viewed through the lens of gender and queer theory. She is a PhD student in Rhetoric at Georgia State University, and she is, like many academics, fond of cats.

STEFFEN HANTKE has edited *Horror*, a special topic issue of *Paradoxa* (2002), *Horror: Creating and Marketing Fear* (2004), *Caligari's Heirs: The German Cinema of Fear after 1945* (2007), *American Horror Film: The Genre at the Turn of the Millennium* (2010), and, with Agnieszka Soltysik-Monnet, *War Gothic in Literature and Culture* (2016). He is also the author of *Conspiracy and Paranoia in Contemporary American Literature* (1994) and *Monsters in the Machine: Science Fiction Film and the Militarization of America after World War II* (2016).

ALEXANDRA HELLER-NICHOLAS is an award-winning Australian film critic who has written five books on cult, horror and exploitation film, including *Ms. 45* from Columbia University Press/Wallflower as part of their *Cultographies* series, *Suspiria* as part of Auteur Publishing's *Devils Advocates* series, and *Rape-Revenge Films: A Critical Study* from McFarland. She was an editor at the film journal *Senses of Cinema* from 2015 to 2018 and is a researcher at the Victorian College of the Arts.

STEVE JONES is Senior Lecturer in Social Sciences at Northumbria University, UK. His research principally focuses on sex, violence, ethics, and selfhood within horror and pornography. He is the author of *Torture Porn: Popular Horror After Saw* (Palgrave-Macmillan, 2013) and his work has been published in journals such as *Feminist Media Studies*, *New Review of Film and Television Studies*, *Sexualities*, and *Film-Philosophy*. For more information, please visit <http://www.drstevejones.co.uk>.

LORNA JOWETT is Reader in Television Studies at the University of Northampton, UK. She is author of *Dancing With the Doctor: Dimensions of Gender in the* Doctor Who *Universe* and *Sex and the Slayer*, co-author with Stacey Abbott of *TV Horror*, and editor of *Time on TV: Narrative Time, Time Travel and Time Travellers in Popular Television Culture*. She has published many articles on television, film and popular culture and her next book is a collection of essays on Joss Whedon and horror, co-edited with Kristopher Woofter.

KAYLA LAR-SON is a Metis woman from Tofield, Alberta, Canada. As an Academic Library Resident at the University of Alberta, and a sessional instructor for the School of Library and Information Studies at the University of Alberta, she specializes in Indigenous initiatives and library engagement, Indigenous LIS, radical librarianship, and diversity studies. She has a strong passion for Indigenous-created graphic novels, comics, and movies.

MURRAY LEEDER holds a PhD from Carleton University and is an adjunct assistant professor at University of Calgary. He the author of *Horror Film: A Critical Introduction* (Bloomsbury, 2018), *The Modern Supernatural and the Beginnings of Cinema* (Palgrave Macmillan, 2017) and *Halloween* (Auteur,

2014), as well as the editor of *Cinematic Ghosts: Haunting and Spectrality from Silent Cinema to the Digital Era* (Bloomsbury, 2015) and *ReFocus: The Films of William Castle* (Edinburgh University Press, 2018).

CHRISTIAN MCCREA is a researcher writing on science fiction, film, videogames, animation and the popular digital arts. He is also a lecturer in the School of Design at RMIT University, Melbourne, Australia.

DANA OCH is Lecturer in English/Film and Media Studies at the University of Pittsburgh, where she also serves as the Director of Undergraduate Studies for the film programme. She writes frequently on questions of Irish cinema, horror, and horror comedy, including publications on Neil Jordan, the postcolonial zombie comedy, *Twin Peaks*, and the neopostmodern horror film. She co-edited the anthology *Transnational Horror Across Visual Media: Fragmented Bodies* (Routledge 2014).

IAN OLNEY is Associate Professor of English at York College of Pennsylvania, where he teaches film studies. He is the author of *Zombie Cinema* (Rutgers University Press, 2017) and *Euro Horror: Classic European Horror Cinema in Contemporary American Culture* (Indiana University Press, 2013), and a co-editor, with Antonio Lázaro-Reboll, of *The Films of Jess Franco* (Wayne State University Press, 2018).

ELIZABETH PARKER is author of *The Forest and the EcoGothic: The Deep Dark Woods* in the Popular Imagination with Palgrave Gothic. She is the founding editor of the journal *Gothic Nature: New Directions in Eco-horror and the EcoGothic* and TV editor of *Irish Gothic Journal*. Her work has featured in such publications as *Plant Horror!: The Monstrous Vegetal* (2016) and *Transecology: Transgender Perspectives on the Environment* (2018). She currently works in Student Engagement at St Mary's University Twickenham.

JULIA ROUND is a Principal Academic at Bournemouth University and edits the *Studies in Comics* journal. Her research focuses on Gothic, comics and children's literature. Her academic books include *Gothic in Comics and Graphic Novels: A Critical Approach* (McFarland, 2014), the co-edited collection *Real Lives Celebrity Stories* (Bloomsbury, 2014), and her new book *Gothic for Girls:*

Misty and British Comics (University Press of Mississippi, 2019). This is accompanied by a searchable database of creators and stories, available at her website <http://www.juliaround.com>.

CRISTINA SANTOS teaches in the Department of Communications, Popular Culture and Film at Brock University. Her book *Unbecoming Female Monsters: Witches, Vampires, and Virgins* (2016) describes the construct of 'monstrous women' in literature, film, television, popular culture and mythology from an intersectional feminist perspective and multi-cultural approach. She also investigates the construct of political and social deviance and trauma in life narratives as the construction of a personal and communal sense of identity that challenges official history and patriarchy.

CARL H. SEDERHOLM is Professor of Interdisciplinary Humanities at Brigham Young University and Chair of the Department of Comparative Arts and Letters. He is the editor of *The Journal of American Culture*. He is co-editor of *The Age of Lovecraft* (2016), *Adapting Poe: Re-Imaginings in Popular Culture* (2012) and *Poe, the 'House of Usher,' and the American Gothic* (2009). He is also the author of multiple essays on authors such as Edgar Allan Poe, H. P. Lovecraft, Stephen King, Jonathan Edwards, Lydia Maria Child, and Nathaniel Hawthorne.

MEHELI SEN is Associate Professor in the Department of African, Middle Eastern, and South Asian Languages and Literatures (AMESALL) at Rutgers University. Her research area is post-independence Indian cinema, particularly Hindi- and Bengali-language films. She co-edited *Figurations in Indian Film* (Palgrave-Macmillan, 2013). Sen's book, *Haunting Bollywood: Gender, Genre and the Supernatural in Hindi Commercial Cinema,* was published in 2017 by the University of Texas Press. She is currently working on a second book on media cultures in South Asia.

JEFFREY ANDREW WEINSTOCK is Professor of English at Central Michigan University, USA, and an editor for *The Journal of the Fantastic in the Arts*. He is an author or editor of twenty-one books, the most recent of which are *Critical Approaches to Welcome to Night Vale: Podcasting Between Weather and the Void* (Routledge 2018), *The Cambridge Companion to the American*

Gothic (2017), *The Age of Lovecraft* (Minnesota 2016), and *Goth Music: From Sound to Subculture* (Routledge 2015). Visit him at <http://www.jeffreyandrewweinstock.com>.

GINA WISKER is Head of University Brighton's Centre for Learning and Teaching, and Professor of Higher Education and Contemporary Literature. She has written twenty-five books (some edited) and published 140 articles, including *The Postgraduate Research Handbook* (2001, 2008), *The Good Supervisor* (2005, 2012), *Getting Published* (2015). She also specializes in twentieth-century women's writing, postcolonial, Gothic and popular fictions. Her publications include *Key Concepts in Postcolonial Writing* (2007), *Horror* (2005), *Margaret Atwood, an Introduction to Critical Views of Her Fiction* (2012), and *Contemporary Women's Gothic Fiction* (2016).

KRISTOPHER WOOFTER, PhD, teaches courses on the American Gothic, weird, and horror traditions in literature and the moving image in the English department at Dawson College, Montréal. He is co-director of the Montréal Monstrum Society and co-editor of its peer-reviewed journal, *MONSTRUM*. His most recent publication is *Joss Whedon vs. the Horror Tradition: The Production of Genre in* Buffy *and Beyond* (co-edited with Lorna Jowett; I. B. Tauris, 2019).

Index

1960s and 1970s 68, 141, 145, 146
1970s 78, 93, 106, 118, 129, 132, 185
1980s 27, 46, 76, 103–9, 127, 129, 144, 191, 214

abjection 2, 3, 8, 13, 27, 30, 48, 50, 114–17, 148, 169, 185, 203, 220, 230
abuse 88, 104, 170, 172, 208, 222–3, 240
abyss 54, 57
affect 2, 3, 4, 5, 27–33, 67, 73, 126
African American 119, 122, 124, 134, 167–74
agency 28, 58, 62
A.I. 112, 201–2, 204, 209
Alien 31, 115, 117
alien (other) 71, 94, 95, 100
alien (outer-space) 1, 19, 20, 23, 24, 68, 96, 100, 238
allegory 16, 198, 207
ambiguity 13, 19, 23, 25, 57, 227, 235, 238, 239
America 37, 47, 64, 76, 95, 103, 106–9, 117, 119, 121, 122, 128, 144, 151, 175, 179, 192, 193, 194, 196, 202, 209, 227, 238
American Horror Story 35–42, 48
American Psycho 106, 115
American Werewolf in London 68, 105
Anglo-American 143, 145, 146, 148
animal 1, 30, 54, 66, 96–7, 140, 163, 171, 193–4, 204, 223–5
Anthropocene 95, 100–1
anthropocentric 94, 213, 215
anthropology 34, 192
anthropomorphize 58, 100

anxiety 5, 8, 16, 57, 167, 182, 184, 215, 229
apocalypse 23, 24, 47, 108, 109, 123, 157, 227
archetype 55
art-horror 2, 3, 7, 28, 146
audience 3, 4, 5, 6, 7, 20, 21, 33–4, 45, 47, 49–50, 63, 70–1, 73, 75, 79, 81, 85–6, 88, 91, 104–7, 119, 121, 126, 127–30, 144–5, 148, 177–8, 183, 185, 186, 191–2, 194–6, 213, 217, 240
aural 5, 48, 67

blood 46, 49, 91, 104, 114, 115, 148, 163, 184
bodily 3, 5, 7, 45, 114, 164
    fluids 49, 184
box office 122, 127, 129, 181, 192
burial 171, 175, 203, 204, 207
Butler, Judith 37, 42

camera 20, 30–1, 49, 50, 63–4, 66, 69, 80, 97, 117, 131, 141, 171, 183, 208, 222
cannibal 49, 106, 109, 145, 148–50, 151
Carroll, Noel 2, 4, 13, 27, 28
Cherry, Brigid 3–4, 33–4, 177
childhood 22, 170, 186
children 16, 23, 54, 55, 58, 71, 79, 80, 153, 159, 169, 170, 172, 177, 178, 182, 193, 195–7, 223
class 13, 34, 47, 122, 124–5, 147, 170, 219, 224–5
Clover, Carol 4, 27, 29, 118
cognitive 3, 4, 5, 27, 29, 30, 31
colonialism 140, 141, 169, 175, 182

comedy 5, 37, 47, 49, 137, 141
comics 3, 53–9, 203
Creed, Barbara 4, 13–14, 27, 57–8, 113, 121, 185
cult horror 36, 38, 41, 144, 146, 159
curse 12–13, 15–16, 76, 113, 153–4, 156, 172

death 15–16, 33, 57, 71, 76, 79, 104, 108, 117, 119, 120, 124, 152, 156, 160, 171, 186, 188, 203–5, 214, 219, 222, 231, 237, 239
dehumanizing 117, 165, 169, 172, 225
Deleuze, Gilles 4, 28
demon 13, 54, 57, 65, 68, 153–4, 170, 177, 186
destiny *see* fate
devil 138, 171, 182, 236
disgust 4, 49, 67, 70, 226
domestic 21–3, 29, 45, 122, 129, 188, 194, 198, 222
Doppelgänger 57
Dracula 39, 53
dread 5, 7, 16, 28, 30–1, 62, 73, 94, 98, 163, 165, 182, 188, 217
dream 1, 25, 54, 69, 78, 146, 204, 207–8, 214, 229

ecology 8, 93–6, 109, 192
environment 3, 62, 64, 65, 89, 93–5, 106–9, 117, 168
epistemology 11, 232
erotic 146, 148, 219, 222
ethnicity 54, 122, 169
existential 2, 5, 14, 54, 116, 142, 175, 178, 188, 205, 228, 232–3, 236

fairy tale 113, 181, 192–3, 196, 198, 229
family 22, 37, 45, 46–8, 50, 55, 57, 71, 73, 117, 121–2, 125, 158, 169, 171, 182, 187, 222, 225, 230
fandom 3, 33, 36, 41–2, 47, 63, 77, 91–2, 127, 134, 145, 149, 204

fantastic, the 59, 96, 143, 228, 230
fantasy 19, 59, 70, 73, 117, 168, 201, 228, 230–3
fate 15, 17, 24, 50, 66, 90, 95, 237
fear 48, 53, 57, 59, 68, 70, 79, 85, 88, 93, 106, 108, 120, 130, 139–40, 141, 157, 161, 162, 163, 172–3, 175, 183, 188, 224, 226
folk-horror 137–9, 140–2
folklore 77, 79, 80, 151, 181, 189, 192, 228, 230
food 107–9, 169, 176, 238
found-footage 20, 30, 41, 76, 79, 120, 145
franchise 20–1, 33, 63, 85, 86, 89, 90–1, 95, 120–1, 123, 124, 126, 129
Frankenstein 53, 111, 113
freak 37, 108, 140, 178, 186
Freak Show 39, 48
Freud, Sigmund 4, 28, 51, 111, 117, 169

games/gaming 7, 21, 30, 61–6, 75, 76, 79, 122, 125, 126, 214
gaze 115, 118, 149
gender 27, 34, 36, 38–9, 42, 45, 48, 49–51, 54, 68, 113, 114, 118, 120, 123, 149, 158, 181, 186, 189
Get Out 6, 119–20, 123, 127, 130–2, 134, 167
ghost 37, 56, 58, 61, 151–2, 154, 156, 160, 163, 164, 165, 169, 177, 203, 206–8, 228, 229, 230, 231, 232
 story 162, 167–73, 176, 228, 231
Ghostbusters 103, 108, 171
globalization 5, 7, 45–6, 112, 120, 121, 140, 181, 198
gore 1, 49, 51, 90, 114, 203
Gothic 2, 29, 38, 40, 41, 47, 48, 53, 55, 57, 58, 111, 117, 138, 144, 145, 146, 160, 182, 201, 203, 206, 207, 219, 220, 223, 226, 227
 horror 36, 112, 113, 159, 167–8, 172
grave 69, 111, 146, 164, 173

haunt 55, 66, 76, 108, 109, 125, 138, 152, 156, 158, 162, 165, 167, 168, 169, 173, 228, 229, 230
haunted house 29, 30, 41, 54, 57–8, 161, 164, 176
Haunting of Hill House, The 53, 227, 228
heteronormative 36, 38–9, 42, 47, 147, 187
Hills, Matt 4–5, 28, 33
Hollywood 5, 128, 130–1, 143, 144–5, 192, 219, 226
horror *see* art-horror, cult horror, folk-horror
horror genre 1, 3, 4, 6, 55, 68, 71, 76, 86, 103, 119, 121, 126, 129, 143, 159, 184, 186, 203, 219, 223, 225
hybridity 6, 11, 41, 97, 100, 115, 122, 150, 192, 193, 198, 203, 227

iconic 37, 39, 42, 45, 78, 103, 116–17, 151, 177, 182, 183, 214, 240
identity 36, 38, 41, 50, 51, 57–8, 120, 141, 223, 232
incest 13, 23, 45, 204
indigenous 138–9, 175–6, 179–80, 223
insect 93, 156
interior 37, 117, 182, 183, 237, 239
internet 75, 77–9, 132, 145, 152, 156–7, 223
intertextual 41, 42, 54, 55, 58, 104, 112, 114, 117, 128, 227
invisible 13, 65, 182
It Follows 12–17, 124, 127, 129, 189

Japan 62, 120, 151, 154, 158, 175
justice 152, 159, 176, 172, 224–5, 237

killer 1, 31, 105–6, 123, 205, 206
    serial 54, 105, 115, 151, 204, 235, 237
King, Stephen 13, 46, 54, 55, 103, 108, 235–40
Kristeva, Julia 2, 8, 114–16, 169–70, 185

Lacan, Jacques 4, 28, 169
Latin America 159–61, 165, 219, 223, 226
legend 67, 77, 176–7, 217
liminal 73, 152, 162, 172, 229
Lovecraft, H. P. 11–12, 14, 16, 17, 55, 211–18

magic 168, 188
masculinity 25, 50, 113, 149, 186, 194, 195, 223
maternal 184, 185
melodrama 36, 37, 47, 181
memory 12, 33, 161, 173, 229
menstrual 172, 185
metamorphosis 6, 171
millennial 14, 157–8
    post- 119
mobile phones 30, 32, 66, 120, 157
monsters 1, 6, 13, 14, 19, 20–1, 24, 28, 29–30, 33, 50, 62, 68, 70, 94–6, 100, 108, 111–12, 113, 115, 117, 119, 120, 128, 151, 156, 162, 172, 188, 212, 213, 214, 220, 230, 236, 237, 239, 240
monstrous feminine 27, 50, 114, 121, 141, 184, 185, 228
moon 69, 172, 230
music 1, 7, 16, 30, 37–9, 46, 59, 65, 67–74, 106, 142, 149–50, 151, 183, 191, 203, 211–12, 214–15, 218, 222
mutation 1, 95–6, 153, 154, 158
myth 77, 79, 80, 81, 96, 111, 134, 142, 175, 193, 214, 217, 228, 230, 231, 236

narrative 5, 7, 14, 20, 24, 30, 31, 35, 36–9, 41, 46, 47–8, 62, 63–4, 68, 69, 70, 76, 79–80, 85, 88–9, 91, 93, 94, 95, 101, 103, 117, 121, 125, 127, 145, 153–4, 162, 163, 167, 168, 172, 176–7, 180, 181–2, 188, 189, 191, 196, 213, 228, 229, 233, 236, 239
Netflix 20, 31, 35, 45–7, 103, 227
network 15, 48, 50, 152, 157

new media 46, 76–9, 81, 118, 125–6, 157, 163, 192, 194, 203, 213–14
nightmare 11, 23, 41, 54, 103, 123, 125, 132, 141, 160, 206
Nightmare on Elm Street 46, 103, 105, 108, 125, 129
non-diegetic 16, 73
nonhuman 93, 95, 97, 100, 224
non-normative 35, 47, 51
nostalgia 36, 37, 46, 103–4, 109, 137, 141, 158, 239–40

pagan 192, 198
paranoia 23, 79, 112, 117–18, 162, 228, 229
paranormal 41, 75, 235, 238
Paranormal Activity 76, 121, 129
patriarchy 16, 51, 57, 117, 121, 146, 149, 193–4, 195
performative 35–42, 50, 139, 151–2, 172
phantasy 57, 128
philosophy 7, 11, 12, 13–4, 16–17, 149, 213, 217, 220, 227
plague 2, 80, 139, 141, 204, 226
plants 96, 98, 108
Poe, Edgar Allan 201–9, 221
political 3, 37, 63, 107, 118, 123, 124–6, 140, 160–5, 167, 180, 187, 194
post-industrial 12, 117, 188
postmodern 5, 128, 129, 145, 162, 227
privilege 13, 122, 124–5, 134, 167
Psycho 39, 48, 70
psychoanalytic 4, 5, 27, 28, 29, 32, 53, 58, 169, 228, 232
psychological 3, 19, 48, 53, 54, 59, 62, 71, 115, 127, 129, 154, 160–1, 164, 168, 206, 222
psychosexual 27, 30

queer 4, 7, 35–42, 48, 147, 228

racism 168, 179, 222
Radcliffe, Ann 2, 53

rage 23, 146, 154, 186, 195, 220, 221, 222, 225, 226
rape-revenge 50, 55, 156, 220, 235
reality 30, 36, 37, 41, 75, 92, 159, 160, 163–5, 168, 179, 211, 213, 214, 228–32, 236
remake 5, 76, 91, 119, 130, 151, 153
repression/repressed 4, 27, 59, 75, 112, 161, 167, 173, 206, 220, 228, 232
reproduce 92, 117, 152–3, 154, 158, 178
revenge 93–4, 122, 146, 220, 223–5, 235–6
robot 63, 111–18
Romero, George A. 47, 54, 76, 120, 134

savage 106, 141, 175, 223, 224, 225
Schneider, Steven Jay 27, 52
science 31, 213, 224
science fiction 19–21, 24, 25, 63, 66, 75, 101, 103, 111–15, 122, 168, 203
sex 15, 49, 50, 80, 88, 145, 148, 153, 170–1, 178, 185, 202, 203, 222
sexism 118
sexuality 1, 15, 35–7, 43, 47, 58, 116, 121, 146, 186–7, 189
slasher 1, 33, 35, 106, 107, 122–3, 129–3, 177
slavery 168–73
somatics 4, 28–9, 30–2
soundtrack 16, 20, 28–30, 39, 67, 69, 70–1, 73, 143, 163, 183, 191, 220
sublimate 4, 112
sublime 2, 71, 114, 139
suburbs 12, 15, 16, 23, 45–7, 104–5, 106–7, 117, 131–2
suicide 154, 228, 230, 235
supernatural 13, 16, 47–8, 50, 61, 62, 66, 68, 70, 73, 75, 77, 103, 143, 146, 151, 154, 159, 162–4, 175, 176, 181, 188, 228, 235–6, 238–40
symbolism 1, 4, 35, 53–5, 57–9, 96, 128, 198, 224

technology 7, 21, 29–31, 46, 65, 66, 75–6, 79, 80, 105, 108, 111, 117–18, 120, 126, 129, 152, 157–8, 179–80
terror 2, 11, 19, 24, 28, 53, 57, 68, 70, 75, 140, 143, 146, 160, 161, 165, 172–3, 220, 222
terrorism 2, 120, 137
terrorize 23, 96, 123
torture 58, 120, 140, 159, 162, 164–5, 182, 184, 186, 203–4, 224
  porn 85–92, 130, 134, 188
trans-
  media 46, 79, 125–6
  national 79, 144, 191–8
transcend 79, 114, 129, 222, 231
transform 6, 8, 24, 41, 42, 54, 56, 59, 69–70, 94–5, 105, 109, 125, 139, 156, 158, 162, 171, 220–1
transgressive 1, 3, 15, 45, 47, 48, 50–1, 146, 162
transition 47, 48, 49, 68, 157
transmission 15, 152, 154, 175
trauma 22, 146, 161, 164–5, 178–9, 182, 228, 231, 235
tropes 3, 5, 24, 29, 35, 42, 54–6, 63, 89, 95, 107, 109, 115, 127, 132, 137, 141, 175, 183, 194, 203, 220, 223
TV horror 30, 35–6, 42, 45–7, 51, 239

uncanny 21, 27, 40–1, 48, 54–5, 57–8, 111, 118, 139, 143, 154, 204, 211, 239

universal 32, 176
Universal Studios 38, 121, 125, 143
universe 64, 65, 153, 162, 213, 215
urban 12, 106, 121, 123, 222, 223
utopia 15, 24

vampires 1, 5–6, 14, 36, 55, 120, 140, 144, 146, 151, 219, 223, 224
video 15, 30, 33, 63, 65, 67–8, 70, 71, 76, 77, 79–80, 86, 105, 120, 144–5, 152–3, 157, 171, 194, 195
violence 1, 2, 8, 53, 70, 80, 85–6, 90, 91, 93, 104–5, 109, 112–13, 117, 123, 138, 139, 145–9, 159, 161–2, 170–1, 176, 178–9, 186, 188, 193, 202–4, 209, 220, 222–5, 230, 239
virus 152–4, 158

war 23, 25, 54, 144, 188, 191
web series 46, 77, 78, 191, 194
website 77, 157, 194
weird 11, 211–18, 228
werewolves 6, 14, 55, 69, 172–3, 223–4
witches 37, 39, 47, 76, 121, 123, 127, 137, 151, 207

YouTube 46, 63, 66, 77, 79, 81

zombies 29–30, 39, 45–51, 61, 62, 69, 107, 120, 145–6, 150, 167, 198, 226